POLITICAL CAMPAIGN COMMUNICATION

A Bibliography and Guide
to the Literature
1973-1982

by
Lynda Lee Kaid
and
Anne Johnston Wadsworth

The Scarecrow Press, Inc.
Metuchen, N.J., & London 1985

Library of Congress Cataloging in Publication Data

Kaid, Lynda Lee.
  Political campaign communication.

  Bibliography: p.
  Includes index.
  1. Electioneering--United States--Bibliography.
2. Advertising, Political--United States--Bibliography.
3. Communication--United States--Political aspects--
Bibliography.   I. Wadsworth, Anne.   II. Title.
Z7164.R4K34 1985 [JK1976]   016.3247'0973   84-23508
ISBN 0-8108-1764-0

Copyright © 1985 by Lynda Lee Kaid
and Anne Johnston Wadsworth
Manufactured in the United States of America

ACKNOWLEDGEMENTS

Several people were very helpful in assisting with the compilation of this bibliography. Anne's parents (Col. and Mrs. Johnston) offered their encouragement and assistance at the very start, making the project so much easier. To Jeannine Freeman, a hardworking student assistant, we express our appreciation for the long hours she spent in front of the computer.

The authors are also grateful to Keith Sanders, Dean of the College of Communications and Fine Arts at Southern Illinois University, for his vision and for his long-term commitment to developing thorough bibliographic skills in his students.

Finally, a very special thanks to Charlie for his moral support and cheap labor and to Cliff for his encouragement and understanding.

TABLE OF CONTENTS

Introduction	1
Bibliography	9
Guide to the Literature	197
Index	203

INTRODUCTION

In the past decade, the growth of political campaign communication as an area of study has been nothing short of astounding. When the first volume of this bibliography[1] was published in 1974, the book contained just over 1500 entries related to political campaign communication between 1950 and 1972. Only a decade later, this current volume contains 2461 entries over a time span only half as long (1973 through 1982).

Political campaign communication is the primary subject matter of the developing field known simply as political communication. At one time a field tied to the broader disciplines of communication and political science, political communication has unquestionably emerged as a legitimate and separate field of inquiry.[2] The emergence of political communication as a distinct discipline has been evidenced not only by the burgeoning literature catalogued in this volume, but also by the formation of the Political Communication Division, and its accompanying journal Political Communication Review, as a separate unit within the International Communication Association. The growth of course offerings at major universities and the publication of specialized handbooks such as Nimmo and Sanders' Handbook of Political Communication[3] offer further documentation.

Despite this rapid growth, researchers continue to be hampered by the scarcity of good reference materials. The researcher's job is made particularly difficult because the field of political campaign communication is truly an interdisciplinary one, including literature published in the journals of communication, political science, journalism, mass communication, sociology, psychology, history, film, English, and others. However, since the publication of the first volume of the bibliography, a few specialized reference materials have appeared.

On a very broad level, several recent bibliographies by Goehlert[4] and by Goudy[5] address the general field of political behavior, encompassing all aspects of that field including political communication. A more specific bibliography on American presidential campaign biographers was published in 1979 by William Miles[6] and contains literature on the more practical views of campaign management and image-making.

Regular, annotated bibliographies and book reviews have been published in Political Communication Review since 1975. This journal also has published occasional articles on non-print resources useful to scholars of political campaign communication.[7] A recent issue of Campaigns and Elections, a journal on the more practical aspects of politics, offered a guide to archival collections of television news coverage of elections.[8]

More comprehensive collections of relevant work have been contained in recent master's theses. Using a very broad definition of political communication, Jenkins compiled a bibliography which included works on the Canadian and British, as well as American, electoral processes.[9] Finally, Wadsworth has completed a bibliography[10] which includes recent scholarly work in political campaign communication and identifies trends in the direction of research about this important topic.

Definition

A careful definition of material to be included and excluded is an important prerequisite to any bibliographic effort. The basic definition used here is identical to that used in the first volume of this work, except for the new time period. That is:

This bibliography consists of entries relevant to the communications process as it operates in a political campaign or similar context in the United States from 1973 through 1982.

The entries include books, pamphlets, articles in scholarly journals, dissertations, and theses. This volume does not include articles in popular magazines or newspapers, government documents, or unpublished papers presented at meetings or conferences.

Communication is defined in terms of the traditional communication variables of sources, messages, channels, and receivers. As indicated in the earlier volume of this book: "Communication variables can function in ways very similar to their operation in an actual political campaign without being in a campaign."[11] For this reason, citations which relate to communication functions in contexts which are similar to or may affect campaign processes are included. For instance, studies of how the media affect a president's approval rating may have implications for his electoral image, even though the study may not have occurred during an actual political campaign.

The material contained in this work is limited to American campaign processes between 1973 and 1982. The time period was chosen simply to provide a ten-year update of the earlier volume which covered 1950 through 1972. Material which was published after 1973 but which dealt with political figures or events prior to the original 1950 time period was usually excluded.

Introduction 3

It was necessary in the citation-gathering process to provide more specific operating procedures for this general definition. In doing so, this work parallels the guidelines for inclusion and exclusion formulated in the first volume. Thus, the volume includes:

1. Descriptive, analytical, and evaluative works on actual political campaigns, including campaigns at local, state, and national levels.
2. Works on the role and effects of the communications media in political campaigns and on the relative use and credibility of the mass media as information sources in political campaigns and in other relevant contexts.
3. Works on the flow of information in political contexts, particularly items on the multi-step flow of communication and on interpersonal communication.
4. Works on public opinion polling and computers when related to political campaigns.
5. Works on public opinion and political attitudes of communications receivers, including works on psychological factors related to receiver perceptions of communications.
6. Works related to the role and effects of public speaking and debating in political campaigns.
7. Works related to the general messages and content of political communication, especially in the context of "issue" versus "image" of political candidates and parties.
8. Works on "practical politics" when related to the role of communication.
9. Works on the financing and high cost of political campaigning, including works discussing governmental regulation of campaign expenditures, media expenditures, and media use in political campaigns (equal time).

The following were excluded:

1. Works on political parties and demographic characteristics of the electorate except when they are related to a communication variable.
2. Works on methodologies used in research in political campaign communication unless the material itself provides information on the operation of a communication variable in a political campaign context.

Procedure for Collecting Citations

The primary method of collecting entries involved reliance on traditional indexes and abstracting services. These, along with the headings consulted under each, are listed below:

Books in Print, Subject Index, 1982-1983 (under advertising campaigns, campaign management, communication, elections--U. S., campaign funds, executive ability, executive power, government and the press, legislators, lobbying, mass media--social aspects, political conventions, political ethics, political participation, political parties, political psychology, presidents, public opinion, public opinion polls, public policy, public relations and politics, radio in politics, television in politics, and voting).

Communication Booknotes (formerly Mass Media Booknotes), 1975-1983 (entire contents).

Psychological Abstracts, Vol. 49, 1973--Vol. 68, 1982 (under advertising, communications media, government personnel, mass media, newspapers, political attitudes, political campaigns, political candidates; political elections, political issues, political processes, politics, public opinion, radio, television, and voting behavior).

Social Science Index, Vol. 1, 1974/75--Vol. 9, 1982/83 (under advertising, political; campaign funds; communication, political aspects; election forecasting; government and press; journalism and politics; legislators; legitimacy of governments; mass media, political aspects; persuasion; political--attitudes, campaigns, candidates, conventions, psychology; presidential campaigns; presidential candidates; primaries; representative; radio and politics; television and politics; and voting).

Humanities Index, Vol. 1, 1975/76--Vol. 9, 1982/83 (under advertising, political; communication in politics; elections; government and press; journalism and politics; journalism and public opinion; mass media, political aspects; mass media and public opinion; persuasion; political campaigns; politicians; presidential campaigns; presidents; public opinion polls; radio and politics; television and politics; voting).

Sociological Abstracts, 1974--April, 1983 (under advertising, campaign, candidate, elections, electoral, electorate, mass media, news, newspapers, political, politics, public opinion, radio, television, and voting).

British Humanities Index, 1974--1982 (under communications, elections, media, political, politics, public opinion, public opinion polls, television and politics, United States--politics and government, voting, and women and/in politics).

Education Index, 1973/74--1982/83 (under advertising, political; campaign funds; communication, political aspects; elections; journalism and politics; mass media; political--attitudes, campaigns, conventions, and psychology; presidential campaigns; presidents; public opinion; public opinion polls; radio in politics; rhetoric in politics; television in politics; voting; and women in politics).

Dissertation Abstracts International A, Vol. 34, 1973--Vol. 43, 7-9, 1982 (under journalism; mass communication; speech/speech communication; and political science, general).

Introduction 5

Journalism Abstracts, Vol. 11, 1973--Vol. 19, 1981 (under all headings).

Communication Abstracts, Vol. 1, 1978--Vol. 5, 1982 (under all headings).

Masters Abstracts, 1973-1983.

Political Communication Review, Vol. 1, 1975--Vol. 7, 1982 (all articles, book reviews, and bibliographies).

Because indexes such as those above often are not comprehensive, other sources were checked to insure thorough collection of citations. These included the following:

1. Every issue of major relevant journals during the appropriate time span was checked. These included Quarterly Journal of Speech, Southern Speech Communication Journal, Central States Speech Journal, Communication Research, Mass Comm Review, Journal of Communication, Human Communication Research, Communication Monographs, Western Journal of Speech Communication, Legislative Studies Quarterly, Presidential Studies Quarterly, Political Behavior, Women and Politics, Quarterly Journal of Speech, Operant Subjectivity, American Political Science Review, Public Opinion Quarterly, Journalism Quarterly, and Journal of Broadcasting.

2. Book review and booknote sections were checked in several major periodicals. These included Journal of Communication, Western Political Quarterly, American Politics Quarterly, Journal of Broadcasting, Journalism Quarterly, and Campaigns and Elections.

3. Finally, reference sections were checked in several important books in the field, including The Handbook of Political Communication, Communication Yearbooks, and Mass Communication Review Yearbooks.

Method of Indexing Citations

The indexing system employed here can best be described as a "modified key word" indexing system. All bibliographers are aware of the problems inherent in strict reliance on a key-word index system. The index here sought to minimize the primary problem of key-word indexing by indexing entry content and context as well as key words in the title of the entry.

Any such system is obviously limited by the compilers' knowledge and information about each entry. However, the index employed here provides a much more comprehensive guide to the contents of the bibliography than a simple title key-word index. The accuracy and the completeness of the indexing process were aided considerably by the fact that whenever possible, brief notes on entry content were taken during the collection process. This information, along with the general familiarity of the compilers with the subject matter, was invaluable in the indexing process.

The compilers wish, however, to caution the user about reliance on the indexing system. While the index provides a good general guide to political campaign communication entries contained herein, it is by no means exhaustive.

Notes

1. Lynda Lee Kaid, Keith R. Sanders, and Robert O. Hirsch. Political Campaign Communication: A Bibliography and Guide to the Literature. Metuchen, NJ: Scarecrow Press, 1974.

2. Dan Nimmo and Keith R. Sanders, Eds. The Handbook of Political Communication. Beverly Hills, CA: Sage Publications, 1981.

3. Nimmo and Sanders.

4. B. Goehlert. Political Behavior: A Bibliography. Monticello, IL: Vance Bibliography, 1981.

5. F. W. Goudy. "American Political Behavior and the Election Process: A Bibliographic Essay," American Library Association, 19 (1980), 237-244.

6. William Miles. The Image Makers: A Bibliography of American Presidential Campaign Biographers. Metuchen, NJ: Scarecrow Press, 1979.

7. Lynda Lee Kaid. "Non-Print Materials in Presidential Libraries," Political Communication Review, 1 (1975), 8-9; H. Eugene Dybvig. "Some Non-Print Resources on Political Campaign Communication," Political Communication Review, 1 (1975), 6-7.

8. Faye Schreibman. "TV News Coverage of Elections: A Guide to Archival Collections," Campaigns and Elections, 2 (1981), 27-29.

9. Linda L. Jenkins. "Political Communication: A Bibliography, 1973-1981" (Unpublished Master's thesis, Southern Illinois University, 1982).

10. Anne Marie Wadsworth. "Communication and the Electoral Process: A Selected Bibliography and Guide to the Liter-

ature, 1973 to 1982" (Unpublished Master's thesis, University of Oklahoma, 1983).

11. Kaid, Sanders, and Hirsch, p. 3.

BIBLIOGRAPHY

1. Abbey, Alan D. "Newspaper Columnist Coverage of the 1960 and 1976 'Great Debates'" (Master's thesis, University of Oregon, 1977), Journalism Abstracts, 15 (1977), 33.

2. Abel, Elie (ed.). What's News: The Media in American Society. New Brunswick, NJ: Transaction Books, 1981.

3. Abelson, R. P.; Kinder, D. R.; Peters, M. D.; and Fiske, S. T. "Affective and Semantic Components in Political Person Perceptions," Journal of Personality and Social Psychology, 42 (1982), 19-30.

4. Abrahamsen, D. Nixon vs. Nixon: An Emotional Tragedy. New York: Farrar, Straus & Giroux, 1977.

5. Abramowitz, Alan I. "Impact of a Presidential Debate on Voter Rationality," American Journal of Political Science, 22 (1978), 680-690.

6. _____. "Name Familiarity, Reputation, and the Incumbency Effect in a Congressional Election," Western Political Quarterly, 28 (1975), 668-684.

7. Abrams, B. A.; and Settle, R. F. "Broadcasting and the Political Campaign Spending Arms Race," Journal of Broadcasting, 21 (1977), 153-162.

8. _____; and _____. "Economic Theory of Regulations and Public Financing of Presidential Elections," Journal of Political Economy, 86 (1978), 245-257.

9. _____; and _____. "Effect of Broadcasting on Political Campaign Spending: An Empirical Investigation," Journal of Political Economy, 84 (1976), 1095-1107.

10. Abramson, Paul R. "Developing Party Identification: A Further Examination of Life-Cycle, Generational and Period Effects," American Journal of Political Science, 23 (1979), 78-96.

11. _____. Political Socialization of Black Americans: A Critical Evaluation of Research on Efficacy and Trust. New York: Free Press, 1977.

12 _____; and Aldrich, John H. Change and Continuity in the 1980 Elections. Washington, D. C.: Congressional Quarterly Press, 1982.

13 Abravanale, M. D.; and Buoch, R. J. "Political Competence, Political Trust and the Action Orientations of University Students," Journal of Politics, 37 (1975), 57-82.

14 "Abstracts of Studies of the 1976 Presidential Debates," Political Communication Review, 3 (1978), 2-11.

15 Achen, C. H. "Mass Political Attitudes and the Survey Response," American Political Science Review, 69 (1975), 1218-1231.

16 Adam, G. Stuart (ed.). Journalism, Communication and the Law. Scarborough, Ontario: Prentice-Hall of Canada Ltd., 1976.

17 Adamany, David W. "Financing National Politics," The New Style in Election Campaigns (2nd ed.), ed. Robert Agranoff. Boston, MA: Holbrook Press, 1976.

18 _____. "Money, Politics, and Democracy: A Review Essay," American Political Science Review, 71 (1977), 289-304.

19 _____; and Agree, George E. Political Money: A Strategy for Campaign Financing in America (2nd ed.). Baltimore, MD: Johns Hopkins University Press, 1975.

20 _____; and Dubois, P. "The 'Forgetful' Voter and Underreported Vote," Public Opinion Quarterly, 34 (1975), 227-231.

21 Adams, Michael F. "A Critical Analysis of the Rhetorical Strategies of Senator Howard H. Baker, Jr., in His 1972 Campaign for Re-Election" (Ph.D. dissertation, The Ohio State University, 1973), Dissertation Abstracts International A 34 (1974), 5361.

22 Adams, R. C. "Newspapers and Television as News Information Media," Journalism Quarterly, 58 (1981), 627-629.

23 _____; et al. "The Effect of Framing on Selection of Photographs of Men and Women," Journalism Quarterly, 57 (1980), 463-467.

24 Adams, William C. "Candidate Characteristics, Office of Election, and Voter Responses," Experimental Study of Politics, 4 (1975), 76-91.

25 _____. "Local Public Affairs Content of TV News," Journalism Quarterly, 55 (1978), 690-695.

Bibliography

26 _____. "Local Television News Coverage and the Central City," Journal of Broadcasting, 24 (1980), 253-265.

27 _____. "Television as a Source of Local Political News" (Ph. D. dissertation, The George Washington University, 1977), Dissertation Abstracts International A, 38 (1978), 5679-5680.

28 _____ (ed.). Television Coverage of International Affairs. Norwood, NJ: Ablex Publishing Co., 1982.

29 _____; and Ferber, Paul H. "Television Interview Shows: The Politics of Visibility," Journal of Broadcasting, 21 (1977), 141-151.

30 _____; and Schreibman, F. (eds.). Television Network News: Issues in Content Research. Washington, D.C.: George Washington University Press, 1978.

31 _____; and Smith, Dennis J. "Effects of Telephone Canvassing on Turnout and Preferences: A Field Experiment," Public Opinion Quarterly, 44 (1980), 389-395.

32 Adoni, Hanna. "The Functions of Mass Media in the Political Socialization of Adolescents," Communication Research, 6 (1979), 84-106.

33 Agnir, F. "Testing New Approaches to Agenda-Setting: A Replication and Extension," Studies in Agenda-Setting, eds. Maxwell McCombs and G. Stone. Syracuse, NY: Newhouse Communication Research Center, 1976.

34 Agranoff, Robert. The Management of Election Campaigns. Boston, MA: Holbrook Press, 1976.

35 _____ (ed.). The New Style in Election Campaigns (2nd ed.). Boston, MA: Holbrook Press, 1976.

36 Alderson, George; and Sentman, Everett. How You Can Influence Congress: The Complete Handbook for the Citizen Lobbyist. New York: E. P. Dutton, 1979.

37 Aldous, E. R.; and Johnson, W. G. "Interpersonal Trust and Reactions to the Senate Watergate Committee," Personality and Social Psychology Bulletin, 1 (1974), 166-167.

38 Aldrich, John H. Before the Convention: Strategies and Choices in Presidential Nomination Campaigns. Chicago, IL: University of Chicago Press, 1980.

39 _____. "Dynamic Model of Presidential Nomination Campaigns," American Political Science Review, 74 (1980), 651-669.

40 _____; and Woy, Jean. Nineteen Eighty Elections. Washington, D.C.: Congressional Quarterly, 1982.

41 Aldrich, Pearl. The Impact of Mass Media. Montclair, NJ: Boynton Cook Publishers, 1975.

42 Alexander, Herbert E. Campaign Money: Reform and Reality in the States. New York, NY: Free Press, 1976.

43 _____. "Financing American Politics," Political Quarterly, 45 (1974), 439-448.

44 _____. "Financing Gubernatorial Election Campaigns," State Government, 53 (1980), 140-143.

45 _____. Financing Politics: Money, Elections, and Political Reform. Washington, D.C.: Congressional Quarterly Press, 1976.

46 _____. Financing the 1976 Election. Washington, D.C.: Congressional Quarterly Press, 1979.

47 _____ (ed.). Political Finance. Beverly Hills, CA: Sage Publications, 1979.

48 _____. "Rethinking Election Reform," The Annals of the American Academy of Political and Social Science, 427 (1976), 1-16.

49 _____; and Haggerty, Brian A. The Federal Election Campaign Act: After a Decade of Political Reform. Santa Barbara, CA: ABC-Clio, 1981.

50 _____; and Margolies, J. "The Making of the Debates," The Presidential Debates: Media, Electoral, and Policy Perspectives, eds. George F. Bishop, Robert G. Meadow, and Marilyn Jackson-Beeck. New York: Praeger Publishers, 1978.

51 _____; et al. Financing the 1972 Election. Lexington, MA: Lexington Books, 1976.

52 Alfred, Deanna D. "A Study of George McGovern's Rhetorical Strategy in Handling the Eagleton Affair" (Master's thesis, North Texas State University, 1976), Masters Abstracts, 14 (1976), 258-259.

53 Allen, C.T., and Weber, J.D. "How Presidential Media Use Affects Individuals' Beliefs about Conversation," Journalism Quarterly, 60 (1983), 98-104.

54 Allen, R.L.; and Chaffee, Steven H. "Mass Communication and the Political Participation of Black Americans," Communication

Bibliography 13

Yearbook 3, ed. Dan D. Nimmo. New Brunswick, NJ: Transaction Books, 1979, 407-522.

55 Alley, R.; and Gladhart, S. C. "Political Efficacy of Junior High Youth: Effects of a Mayoral Election Simulation," Simulation and Games, 6 (1975), 73-83.

56 Altenberg, L.; and Cathcart, R. "Jimmy Carter on Human Rights: A Thematic Analysis," Central States Speech Journal, 33 (1982), 446-457.

57 Altheide, David L. Creating Reality: How TV News Distorts Events. Beverly Hills, CA: Sage Publications, Inc., 1976.

58 _____. "Mental Illness and the News: The Eagleton Story" Sociology and Social Research, 61 (1977), 138-155.

59 _____. "Three-in-One News: Network Coverage of Iran," Journalism Quarterly, 59 (1982), 482-486.

60 _____; and Snow, Robert P. Media Logic. Beverly Hills, CA: Sage Publications, 1979.

61 Altschuler, Bruce E. Keeping A Finger on the Public Pulse. Westport, CT: Greenwood Press, 1982.

62 _____. "Political Polling and Presidential Elections" (Ph. D. dissertation, City University of New York, 1980), Dissertation Abstracts International A, 41 (1980), 1745.

63 Andersen, Peter A. "The Effect of Source Credibility, Attraction, and Homophily on Voter Preference" (Ph. D. dissertation, Florida State University, 1975), Dissertation Abstracts International A, 36 (1975), p. 3208.

64 _____; and Garrison, John P. "Media Consumption and Population Characteristics of Political Opinion Leaders," Communication Quarterly, 26 (1978), 40-50.

65 _____; and Kibler, Robert J. "Candidate Valence as a Predictor of Voter Preference," Human Communication Research, 5 (1978), 4-14.

66 _____; and Todd de Mancillas, William R. "Scales for the Measurement of Homophily with Public Figures," Southern Speech Communication Journal, 43 (1978), 169-179.

67 Anderson, Hayes L. "The Effects of Filming a Television News Source by Vertical Camera Angle, Horizontal Camera Angle, and Source Eye Contact on Source Credibility and Audience Attitude Toward the Televised Message" (Ph. D. dissertation, Michigan State University, 1973), Dissertation Abstracts International A, 34 (1973), 1305.

68 Anderson, James A.; and Avery, Robert K. "An Analysis of Changes in Voter Perceptions of Candidates' Positions," Communication Monographs, 45 (1978), 354-361.

69 Anderson, Judith. "Sexual Politics: Chauvinism and Backlash," Today's Speech, 21 (1973), 11-16.

70 Anderson, Robert O. "The Characterization Model for Rhetorical Criticism of Political Image Campaigns," Western Speech, 37 (1973), 75-86.

71 Anderson, V. F.; and Van Winkle, R. A. In the Arena. New York: Harper and Row, 1976.

72 Andreoli, Virginia; and Worchel, Stephen. "Effects of Media, Communicator, and Message Position on Attitude Change," Public Opinion Quarterly, 42 (1978), 59-70.

73 Andres, Gary J. "Corporate Involvement in Campaign Finance During the 1970s" (Ph.D. dissertation, University of Illinois at Chicago Circle, 1982), Dissertation Abstracts International A, 43 (1982), 2079.

74 Andrews, Kenneth H. "Political Beliefs and Political Experience: Efficacy, Trust, Participation, and Governmental Treatment" (Ph.D. dissertation, Columbia University, 1977), Dissertation Abstracts International A, 38 (1978), 6281.

75 Ankrom, Reginald R. "Coverage of Mayor Richard J. Daley During the 1968 Democratic National Convention by the Chicago Tribune and the Chicago Daily News" (Master's thesis, University of Kansas, 1973), Journalism Abstracts, 11 (1973), 69.

76 Apple, R. W. (ed.). The Watergate Hearings. New York: Viking Press, 1973.

77 Arcelus, F.; and Meltzer, A. H. "Effect of Aggregate Economic Variables on Congressional Elections," American Political Science Review, 69 (1975), 1232-1269.

78 Ardoin, Birthney. "A Content Analysis of Mississippi Daily Newpaper Coverage of the Waller-Evers Political Campaign," The Southern Quarterly, 11 (1973), 207-220.

79 Arnold, S. N. I Ran Against Jimmy Carter. New York: Manor Books, 1979.

80 Arnston, Paul H.; and Smith, Craig R. "News Distortion as a Function of Organizational Communication," Communication Monographs, 45 (1978), 371-381.

81 Arnoff, Myron J. (ed.) Culture and Political Change. New

Bibliography

Brunswick, NJ: Transaction Books, 1982.

82 Arrington, T. S. "Some Effects of Political Experience on Issue Consciousness and Issue Partisanship Among Tuscon Party Activists," American Journal of Political Science, 19 (1975), 695-702.

83 Arterton, F. Christopher. "Campaign Organizations Confront the Media-Political Environment," Race for the Presidency: The Media and the Nominating Process, ed. James D. Barber. Englewood Cliffs, NJ: Prentice-Hall, 1978.

84 _____. "The Impact of Watergate on Children's Attitudes Toward Political Authority," Political Science Quarterly, 89 (1974), 269-288.

85 _____. "The Media Politics of Presidential Campaigns," Race for the Presidency: The Media and the Nominating Process, ed. James D. Barber. Englewood Cliffs, NJ: Prentice-Hall, 1978.

86 _____. "Strategies and Tactics of Candidate Organizations," Political Science Quarterly, 92 (1977-78), 663-672.

87 _____. "Watergate and Children's Attitudes Toward Political Authority Revisited," Political Science Quarterly, 90 (1975), 477-496.

88 Ashenfelter, O.; and Kelley, S., Jr. "Determinants of Participation in Presidential Elections," Journal of Law and Economics, 18 (1975), 695-744.

89 Asher, Herbert. Presidential Elections and American Politics: Voters, Candidates, and Campaigns Since 1952. Homewood, IL: Dorsey Press, 1980.

90 Asher, Thomas R., and Hahn, J. Victor. Broadcast Media Guide for Candidates. Washington, D.C.: Media Access Projects, 1974.

91 Ashford, D. E. Ideology and Participation. Beverly Hills, CA: Sage Publications, Inc., 1973.

92 Ashworth, W. Under the Influence: Congress, Lobbies, and the American Pork-Barrel System. New York: Hawthorn and Dutton, 1981.

93 Atkin, Charles K. "Communication and Political Socialization," Handbook of Political Communication, eds. Dan D. Nimmo and Keith R. Sanders. Beverly Hills, CA: Sage Publications, 1981, 299-328.

94 _____. "Communication and Political Socialization," Political Communication Review, 1 (1975), 2-6.

95 _____. "Effects of Campaign Advertising and Newscasts on Children," Journalism Quarterly, 54 (1977), 503-508.

96 _____. "Instrumental Utilities and Information Seeking," New Models for Mass Communication Research, ed. Peter Clarke. Beverly Hills, CA: Sage Publications, 1980, 205-242.

97 _____. "Mass Media Effects on Voting: Recent Advances and Future Priorities," Political Communication Review, 6 (1981), 13-26.

98 _____. "Political Campaigns: Mass Communication and Persuasion," Persuasion: New Directions in Theory and Research, eds. Michael E. Roloff and Gerald Miller. Beverly Hills, CA: Sage Publications, 1980, 285-306.

99 _____. "Television Advertising and Consumer Role Socialization," Television and Behavior: Ten Years of Scientific Progress. Washington, D.C.: Government Printing Office, 1982.

100 _____; Bowen, Lawrence; Nayman, Oguz B.; and Sheinkopf, Kenneth C. "Quality Versus Quantity in Televised Political Ads," Public Opinion Quarterly, 37 (1973), 209-224.

101 _____; Galloway, John; and Nayman, Oguz B. "News Media Exposure, Political Knowledge and Campaign Interest," Journalism Quarterly, 53 (1976), 231-237.

102 _____; and Gantz, Walter. "Television News and Political Socialization," Public Opinion Quarterly, 42 (1978), 183-198.

103 _____; and Greenberg, B. "Public Television and Political Socialization," Congress and Mass Communication (appendix to hearings before the Joint Committee on Congressional Operations). Washington, D.C.: Government Printing Office, 1974.

104 _____; and Heald, Gary. "Effects of Political Advertising," Public Opinion Quarterly, 40 (1976), 216-228.

105 Atkins, C. G. Getting Elected: A Guide to Winning State and Local Office. Boston, MA: Houghton Mifflin, 1973.

106 Atwan, Robert, et al. American Mass Media (2nd ed.) New York: Random House, 1982.

107 Atwood, L. Erwin. "From Press Release to Voting Reasons: Tracing the Agenda in a Congressional Campaign," Communication Yearbook 4, ed. Dan D. Nimmo. New Brunswick, NJ: Transaction Books, 1981.

108 _____; and Sanders, Keith R. "Information Sources and Voting in Primary and General Election," Journal of Broadcasting, 20 (1976), 291-302.

109 _____; and _____. "Perceptions of Information Sources and Likelihood of Split Ticket Voting," Journalism Quarterly, 52 (1975), 421-428.

110 Auh, Taik S. "Issue Conflict and Mass Media Agenda-setting During the 1974 Indiana Senatorial Campaign" (Ph.D. dissertation, Indiana University, 1977), Dissertation Abstracts International A, 38 (1978), 5107-5108.

111 Ault, Wayne H. "Show Business and Politics: The Influence of Television, Entertainment Celebrities, and Motion Pictures on American Public Opinion and Political Behavior" (Ph.D. dissertation, Saint Louis University, 1981), Dissertation Abstracts International A, 43 (1982), 1665.

112 Baas, Larry R.; and Thomas, Dan B. "Dissonance and Perception during a Presidential Campaign: Pre-and Postelection Findings from the Ford-Carter Contest," Journal of Social Psychology, 112 (1980), 305-306.

113 _____; and _____. "The Impact of the Election and the Inauguration on Identification with the President," Presidential Studies Quarterly 10 (1980), 544-549.

114 Babad, Elisha Y. "Voting for Unknown Candidates: Distortions in Post Factum Explanations," Personality and Social Psychology Bulletin, 6 (1980), 460-466.

115 Bacus, Karen P. "The Rhetoric of the Press: Newspaper Treatment of Richard Nixon's Major Statements on Vietnam, 1969-1970" (Ph.D. dissertation, University of Kansas, 1974), Dissertation Abstracts International A, 36 (1975), 593-594.

116 Baer, Dennis L.; Bositis, David A.; and Miller, Roy E. "A Field Experimental Study of a Precinct Committeeman's Canvassing Efforts in a Primary Election: Cognitive Effects," Communication Yearbook 5, ed. Michael Burgoon. New Brunswick, NJ: Transaction Books, 1982, 651-666.

117 Baer, Michael A.; and Jaros, Dean. "Participation as Instrument and Expression: Some Evidence from the States," American Journal of Political Science, 18 (1974), 365-383.

118 Bagdikian, B. H. "Election Coverage '72: The Fruits of Agnewism," Columbia Journalism Review, 11 (1978), 9-30.

119 Bailey, G. "How Newsmakers Make the News: Covering the Political Campaign," Journal of Communication, 28 (1978), 80-83.

120 Bailey, K. D. "Political Learning and Development: Continuity and Change in Childhood Political Orientations, 1973-1975" (Ph. D. dissertation, University of Maryland, 1975), Dissertation Abstracts International A, 37 (1976), 1188.

121 Bainter, Wendell D. "Grass Roots Campaigning: A Case Study" (Master's thesis, California State University, Long Beach, 1976), Masters Abstracts, 15 (1977), 46.

122 Baker, Howard H., Jr. No Margin for Error: America in the Eighties. New York: Time Books, 1980.

123 Baker, Kendall L.; and Walter, B. Oliver. "The Press as a Source of Information about Activities of a State Legislature," Journalism Quarterly, 52 (1975), 735-740, 761.

124 Baker, Mary L. "A Socio-Political Behavior as a Function of Ideology and Moral Judgment" (Master's thesis, California State University, Fullerton, 1972) Masters Abstracts, 11 (1973), 76.

125 Ballenger, G.; and Hennessey, G. "Door to Door Canvassing Pays Off: An Experimental Study in a Nonpartisan Suburb," Experimental Study of Politics, 3 (1974), 1-14.

126 Ball-Rokeach, Sandra J.; and DeFleur, Melvin L. "A Dependency Model of Mass Media Effects," Communication Research, 3 (1976), 3-21.

127 Balof, Eugene H. "A Rhetoric of Political Ideology" (Ph. D. dissertation, University of Missouri-Columbia, 1975), Dissertation Abstracts International A, 36 (1976), 6363-6364.

128 Balutis, Alan P. "Congress, The President and the Press," Journalism Quarterly, 53 (1976), 509-515.

129 _____. "The Presidency and the Press: The Expanding Presidential Image," Presidential Studies Quarterly, 7 (1977), 244-251.

130 Balz, D. J. Interest Groups: Who They Are and How They Influence. Washington, D. C.: Government Research Corp., 1977.

131 Bantz, Charles R. "The Critic and the Computer: A Multiple Technique Analysis of the ABC Evening News," Communication Monographs, 46 (1979), 27-39.

132 Baran, S. J.; and Davis, D. K. "The Audience of Public Television: Did Watergate Make a Difference," Central States Speech Journal, 26 (1975), 93-98.

133 Barber, James D. "Characters in the Campaign: The Educa-

tional Challenge," Race for the Presidency, ed. James D. Barber. Englewood Cliffs, NJ: Prentice-Hall, 1978.

134 _____. "Characters in the Campaign: The Literacy Problem," Race for the Presidency, ed. James D. Barber. Englewood Cliffs, NJ: Prentice-Hall, 1978.

135 _____ (ed.). Choosing the President. Englewood Cliffs, NJ: Prentice-Hall, 1974.

136 _____. "Nixon Brush with Tyranny," Political Science Quarterly, 92 (1977-78), 581-605.

137 _____. The Presidential Character: Predicting Performance in the White House. Englewood Cliffs, NJ: Prentice-Hall, 1977.

138 _____. The Pulse of Politics: Electing Presidents in the Media Age. New York: W. W. Norton, 1980.

139 _____ (ed.). Race for the Presidency: The Media and the Nominating Process. Englewood Cliffs, NJ: Prentice-Hall, 1978.

140 _____. "Strategies for Understanding Politicians," American Journal of Political Science, 18 (1974), 103-137.

141 _____. "What Network News Should Be," Television Quarterly, 16 (1979), 47-56.

142 Barger, Harold M. "Images of Political Authority in Four Types of Black Newspapers," Journalism Quarterly, 50 (1973), 645-651.

143 Barkin, Steve M. "The Making of a Public: A Participant Observation Study of Audience Formation in a Gubernatorial Primary" (Ph.D. dissertation, The Ohio State University, 1979), Dissertation Abstracts International A, 40, (1979), 1733.

144 Barlett, Dorothy L., et al. "Selective Exposure to a Presidential Campaign Appeal," Public Opinion Quarterly, 38 (1974), 264-270.

145 Barnard, R. E. "Children's Images of Political Authority Figures as Potent and Benevolent" (Ph.D. dissertation, Cornell University, 1973), Dissertation Abstracts International A, 34 (1973), 81-82.

146 Barnett, George A. "A Multidimensional Analysis of the 1976 Presidential Campaign," Communication Quarterly, 29 (1981), 156-165.

147 _____; Serota, Kim B.; and Taylor, James A. "Campaign

Communication and Attitude Change: A Multidimensional Analysis," Human Communication Research, 2 (1976), 227-244.

148 Barnett, William L. "An Analysis of the Rhetorical Effectiveness of the 1972 Presidential Primary Election Campaign of Senator Edmund S. Muskie" (Ph.D. dissertation, University of Pittsburgh, 1976), Dissertation Abstracts International A, 38 (1977), 22-23.

149 Baron, A. "1979 Conventional Wisdom About the 1980 Conventions," Politics Today, (1979), 32-33.

150 _____; and Schneider, B. "Polls and Polling in Campaign '80," Washington Journalism Review, 2 (1980), 43-45.

151 Barrett, L. I. "Polls: How Do You Feel About How You Feel," Columbia Journalism Review, 15 (1977), 36-37.

152 Barrett, M. "Supplement: Broadcast Journalism Since Watergate," Columbia Journalism Review, 14 (1976), 73-83.

153 Barrett, Marvin (ed.). Broadcast Journalism 1979-1981, The Eighth Alfred I. du Pont/Columbia University Survey. New York: Everest House Publishers, 1982.

154 _____. Rich News, Poor News: The Sixth Alfred I. du Pont/Columbia University Survey of Broadcast Journalism. New York: Crowell, 1978.

155 Bartell, Ted; and Bouxsein, Sandra. "The Chelsea Project: Candidate Preference, and Turnout Effects of Student Canvassing," Public Opinion Quarterly, 37 (1973), 268-275.

156 Bartlett, F. C. Political Propaganda. New York: Farrar, Straus Publishing, 1973.

157 Barton, Allen H. "Consensus and Conflict Among American Leaders," Public Opinion Quarterly, 38 (1974-75), 507-530.

158 Baskin, Otis W. "The Effects of Televised Political Advertisements on Voters' Perceptions about Candidates" (Ph.D dissertation, University of Texas at Austin, 1975), Dissertation Abstracts International A, 36 (1976), 6355.

159 Bass, J. D.; and Cherwitz, R. "Imperial Mission and Manifest Destiny: A Case Study of Political Myth in Rhetorical Discourse," Southern Speech Communication Journal, 43 (1978), 213-232.

160 Baudhuin, Scott. "From Campaign to Watergate: Nixon's Communication Image," Western Speech, 38 (1974), 182-189.

Bibliography

161 Bauer, Robert; and Kafka, Doris. U.S. Federal Election Law. Dobbs Ferry, NY: Oceana Publications, 1982.

162 Baums, Roosevelt. A Minority View of How to Campaign for Political Office, eds. Nancy Augst and Michelle Mathews. Syracuse, NY: Rosey-Royce Publishing, Co., 1982.

163 Baxter, Sandra; and Lansing, Marjorie. Women and Politics: The Invisible Majority. Ann Arbor, MI: University of Michigan Press, 1980.

164 Bay, Deborah L. "The Influence of Television on Press Coverage of the Presidency" (Master's thesis, University of Texas, 1981), Journalism Abstracts, 19 (1981), 25.

165 Bayley, Edwin R. Joe McCarthy and the Press. Madison, WI: University of Wisconsin Press, 1981.

166 Beatty, J. Michael; and Kruger, Michael W. "The Effects of Heckling on Speaker Credibility and Attitude Change," Communication Quarterly, 26 (1978), 46-50.

167 Beatty, Vander L. "Political Candidates' Perceptions of Barriers to Elective Public Office" (Ph.D. dissertation, New York University, 1980), Dissertation Abstracts International A, 41 (1981), 5228.

168 Bechtolt, Warren E., Jr.; Ailyard, Joseph; and Bybee, Carl R. "Agenda Control in the 1976 Debates: A Content Analysis," Journalism Quarterly, 54 (1977), 674-681.

169 Beck, N.; and Pierce, J. C. "Political Involvement and Party Allegiances in Canada and the United States," International Journal of Comparative Sociology, 18 (1977), 23-43.

170 Beck, Paul A.; and Jennings, M. Kent; "Pathways to Participation," American Political Science Review, 76 (1982). 94-108.

171 Becker, Lee B. "The Impact of Issue Saliences," The Emergence of American Political Issues: The Agenda-Setting Function of the Press, eds. Donald L. Shaw and Maxwell E. McCombs. St. Paul, MN: West, 1977.

172 _____. "The Mass Media and Citizen Assessment of Issue Importance: A Reflection on Agenda-Setting Research," Mass Communication Yearbook 3, eds. D. Charles Whitney, Ellen Wartella, and Sven Windahl. Beverly Hills, CA: Sage Publications, 1982, 521-536.

173 _____. "Measurement of Gratifications," Communication Research, 6 (1979), 54-73.

174 _____. "Methodological Advances in Uses and Gratifications Research," Political Communication Review, 3 (1978), 18-20.

175 _____. "Two Tests of Media Gratifications: Watergate and the 1974 Election," Journalism Quarterly, 53 (1976), 28-33.

176 _____; Cobbey, Robin E.; and Sobowale, Idowa A. "Public Support for the President," Journalism Quarterly, 55 (1978), 421-430.

177 _____; and Doolittle, John C. "How Repetition Affects Evaluations of and Information Seeking About Candidates," Journalism Quarterly, 52 (1975), 611-617.

178 _____; and Dunwoody, S. "Media Use, Public Affairs Knowledge, and Voting in a Local Election," Journalism Quarterly, 59 (1982), 212-218.

179 _____; and McCombs, Maxwell, E. "The Role of the Press in Determining Voter Reactions to Presidential Primaries," Human Communication Research, 4 (1978), pp. 301-307.

180 _____; _____; and McLeod, Jack M. "The Development of Political Cognitions," Political Communication: Strategies and Issues in Research, ed. Steven H. Chaffee. Beverly Hills, CA: Sage Publications, 1975.

181 _____; and McLeod, Jack M. "Political Consequences of Agenda-Setting," Mass Comm Review, 3 (1976), 8-15.

182 _____; Sobowale, Idowa A.; and Casey, William E., Jr. "Newspaper and Television Dependencies: Effects on Evaluations of Public Officials," Journal of Broadcasting, 23 (1979), 465-475.

183 _____; _____; Cobbey, R.; and Eyal, C. "Debates' Effects on Voters' Understanding of Candidates and Issues," The Presidential Debates, eds. George Bishop, Robert Meadow, and Marilyn Jackson-Beeck. New York: Praeger, 1978.

184 _____; Weaver, David; Graber, Doris A.; and McCombs, Maxwell. "Influence of the Debates on Public Agenda," The Great Debates: Carter vs. Ford, 1976, ed. Sidney Kraus. Indianapolis, IN: University of Indiana Press, 1978.

185 _____; and Whitney, D. Charles. "Effects of Media Dependencies--Audience Assessment of Government," Communication Research, 7 (1980), 95-120.

186 Becker, Samuel L.; and Kraus, Sidney. "The Study of Campaign '76: An Overview," Communication Monographs, 45 (1978), 265-267.

Bibliography

187 Bedner, Mark A. "A Case Study of Spiro Agnew's Relations with the National News Media" (Master's thesis, University of Kansas, 1975), Journalism Abstracts, 13 (1975), 50.

188 Beldon, Thomas M. "Presidential Press Conferences as Richard Nixon Used Them" (Master's thesis, University of Wisconsin-Madison, 1974), Journalism Abstracts, 13 (1975), 50.

189 Bell, D. Power, Influence and Authority. New York: Oxford University Press, 1975.

190 Bell, Leslie. "Constraints on the Electoral Success of Minor Political Parties in the United States," Political Studies, 25 (1977), 103-109.

191 Bell, Lillian S. "The Role and Performance of Black and Metro Newspapers in Relation to Political Campaigns in Selected Racially Mixed Congressional Elections: 1960-1970" (Ph.D. dissertation, Northwestern University, 1973), Journalism Abstracts, 11 (1973), 4-5.

192 Belmont, Perry. Return to Secret Party Funds. New York: Arno Press, 1974.

193 Bender, John R. "A Conservative View of the Kennedy-Nixon Campaign: National Review's Coverage of the 1960 Presidential Election" (Master's thesis, University of Kansas, 1977), Journalism Abstracts, 15 (1977), 39.

194 Beniger, James R. "Winning the Presidential Nomination: National Polls and State Primary Elections, 1936-1972," Public Opinion Quarterly, 40 (1976), 22-38.

195 Bennett, George, C. "The Heckler and the Heckled in the Presidential Campaign of 1968," Communication Quarterly, 27 (1979), 28-37.

196 Bennett, Michael J. "The 'Imperial' Press Corps," Public Relations Journal, 38 (1982), 10-13.

197 Bennett, W. Lance. "Assessing Presidential Character: Degradation Rituals in Political Campaigns," Quarterly Journal of Speech, 67 (1981), 310-321.

198 _____. "Imitation, Ambiguity, and Drama in Political Life: Civil Religion and the Dilemmas of Public Morality," Journal of Politics, 41 (1979), 106-133.

199 _____. "Myth, Ritual, and Political Control," Journal of Communication, 30 (1980), 166-179.

200 _____. The Political Mind and the Political Environment:

An Investigation of Public Opinion and Political Consciousness. Lexington, MA: D. C. Health & Co., 1975.

201 _____. "Political Scenarios and the Nature of Politics," Philosophy of Rhetoric, 8 (1975), 23-42.

202 _____. Public Opinion in American Politics. New York: Harcourt Brace Jovanovich, 1980.

203 _____. "The Ritualistic and Pragmatic Bases of Political Campaign Discourse," Quarterly Journal of Speech, 63 (1977), 219-238.

204 _____. "When Politics Becomes Play," Political Behavior, 1 (1979), 331-359.

205 Benoit, William L. "Richard Nixon's Rhetorical Strategies in his Public Statements on Watergate," Southern Speech Communication Journal, 47 (1982), 192-211.

206 Benson, T. W. "Another Shooting in Cowtown," Quarterly Journal of Speech, 67 (1981), 347-406.

207 Bentley, Catherine. "The Social Psychology of the Political Market Place: An Empirical Investigation of the Relationship between Candidate-Voter Interpersonal Similarity/ Dissimilarity, Candidate Attention-Getting Ability and Voter Preference" (Ph. D. dissertation, University of Texas at Austin, 1977), Dissertation Abstracts International A, 38 (1978), 7525.

208 Benton, M.; and Frazier, P. J. "The Agenda-Setting Function of Mass Media at Three Levels of 'Information Holding'," Communication Research, 3 (1976), 261-274.

209 Berger, Arthur A. Media Analysis Techniques. Beverly Hills CA: Sage Publications, 1982.

210 Berman, David R.; and Stookey, John A. "Adolescents, Television, and Support for Government," Public Opinion Quarterly, 44 (1980), 330-340.

211 Bernick, E. Lee. "Gubernatorial Tools: Formal vs. Informal," Journal of Politics, 41 (1979), 656-664.

212 Berns, L. "Rational Animal-Political Animal: Nature and Convention in Human Speech and Politics," Review of Politics, 38 (1976), 177-189.

213 Bernstein, Richard J. The Restructuring of Social Political Theory. New York: Harcourt Brace Jovanovich, Inc., 1976.

214 Berquist, Goodwin F.; and Golden, James L. "Media Rhetoric, Criticism, and the Public Perception of the 1980 Presidential Debates," Quarterly Journal of Speech, 67 (1981), 125-137.

215 Berry, Jeffrey M. Lobbying for the People: The Political Behavior of Public Interest Groups. Princeton, NJ: Princeton University Press, 1977.

216 Berthold, Carol A. "The Image and Character of President John F. Kennedy: Rhetorical-Critical Approach" (Ph.D. dissertation, Northwestern University, 1975), Dissertation Abstracts International A, 36 (1976), 7727-7728.

217 Besen, Stanley M.; and Mitchell, Bridger M. "Watergate and Television: An Economic Analysis," Communication Research, 3 (1976), 243-260.

218 _____; and _____. Watergate and Television: An Economic Analysis. Santa Monica, CA: Rand, 1975.

219 Best, J. Case Against Direct Election of the President: A Defense of the Electoral College. Ithaca, NY: Cornell University Press, 1975.

220 Best, J. J. Public Opinion: Micro and Macro. Homewood, IL: Dorsey, 1973.

221 Beth, Richard S. "Analysis of Political Interaction Through Communication Theory" (Ph.D. dissertation, Yale University, 1976), Dissertation Abstracts International A, 38 (1977), 451.

222 Bicker, W. E. "Network Television News and the 1976 Presidential Primaries," Race for the Presidency, ed. James D. Barber. Englewood Cliffs, NJ: Prentice-Hall, 1978.

223 Bingham, R. D. "Nominating Process in Nonpartisan Elections: Petition Signing as an Act of Support," Journal of Politics, 40 (1973), 1044-1053.

224 Birch, A. L., and Schmidt, A. A. "Public Opinion Surveys as Guides to Public Policy and Spending," Social Indicators Research, 7 (1980), 299-311.

225 Bird, A. T. "Women in Politics: Changing Perceptions," Journal of the Association for the Study of Perception, 10 (1975), 1-9.

226 Bishop, George F. "Resolution and Tolerance of Cognitive Inconsistency in a Field Situation: Change in Attitudes and Beliefs Following the Watergate Affair," Psychological Reports, 36 (1975), 747-753.

227 _____. "Survey Research," Handbook of Political Communication, ed. Dan D. Nimmo and Keith R. Sanders. Beverly Hills, CA: Sage Publications, 1981, 591-626.

228 _____; Meadow, Robert G.; and Jackson-Beeck, Marilyn. The Presidential Debates: Media, Electoral, and Policy Perspectives. New York: Praeger, 1978.

229 _____; Oldendick, Robert W.; and Tuchfarber, Alfred J. "Debate Watching and the Acquisition of Political Knowledge," Journal of Communication, 28 (1978), 99-113.

230 _____; _____; and _____. "Effects of Question Wording and Format on Political Attitude Consistency," Public Opinion Quarterly, 42 (1978), 81-92.

231 _____; _____; and _____. "Experiments in Filtering Political Opinions," Political Behavior, 2 (1980), 339-369.

232 _____; _____; and _____. "The Presidential Debates as a Device for Increasing the 'Rationality' of Electoral Behavior," The Presidential Debates, eds. George Bishop, Robert Meadow, and Marilyn Jackson-Beeck. New York: Praeger, 1978.

233 _____; _____; and _____. "Change in the Structure of American Political Attitudes: The Nagging Question of Question Wording," American Journal of Political Science, 22 (1978), 250-269.

234 _____; _____; _____; and Bennett, S. "Pseudo-opinions on Public Affairs," Public Opinion Quarterly, 44 (1980), 198-209.

235 Bittner, John R. "Politics and Information Flow: The Oregon Shield Law," Western Speech, 39 (1975), 51-59.

236 Bitzer, Lloyd. "Political Rhetoric," Handbook of Political Communication, eds. Dan D. Nimmo and Keith R. Sanders. Beverly Hills, CA: Sage Publications, 1981, 225-248.

237 _____; and Reuter, Theodore. Carter vs. Ford: The Counterfeit Debates of 1976. Madison, WI: University of Wisconsin Press, 1980.

238 Black, Edwin R. "Electing Time," Quarterly Journal of Speech, 59 (1973), 125-129.

239 _____. Politics and the News: The Political Functions of the Mass Media. Toronto: Butterworths, 1982.

240 Black, J. "Opinion Leaders: Is Anyone Following?" Public Opinion Quarterly, 46 (1982), 169-176.

Bibliography

241 Blake, Joan S. "An Analysis of Criticism of Political Public Relations Propaganda in Presidential Campaigns: 1952 and 1972" (Master's thesis, California State University, Fullerton, 1978).

242 Blanchard, Robert O. (ed). Congress and the News Media. New York: Hastings House, 1974.

243 _____. "Congress and the Press: An Historical Sketch," Journal of Communication, 24 (1974), 78-81.

244 _____; and Wolfson, L. "Courses on the Media, Government, and Public Policy," News for Teachers of Political Science, 25 (1980), 14-15.

245 Blankenburg, William B. "Nixon vs. the Networks: Madison Avenue and Wall Street," Journal of Broadcasting, 21 (1977), 163-175.

246 Blankenship, Albert B. Consumer and Opinion Research. eds. Henry Assael. New York: Arno Press, 1978.

247 Blechman, Robert K. "Myth as Advertising: An Analysis of Prime-Time American Television Advertising Using a Structural Methodology Based on the Theories of Claude Levi-Strauss" (Ph.D. dissertation, New York University, 1978).

248 Bloch, M. Political Language and Oratory in Traditional Society. New York: Academic Press, 1975.

249 Blomquist, David. Setups: Elections and the Mass Media. Washington, D.C.: American Political Science Association, 1982.

250 Bloom, Melvyn. Public Relations and Presidential Campaigns: A Crisis in Democracy. New York: Thomas Y. Crowell, 1973.

251 Blumenthal, Sidney. "The Candidate Makers," Politics Today, (March 1980), 27-31.

252 _____. The Permanent Campaign: Inside the World of Elite Political Operatives. Boston, MA: Beacon Press, Inc., 1980.

253 Blumler, Jay G. "The Media and the Election," New Society, 7 (1974), 570-572.

254 _____. "Political Communication: Democratic Theory and Broadcast Practice," Mass Communication Yearbook, 3, eds. D. Charles Whitney, Ellen Wartella, and Sven Windahl. Beverly Hills, CA: Sage Publications, 1982, 621-636.

255 _____. "The Role of Theory in Uses and Gratifications Studies," Communication Research, 6 (1979), 9-36.

256 _____; and Gurevitch, Michael. "Politicians and the Press: An Essay on Role Relationships," Handbook of Political Communication, eds. Dan Nimmo and Keith R. Sanders. Beverly Hills, CA: Sage Publications, 1981, 467-493.

257 _____; and _____. "The Reform of Election Broadcasting: A Reply to Nicholas Garnham," Media, Culture and Society, 1 (1979), 211-219.

258 _____; and _____. "Toward a Comparative Framework for Political Communication Research," Political Communication, ed. Steven H. Chaffee. Beverly Hills, CA: Sage Publications, 1975.

259 _____; and _____; and Ives, J. The Challenge of Election Broadcasting. Leeds: Leeds University Press, 1978.

260 _____; and Katz, Elihu (eds.). The Uses of Mass Communications: Current Perspectives on Gratifications Research. Beverly Hills/London: Sage Publications, 1974.

261 _____; _____; and Gurevitch, Michael. "Utilization of Mass Communication by the Individual," The Uses of Mass Communications, eds. Jay G. Blumler and Elihu Katz. Beverly Hills, CA: Sage Publications, 1974.

262 Blydenburgh, John C. "An Application of Game Theory to Political Campaign Decision-Making," American Journal of Political Science, 20 (1976), 51-65.

263 _____. "The Effect of Ballot Form on City Council Elections," Political Science, 26 (1974), 47-55.

264 Bobrow, D. B. "Mass Communication and Political System," Public Opinion Quarterly, 37 (1973-74), 551-568.

265 Bogart, Leo. Premises for Propaganda. New York: Free Press, 1976.

266 Bohn, Thomas W. "Broadcasting National Election Returns, 1952-1976," Journal of Communication, 30 (1980), 140-153.

267 Boland, J. E., et al. Deciding How to Act in a Political Society. Evanston, IL: McDougal, Littell & Co., 1975.

268 Bollens, John C.; and Geyer, Grant B. Yorty: Politics of a Constant Candidate. Pacific Palisades, CA: Palisades Publishers, 1973.

269 Bonafede, Dom. "The New Political Power of the Press," Washington Journalism Review, 2 (1980), 25-27.

270 _____. "The Press and the Hollywood Presidency," Washington Journalism Review, 3 (1981), 27-31.

271 Bone, H. A.; and Ranney, A. Politics and Voters. New York: McGraw-Hill, 1981.

272 Boneparth, Ellen. "Women in Campaigns: From Lickin' and Stickin' to Strategy," American Politics Quarterly, 5 (1977), 289-300.

273 Boor, Myron. "Effect of Candidate's Psychotherapy Treatment on the Choices of Simulated Voters," Journal of Social Psychology, 110 (1980), 299-300.

274 _____. "Effect of Vindicated Criminal Charges on the Choices of Simulated Voters," Journal of Social Psychology, 106 (1978), 289-290.

275 Bordwich, F. M. "Press Harmonizes on a Presidential Theme," Columbia Journalism Review, 16 (1977), 36-37.

276 Bormann, Ernest G. "The Eagleton Affair: A Fantasy Theme Analysis," Quarterly Journal of Speech, 57 (1973), 143-159.

277 _____. "A Fantasy Theme Analysis of the Television Coverage of the Hostage Release and the Reagan Inaugural," Quarterly Journal of Speech, 68 (1982), 133-145.

278 _____; Koester, John; and Bennett, Janet. "Political Cartoons and Salient Rhetorical Fantasies: An Empirical Analysis of the '76 Presidential Campaign," Communication Monographs, 45 (1978), 317-329.

279 Bortz, Jurgen; and Braune, Paul. "The Effects of Daily Newspapers on their Readers: Exemplary Presentation of a Study and Its Results," European Journal of Social Psychology, 10 (1980), 165-193.

280 Bositis, David A. "Turnout, Information, Preference and Precinct-Level Canvassing: What Effects" (Ph.D. dissertation, Southern Illinois University at Carbondale, 1982), Dissertation Abstracts International A, 43 (1982), 1666.

281 _____; and Miller, Roy E. "The Successful Communication of Cognitive Information: A Study of a Precinct Committeeman," Communication Yearbook 6, ed. Michael Burgoon. Beverly Hills, CA: Sage Publications, 1982.

282 Boss, G. P. "Essential Attributes of the Concept of Charisma,"

Southern Speech Communication Journal, 41 (1976), 300-313.

283 Botein, N. "Ventilation of the President, 1972: Political Broadcasting Under the Campaign Communications Reform Act," Tennessee Law Review, 40 (1973), 361.

284 Bower, Robert T. Television and the Public. New York: Holt, Rinehart & Winston, 1973.

285 Bowers, Thomas A. "Candidate Advertising: The Agenda is the Message," The Emergence of American Political Issues, eds. Donald L. Shaw and Maxwell E. McCombs. St. Paul, MN: West Publishing, 1977.

286 _____. "The Coverage of Political Advertising by the Prestige Press in 1972," Mass Comm Review, 2 (1975), 19-24.

287 _____. "Issue and Personality Information in Newspaper Political Advertising," Journalism Quarterly, 49 (1973), 446-452.

288 _____. "Newspaper Political Advertising and the Agenda Setting Function," Journalism Quarterly, 50 (1973), 552-555.

289 Bowes, J. E. "Stereotyping and Communication Accuracy," Journalism Quarterly, 54 (1977), 70-76.

290 _____; and Strentz, H. "Candidate Images: Stereotyping and the 1976 Debates," Communication Yearbook 2, ed. Brent D. Ruben. New Brunswick, NJ: Transaction Books, 1978, 391-406.

291 Bowman, L.; and Boynton, G. R. Political Behavior and Public Opinion: Comparative Analysis. Englewood Cliffs, NJ: Prentice-Hall, 1974.

292 Boyarsky, B., and Boyarsky, N. Backroom Politics: How Your Local Politicians Work, Why Your Government Doesn't, And What You Can Do About It. New York: Hawthorn Books, 1974.

293 Boyd, Forrest. Instant Analysis: Confessions of a White House Correspondent. Atlanta, GA: John Knox Press, 1974.

294 Boyd, John M. "An Experimental Analysis of Source Credibility and Message Discrepancy Under Differential Levels of Ego-Involvement in Political Television Commercials" (Ph.D. Dissertation, University of Southern California, 1978), Dissertation Abstracts International A, 38 (1978), 5774.

Bibliography

295 Boyd, Stephen D. "The Campaign Speaking of Frank Clement in the 1954 Democratic Primary: Field Study of Rhetorical Analysis" (Ph. D. dissertation, University of Illinois at Urbana-Champaign, 1972), Dissertation Abstracts International A, 33 (1973), 5863-5864.

296 ———. "Delivery in the Campaign Speaking of Frank Clement," Southern Speech Communication Journal, 39 (1974), 279-290.

297 Braden, W. W. "How TV Has Made the Public Speaker Obsolete," Vital Speeches, 40 (1974), 500-503.

298 Bradley, Bert E. "Jefferson and Reagan: The Rhetoric of Two Inaugurals," Southern Speech Communication Journal, 48 (1982), 119-136.

299 Braithwaite, John E., Jr. "A Content Analysis of the 1979 Louisiana Governor's Race as Covered by Community Newspapers" (Master's thesis, Louisiana State University, 1981), Journalism Abstracts, 19 (1981), 29.

300 Brams, Steven J. The Presidential Election Game. New Haven, CT: Yale University Press, 1978.

301 ———; and Davis, Morton D. "The 3/2's Rule in Presidential Campaigning," American Political Science Review, 68 (1974), 113-134.

302 Brandt, W. People and Politics: The Years 1960-1973. Boston, MA: Little, Brown and Co., Inc., 1978.

303 Branscomb, A. W.; and Savage, M. "The Broadcast Reform Movement: At the Crossroads," Journal of Communication, 28 (1978), 25-34.

304 Brant, William D.; Batres, Alfonso; and Hays, Ron. "Authoritarian Traits as Predictors of Preference for Candidates in 1980 United States Presidential Election," Psychological Reports, 47 (1980), 416-418.

305 ———; Larsen, Knud S.; and Langenberg, Don. "Authoritarian Traits as Predictors of Candidate Preference in 1976 United States Presidential Election," Psychological Reports, (1978), 313-314.

306 Brantley, D. "The Charismatic Political Leader: A Study in Political Authority and Leadership" (Ph. D. Dissertation, Howard University, 1979), Dissertation Abstracts International A, 40 (1980), 6040.

307 Brauen, M.; and Harmon, K. N. "Political Socialization: A Topical Bibliography," Youth and Society, 8 (1977), 299-320.

308 Braungart, Richard G.; and Braungart, Margaret M. "Family, School, and Personal Political Factors in Student Politics: A Case Study of the 1972 Presidential Election," *Journal of Marriage and the Family*, 37 (1975), 823-839.

309 Brayman, H. *The President Speaks Off the Record.* Princeton, NJ: Dow Jones Books, 1976.

310 Breckenridge, Adam C. *Electing the President.* Washington, D.C.: University Press of America, 1982.

311 Bremmer, Dorothy M. "Polarization in Three of Spiro T. Agnew's Speeches" (Master's thesis, California State University, Long Beach, 1974), *Masters Abstracts*, 12 (1974), 168-169.

312 Brennan, T. "Television and Politics," *Political Quarterly*, 49 (1978), 94-99.

313 Brent, Edward; and Granberg, Donald. "Subjective Agreement With the Presidential Candidates of 1976 and 1980," *Journal of Personality and Social Psychology*, 42 (1982), 393-403.

314 Brewer, G. D. *Politicians, Bureaucrats, and the Consultant.* New York: Basic Books, 1974.

315 Brigham, John C.; and Severy, Lawrence J. "Personality and Attitude Determinants of Voting Behavior," *Social Behavior and Personality*, 4 (1976), 127-139.

316 Broder, David S. *Changing of the Guard: Power and Leadership in America.* New York: Simon and Schuster, 1980.

317 _____; and Harwood, R. *The Pursuit of the Presidency 1980 and the Staff of the Washington Post.* New York: Berkley Publishing, 1980.

318 Brody, Richard A., and Page, Benjamin I. "The Impact of Events on Presidential Popularity: The Johnson and Nixon Administrations," *Perspectives on the Presidency*, ed. A. Wildavsky. Boston, MA: Little, Brown, 1975.

319 _____; and _____. "Indifference, Alienation and Rational Decisions: The Effects of Candidate Evaluations on Turnout and the Vote," *Public Choice*, 15 (1973), 1-17.

320 Broh, C. A. "Horserace Journalism: Reporting the Polls in the 1976 Presidential Election," *Public Opinion Quarterly*, 44 (1980), 514-529.

321 _____. "Issue Attitudes, Conceptualization and Perception: Toward a Theory of Issue Voting" (Ph.D. dissertation,

Bibliography

University of Wisconsin, 1972), Dissertation Abstracts International A, 33 (1973), 6977-6978.

322 _____. "Whether Bellwethers or Weather-Jars Indicate Election Outcomes," Western Political Quarterly, 33 (1980), 564-570.

323 Brooks, Charles (ed.). Best Editorial Cartoons of the Year: 1982 Edition. Gretna, LA: Pelican Publishing Co., 1982.

324 Brooks, R. S. "Differentiation of Adults on the Basis of Political Self Stages" (Ph.D. dissertation, University of Missouri-Columbia, 1974), Dissertation Abstracts International A, 36 (1975), 1767-1768.

325 _____. "Political Broadcasting After Ruling: Legislative Reform of Section 315(a) of the Communications Act of 1934," University of Michigan Journal of Law Reform, 13 (1979), 53-65.

326 Brown, C. W., Jr., et al. "Modes of Elite Political Participation: Contributors to the 1972 Presidential Candidates," American Journal of Political Science, 24 (1980), 259-290.

327 Brown, Charlene, et al. The Media and the People. Melbourne, FL: Robert E. Krieger Publishing Co., 1978.

328 Brown, J.; and Seib, P. M. The Art of Politics. Washington, D.C.: Alfred Publishing Co., 1976.

329 Brown, J. M. "An Experiment on the Role of Instructional Television as an Agent of Political Socialization," (Ph.D. dissertation, Columbia University, 1976), Dissertation Abstracts International A, 37 (1977), 6717-6718.

330 Brown, James; and Hain, Paul L. "Reporting the Vote on Election Night," Journal of Communication, 28 (1978), 132-138.

331 Brown, Janellen H. "An Investigation of the Effects of News and Public Affairs Media Consumption on Individuals' Issue Accuracy and Political Discussion" (Ph.D. dissertation, University of Oregon, 1978), Dissertation Abstracts International A, 39 (1979), 5783.

332 Brown, Stephen P. "Competition, Activism and the Vote: An Empirical Assessment of the Effectiveness of Local Party Campaign Activity" (Ph.D. dissertation, University of Rochester, 1976), Dissertation Abstracts International A, 38 (1977), 991-992.

333 Brown, Steven R. "The Importance of Factors in Q-Methodology: Statistical and Theoretical Considerations," Operant

Subjectivity, 1 (1978), 117-124.

334 _____. "Intensive Analysis of Political Communication," Handbook of Political Communication, eds. Dan D. Nimmo and Keith R. Sanders. Beverly Hills, CA: Sage Publications, 1981, 627-649.

335 _____. "Intensive Analysis in Political Research," Political Methodology, 1 (1974), 1-25.

336 _____. "Perspective, Transfiguration, and Equivalence in Communication Theory: Review and Commentary," Communication Yearbook 3, ed. Dan D. Nimmo. New Brunswick, NJ: Transaction Books, 1979.

337 _____. "Political Literature and the Response of the Reader: Experimental Studies of Interpretation, Imagery and Criticism," American Political Science Review, 71 (1977), 567-584.

338 _____. Political Subjectivity: Applications of Q-Methodology in Political Science. New Haven, CT: Yale University Press, 1980.

339 _____. "Three's a Crowd: Jimmy Carter, Ronald Reagan, and the Invisibility of John Anderson," Operant Subjectivity, 4 (1981), 54-60.

340 Brownstein, Charles N. "The Effect of Media, Message, and Interpersonal Influence on the Perception of Political Figures" (Ph.D. dissertation, Florida State University, 1971), Dissertation Abstracts International A, 34 (1974), 6059.

341 Bruce, A.; and Lee, G. "Local Election Campaigns," Political Studies, 30 (1982), 247-261.

342 Brucker, H. Communication is Power: Unchanging Values in a Changing Journalism. New York: Oxford University Press, 1973.

343 Brummett, Barry. "Burkean Scapegoating, Mortification, and Transcendence in Presidential Campaign Rhetoric," Central States Speech Journal, 32 (1981), 254-264.

344 _____. "Gastronomic Reference, Synecdoche, and Political Images," Quarterly Journal of Speech, 67 (1981), 138-145.

345 _____. "Towards a Theory of Silence as a Political Strategy," Quarterly Journal of Speech, 66 (1980), 289-303.

346 Brunk, Gregory G.; and Fishkin, James Andrew. "Media

Bibliography

Coverage of Presidential Candidates: A Study of Popularity Prior to the 1976 National Nominating Conventions," Communication Research, 9 (1982), 525-538.

347 Brydon, Steven R. "The Carter-Ford Television Debates: A Study of Campaign Communication" (Ph. D. dissertation, University of Southern California, 1979), Dissertation Abstracts International A, 40 (1980), 3624-3625.

348 Bryski, B. G. "An Analysis of Evidence in the First Ford/Carter Debate," Journal of Applied Communication Research, 6 (1978), 19-30.

349 Buchanan, Bruce. The Presidential Experience: What the Office Does to the Man. Englewood Cliffs, NJ: Prentice-Hall, Inc., 1978.

350 Buchanan, C. "Reagan Melds Acting Ability with his Prowess in Politics; Accomplished Television User (Campaign Planning and Techniques)," Congressional Quarterly Weekly Reports, 38 (1980), 2759-2765.

351 Buckley, James L. If Men Were Angels . . . A View From the Senate. New York, NY: G. P. Putnam's Sons, 1976.

352 Bull, R.; and Hawkes, C. "Judging Politicians by Their Faces," Political Studies, 30 (1982), 95-101.

353 Bullitt, Stimson. To Be a Politician. New Haven, CT: Yale University Press, 1977.

354 Bullock, Charles S., III. "Explaining Congressional Elections; Differences in Perceptions of Opposing Candidates," Legislative Studies Quarterly, 2 (1977), 295-308.

355 Bundy, M.; and Muskie, E. S. Presidential Promises and Performance. New York: Macmillan, 1981.

356 Burdick, Eugene; and Brodbeck, Arthur J. (eds.). American Voting Behavior. Westport CT: Greenwood Press, 1977.

357 Burgoon, Michael; and Burgoon, J. K. "Predictive Models of Satisfaction with the Newspaper," Communication Yearbook 3, ed. Dan D. Nimmo. New Brunswick, NJ: Transaction Books, 1979.

358 Burkholder, Donald R. "The Caretakers of the Presidential Image" (Ph. D. dissertation, Wayne State University, 1973), Dissertation Abstracts International A, 34 (1974), 7289.

359 Burnet, A. "Election Day on Television," Royal Sociology of Arts Journal, 127 (1979), 349-359.

360 Burnham, Walter D. The Current Crisis in American Politics. New York: Oxford University Press, 1982.

361 Burns, James MacGregor. Edward Kennedy and the Camelot Legacy. New York: W. W. Norton, 1976.

362 _____. Leadership. New York: Harper & Row, 1978.

363 Burstein, Paul. "Social Networks and Voting," Social Forces, 54 (1976), 833-847.

364 Buss, Terry F.; and Hofstetter, C. Richard. "An Analysis of the Logic of Televised Campaign Advertisements: The 1972 Presidential Campaign," Communication Research, 3 (1976), 367-392.

365 _____; and _____. "The Logic of Televised News Coverage of Political Campaign Information," Journalism Quarterly, 54 (1977), 341-349.

366 _____; and Malaney, G. D. "How Broadcasters Feel About the Fairness Doctrine," Journalism Quarterly, 55 (1978), 793-797.

367 Butterfield, D. Anthony; and Powell, Gary N. "Convergent Validity in Students' Perceptions of Jimmy Carter, Ted Kennedy, and the Ideal President," Perceptual and Motor Skills, 52 (1981), 51-56.

368 Bybee, Carl R. "Facilitating Decision-Making Through News Story Organization," Journalism Quarterly, 57 (1980), 624-630.

369 _____; McLeod, Jack M.; Leutscher, W. D.; and Garramone, Gina. "Mass Communication and Voter Volatility," Public Opinion Quarterly, 45 (1981), 69-80.

370 Byrne, Gary C.; and Marx, Paul. The Great American Convention: A Political History of Presidential Elections. Palo Alto, CA: Pacific Books, 1977.

371 _____; and Pueschel, J. K. "But Who Should I Vote for for County Coroner?" Journal of Politics, 36 (1974), 778-784.

372 Caddell, P.; and Wirthlin, R. "Face Off: A Conversation with the Presidents' Pollsters," Public Opinion, 3 (1981), 2-12.

373 Cade, Robert B. "Mass Media Influences in the Candidate Choice, Time of Vote Decision, and Ticket-Splitting Voting Behavior of Jasper County, Mississippi, Voters in the 1975 General Election" (Ph.D. dissertation, University

of Southern Mississippi, 1977), Dissertation Abstracts International A, 38 (1977), 2394.

374 Cahn, Dudley D.; Pappas, Edward J.; and Schoen, Ladene. "Speech in the Senate: 1978," Communication Quarterly, 27 (1979), 50-54.

375 Callahan, Carole R. "Stevenson of Illinois: Identification in the 1970 Senatorial Campaign of Adlai E. Stevenson III," Central States Speech Journal, 24 (1973), 272-277.

376 Calvert, Randall L. "On the Role of Imperfect Information in Electoral Politics," (Ph.D. dissertation, California Institute of Technology, 1980), Dissertation Abstracts International A, 40 (1980), 4208.

377 Campbell, B. A. American Electorate: Attitudes and Action. New York: Holt, Rinehart & Winston, 1979.

378 Campbell, J. Louis, III. "Jimmy Carter and the Rhetoric of Charisma," Central States Speech Journal, 30 (1979), 174-186.

379 Cantor, Robert D. Voting Behavior and Presidential Elections. Itasca, IL: F. E. Peacock Publishers, 1975.

380 Cantrall, William R., II. "The Impact of Issues and Voting on Changing Attitudes Toward Political Institutions in the 1972 Election" (Ph.D. dissertation, University of Illinois at Urbana-Champaign, 1975), Dissertation Abstracts International A, 36 (1976), 3081.

381 Cantril, Albert H. (ed.). Polling on the Issues: Twenty-One Perspectives on the Role of Opinion Polls in the Making of Public Policy. Cabin John, MD: Seven Locks Press, 1980.

382 _____. "The Press and the Pollster," The Annals of the American Academy of Political and Social Science, 427 (1976), 45-52.

383 Carey, James W. "Mass Communication Research and Cultural Studies: An American View," Mass Communication and Society, eds. James Curran, Michael Gurevitch, and Janet Woolacott. London: Edward Arnold, 1977.

384 _____; and Kreiling, Albert L. "Popular Culture and Uses and Gratifications: Notes Toward an Accommodation," The Uses of Mass Communications, eds. Jay G. Blumler and Elihu Katz. Beverly Hills, CA: Sage Publications, 1974.

385 Carey, John. "How Media Shape Campaigns," *Journal of Communication*, 26 (1976), 50-57.

386 ———. "A Micro-Frame Analysis of the On-Camera/On-Mike Paralinguistic Behavior of Three Presidential Candidates" (Ph. D. dissertation, University of Pennsylvania, 1976), *Dissertation Abstracts International A*, 37 (1976), 1856.

387 Carison, R. O. *Communications and Public Opinion: A Public Opinion Quarterly Reader*. New York: Praeger, 1975.

388 Carlson, J. M.; and Boring, M. K. "Androgyny and Politics: The Effects of Winning and Losing on Candidate Image," *International Political Science Review*, 2 (1981), 481-490.

389 Carlson, James M. "Politics and Interpersonal Attraction," *American Politics Quarterly*, 7 (1979), 120-126.

390 ———; and Hyde, Mark S. "Personality and Political Recruitment: Actualization or Compensation," *Journal of Psychology*, 106 (1980), 117-120.

391 Carlson, Jody. *George C. Wallace and the Politics of Powerlessness*. New Brunswick, NJ: Transaction Books, 1981.

392 Carlyle, C. I. "The Role of Imagery in Communication: Susanne Langer's Concept of Presentational Symbols Applied to Intrapersonal and Mass Media Communication" (Ph. D. dissertation, University of Iowa, 1978), *Dissertation Abstracts International A*, 39 (1978), 3200.

393 Carmines, Edward G. "A Competence Theory Versus Need Theory of Political Involvement," *Journal of Political and Military Sociology*, 6 (1978), 17-28.

394 ———. "Decline in Presidential Idealization Among Adolescents: Watergate Created?" *Adolescence*, 16 (1981), 487-492.

395 ———. "Psychological Origins of Adolescent Political Attitudes: Self-Esteem, Political Salience, and Political Involvement," *American Politics Quarterly*, 6 (1978), 167-186.

396 ———; and Gopoian, J. D. "Issue Coalitions, Issueless Campaigns: The Paradox of Rationality in American Presidential Elections," *Journal of Politics*, 43 (1981), 1170-1189.

397 ———; and Stimson, J. A. "Two Faces of Issue Voting," *American Political Science Review*, 74 (1980), 78-91.

398 Carpenter, R. H., and Jordan, W. J. "Style in Discourse as a Predictor of Political Personality for Mr. Carter and Other Twentieth-Century Presidents: Testing the Barber Paradigm," Presidential Studies Quarterly, 8 (1978), 67-78.

399 Carroll, Susan J. "Women as Candidates: Campaigns and Elections in American Politics" (Ph.D. dissertation, Indiana University, 1980), Dissertation Abstracts International A, 41 (1980), 2747.

400 Carter, Jimmy. A Government Is As Good as its People. New York: Simon & Schuster, 1977.

401 Carter, John J. "Voter Images in the 1980 Election: A Panel Study Using Q-technique" (Ph.D. dissertation, University of Missouri-Columbia, 1981), Dissertation Abstracts International A, 43 (1982), 250-251.

402 Carter, R. F. "A Very Peculiar Horse Race," The Presidential Debates: Media, Electoral and Policy Perspectives, eds. George F. Bishop, Robert G. Meadow, and Marilyn Jackson-Beeck. New York: Praeger, 1978.

403 Case, Dale C. "Majority Party Presidential Nominee Acceptance Speeches, 1948-1976: A Rhetorical Analysis" (Ph.D. dissertation, Indiana University, 1979), Dissertation Abstracts International A, 40 (1979), 538.

404 Caspi, Dan. "On Politicians' Criticism of the Mass Media," Journal of Broadcasting, 25 (1981), 181-193.

405 Cassata, Mary B.; and Asnate, Molefi K. (eds.). The Social Uses of Mass Communication. Buffalo, NY: Department of Communication, SUNY at Buffalo, 1977.

406 Cater, Douglass. "A Strategy for Political Broadcasting," Journal of Communication, 26 (1976), 58-61+.

407 _____; and Adler, R. (eds.). Television as a Social Force: New Approaches to TV Criticism. New York: Praeger, 1975.

408 Cavazza, Fabio L., et al. Television and Political Life. State Mutual Book and Periodical Service, Ltd., 1981.

409 Ceaser, J. W. Presidential Selection: Theory and Development. Princeton, NJ: Princeton University Press, 1979.

410 _____; Thurow, G. E.; Tulis, J.; and Bessette, J. M. "The Rise of the Rhetorical Presidency," Presidential Studies Quarterly, 11 (1981), 158-171.

411 Ceci, Stephen J.; and Kain, Edward L. "Jumping on Band-Wagon with the Underdog: The Impact of Attitude Polls on Polling Behavior," Public Opinion Quarterly, 46 (1982), 228-242.

412 Chaffee, Steven H. "Approaches of U.S. Scholars to the Study of Televised Political Debates," Political Communication Review, 4 (1979), 19-33.

413 _____. "The Diffusion of Political Information," Political Communication: Issues and Strategies for Research, ed. Steven H. Chaffee. Beverly Hills, CA: Sage Publications, 1975.

414 _____. "The Mass Media as Agents of Political Socialization," International Journal of Political Education, 1 (1978), 127-142.

415 _____. "Mass Media Effects: New Research Perspective," Communication Research: A Half Century Appraisal, eds. D. Lerner and L. Nelson. Honolulu: University Press of Hawaii, 1977.

416 _____. "Mass Media in Political Campaigns: An Expanding Role," Public Communication Campaigns, eds. Ronald Rice and William J. Paisley. Beverly Hills: Sage Publications, 1981, 181-198.

417 _____ (ed.). Political Communication: Issues and Strategies for Research. Beverly Hills, CA: Sage Publications, 1976.

418 _____. "Presidential Debates--Are They Helpful to Voters?" Communication Monographs, 45 (1978), 330-346.

419 _____; and Becker, Lee B. "Young Voters' Reactions to Early Watergate Issues," American Politics Quarterly, 3 (1975), 360-385.

420 _____; and Choe, Sun Yuel. "Newspaper Reading in Longitudinal Perspective: Beyond Structural Constraints," Journalism Quarterly, 58 (1981), 201-211.

421 _____; and _____. "Time of Decision and Media Use During the Ford-Carter Campaign," Public Opinion Quarterly, 44 (1980), 53-69.

422 _____; and Dennis, Jack. "Legitimation in the 1976 U.S. Election Campaign," Communication Research, 5 (1978), 371-194.

423 _____; Jackson-Beeck, Marilyn; Durall, J.; and Wilson, Donna. "Mass Communication in Political Socialization," Handbook of Political Socialization, ed. S. Renshon. New York: Free Press, 1977.

424 _____; and McLeod, Jack M. "Individual vs. Social Predictors of Information Seeking," Journalism Quarterly, 50 (1973), 237-245.

425 _____; _____; and Wackman, D. "Family Communication Patterns and Adolescent Political Participation," Socialization to Politics: A Reader, ed. Jack Dennis. New York: Wiley, 1973.

426 _____; and Tims, A. R. "News Media Use in Adolescence: Implications for Political Cognitions," Communication Yearbook 6, ed. Michael Burgoon. Beverly Hills, CA: Sage Publications, 1982.

427 _____; and Wilson, Donna G. "Media Rich, Media Poor: Two Studies of Diversity in Agenda-Holding," Journalism Quarterly, 54 (1977), 466-476.

428 Chagall, David. The New Kingmakers. New York: Harcourt Brace Jovanovich, 1981.

429 Chalfa, John J., Jr. "A Multi-Model Examination of Vote Intention in the 1976 Presidential Campaign" (Ph.D. dissertation, Southern Illinois University at Carbondale, 1980), Dissertation Abstracts International A, 41 (1980), 447-448.

430 Chandon, Jean-Louis J. "A Comparative Study of Media Exposure Models" (Ph.D. dissertation, Northwestern University, 1976), Dissertation Abstracts International A, 37 (1977), 4578.

431 Chapel, G. E. "Speechwriting in the Nixon Administration," Journal of Communication, 26 (1976), 65-72.

432 Chapel, Gage W. "Humor in the White House: An Interview with Presidential Speechwriter Robert Orben," Communication Quarterly, 26 (1978), 44-49.

433 Chappell, H. W., Jr. "Campaign Contributions and Congressional Voting: A Simultaneous Probit-Tobit Model," Review of Economics and Statistics, 64 (1982), 77-83.

434 Chase, I. H. "An Affair to Remember: Lessons Learned from Last Year's Eagleton Episode are Sorted Out," Mental Hygiene, 57 (1973), 8-11.

435 Chatmah, Kathleen M. "Political Immorality and Communication Behavior" (Master's thesis, University of Washington, 1975), Journalism Abstracts, 14 (1976), 70-71.

436 Chaudhary, Anju G. "Press Portrayal of Black Officials," Journalism Quarterly, 57 (1980), 636-641.

437 Cheatham, Richard. "An Overview of Contemporary Gubernatorial Inaugurals," Southern Speech Communication Journal, 40 (1975), 191-203.

438 Cherwitz, Richard, et al. "How Voters Process Political Campaign Communications: A Qualitative Study of a Panel of Voters during Campaign '76," Central States Speech Journal, 28 (1977), 258-271.

439 Chesebro, J. W. "Political Communication," Quarterly Journal of Speech, 62 (1976), 189-300.

440 Cheslik, Francis E. "Presidential Influence on the Media: A Descriptive Study of the Administrations of Lyndon B. Johnson and Richard M. Nixon" (Ph.D. dissertation, Wayne State University, 1977), Dissertation Abstracts International A, 38 (1978), 6378.

441 Chester, E. W. "Beyond the Rhetoric: A New Look at Presidential Inaugural Addresses," Presidential Studies Quarterly, 10 (1980), 571-582.

442 _____. "Shadow or Substance: Critiquing Reagan's Inaugural Address," Presidential Studies Quarterly, 11 (1981), 172-176.

443 Chisman, Forrest P. Attitude Psychology and the Study of Public Opinion. University Park, PA: Pennsylvania State University Press, 1977.

444 Chisholm, Shirley. The Good Fight. New York: Harper and Row, 1973.

445 Chodkiewicz, A.; Isert, N; and Pantzer, S. "Media Use: Politics Students," Politics, 10 (1975), 84-87.

446 Christensen, S., and Daugaard Jensen, P. E. "Communication and Political Agendas," Communication, 7 (1982), 59-74.

447 Church, Russell T. "President Richard M. Nixon's Crisis Rhetoric, 1969-1972" (Ph.D. dissertation, Temple University, 1977), Dissertation Abstracts International A, 37 (1977), 7402-7403.

448 Cirino, Robert. Power to Persuade: Mass Media and the News. New York: Bantam Books, 1974.

449 A Citizen's Guide to Winning Elections. Scottsdale, AZ: Faith American Foundation, 1982.

450 Clark, Blair. "Notes on a No-Win Campaign," Columbia Journalism Review, 19 (1980), 36-40.

Bibliography

451 Clark, M. J. (ed). Politics and the Media: Film and Television for the Political Scientist and Historian. Elmsford, NY: Pergamon Press, 1979.

452 Clark, Thomas D. "An Analysis of Recurrent Features of Contemporary American Radical, Liberal, and Conservative Political Discourse," Southern Speech Communication Journal, 44 (1979), 399-422.

453 _____. "An Exploration of Generic Aspects of Contemporary American Campaign Orations," Central States Speech Journal, 30 (1979), 122-133.

454 Clark, William R.; and Ertas, Metin (eds.). "A Comparison of Pupillary Reactions to Visual and Auditory Stimuli in a Test of Preferences for Presidential Candidates," Catalog of Selected Documents in Psychology, 5 (1975), 230.

455 Clarke, Peter; and Evans, Susan H. "All in a Day's Work: Reporters Covering Congressional Campaigns," Journal of Communication, 30 (1980), 112-121.

456 _____; and Fredin, Eric. "Newspapers, Television and Political Reasoning," Public Opinion Quarterly, 42 (1978), 143-160.

457 _____; and Kline, F. Gerald. "Media Effects Reconsidered," Communication Research, 1 (1974), 224-240.

458 Clausen, A. R. "The Accuracy of Leader Perceptions of Constituency Views," Legislative Studies Quarterly, 2 (1977), 361-384.

459 Clemens, John. "The Volatility of Voting Behavior," Journal of the Market Research Society, 16 (1974), 291-301.

460 Clements, Kevin P. "The Citizens for Rowling Campaign: An Insider's View," Political Science, 28 (1976), 81-96.

461 Cleveland, L. "Pressure Groups and Press Councils," Politics, 10 (1975), 79-80.

462 Clor, Harry M. (ed). The Mass Media and Modern Democracy. Chicago, IL: Rand McNally College Publishing Co., 1974.

463 Clotfelter, James; and Prysby, Charles. Political Choices: A Study of Elections and Voters. New York: Holt, Rinehart and Winston, Inc., 1980.

464 Clubb, Jerome M.; Flanigan, William H.; and Zingale, Nancy H. (eds.). Analyzing Electoral History: A Guide to the Study of American Voting Behavior. Beverly Hills, CA: Sage Publications, 1981.

465 Cobb, R.; Ross, J.; and Ross, M. H. "Agenda Building as a Comparative Political Process," *American Political Science Review*, 70 (1976), 126-138.

466 Cobb, Roger W.; and Elder, Charles D. "Communication and Public Policy," *Handbook of Political Communication*, eds. Dan D. Nimmo and Keith R. Sanders. Beverly Hills, CA: Sage Publications, 1981, 391-416.

467 _____; and _____. *Participation in American Politics: The Dynamics of Agenda Building*. Baltimore, MD: The Johns Hopkins University Press, 1975.

468 _____; and _____. "Symbolic Identification and Political Behavior," *American Politics Quarterly*, 3 (1976), 1-11.

469 Coffey, Phillip J. "A Quantitative Measure of Bias in Reporting of Political News," *Journalism Quarterly*, 52 (1975), 551-553.

470 Coffman, Tom. *Catch a Wave: A Case Study of Hawaii's New Politics*. Honolulu: University of Hawaii Press, 1973.

471 Cohen, Akiba A. "Attention to the Mass Media Among Straight and Split Ticket Voters: A Research Note," *Human Communication Research*, 2 (1975), 75-78.

472 _____. "Coping with Uncertainty, Information Usage and Ticket Splitting" (Ph.D. dissertation, Michigan State University, 1973), *Dissertation Abstracts International A*, 34 (1974), 7797.

473 _____. "Radio vs. TV: The Effect of the Medium," *Journal of Communication*, 26 (1976), 29-35.

474 Cohen, Dan. *Undefeated: The Life of Hubert H. Humphrey*. Minneapolis, MN: Lerner, 1978.

475 Cohen, J. "Presidential Personality and Political Behavior: Theoretical Issues and an Empirical Test," *Presidential Studies Quarterly*, 10 (1980), 588-599.

476 Cohen, Stanley; and Young, Jack (eds.). *The Manufacture of News: Deviance, Social Problems, and the Mass Media* (rev. ed.). Beverly Hills, CA: Sage Publications, 1981.

477 Coleman, N. D. "Spending Limitations on State Election Campaigns," *State Government*, 47 (1974), 214-217.

478 Collier, Barney. *Hope and Fear in Washington: The Story of the Washington Press Corp*. New York: Dial Press, 1976.

Bibliography 45

479 Collins, Catherine A. "Kissinger's Press Conference, 1972-1974: An Exploration of Form and Role Relationship on News Management," Central States Speech Journal, 28 (1977), 185-193.

480 Combs, James E. Dimensions of Political Drama. Santa Monica, CA: Goodyear Publishing Co., 1980.

481 _____. "The Dramaturgical Image of Political Man: A Modernist Approach to Political Inquiry" (Ph.D. dissertation, University of Missouri, Columbia, 1973), Dissertation Abstracts International A, 35 (1974), 2349.

482 _____. "Political Advertising as a Popular Mythmaking Form," Journal of American Culture, 2 (1979), 331-340.

483 _____. "A Process Approach," Handbook of Political Communication, eds. Dan D. Nimmo and Keith R. Sanders. Beverly Hills, CA: Sage Publications, 1981, 39-65.

484 _____; and Mansfield, Michael (eds.). Drama in Life: The Uses of Communication in Society. New York: Hastings House, 1976.

485 Commanger, Henry S. The Defeat of America: Presidential Power and the National Character. New York: Simon & Schuster, 1975.

486 Commoner, Barry. "Talking to a Mule," Columbia Journalism Review, 20 (1981), 30-31.

487 Compliance with Federal Election Campaign Requirements: A Guide for Candidates. New York: AICPA, 1976.

488 Comstock, George. "The Impact of Television on American Institutions," Journal of Communication, 28 (Spring, 1978), 12-28.

489 _____. Priorities for Action-Oriented Psychological Studies of Television and Behavior. Santa Monica, CA: Rand Corporation, 1977.

490 _____. Television in America. The Sage Commtext Series, Vol. 1. Beverly Hills, CA: Sage Publications, Inc., 1980.

491 _____; and Cobbey, R. "Watching the Watchdogs: Trends and Problems in Monitoring Network News," Television Network News: Issues in Content Research, eds. W. Adams and F. Schreibman. Washington, D.C.: George Washington University, 1978.

492 _____, et al. Television and Human Behavior, Vols. 1, 2, 3. Santa Monica, CA: Rand Corporation, 1975.

493 Connor, Susan. "Nixon and Newspaper Coverage: A Comparison of Political Endorsements, 1972, and Watergate Coverage, 1973" (Master's thesis, Indiana University, 1977), Journalism Abstracts, 16 (1978), 44.

494 Conover, Pamela J. "The Nature and Sources of Candidate Images: A Social Psychological Approach" (Ph.D. dissertation, University of Minnesota, 1979), Dissertation Abstracts International A, 40 (1979), 3503.

495 _____. "Political Cues and the Perception of Candidates," American Politics Quarterly, 9 (1981), 427-448.

496 _____; and Feldman, Stanley. "Projection and the Perception of Candidates' Issue Positions," Western Political Quarterly, 35 (1982), 228-244.

497 Conrad, Roan. "TV News and the 1976 Election: A Dialogue," Wilson Quarterly (Spring 1977), 83-85.

498 Converse, Philip E. "Plus ça Change . . . The New CPS Election Study Panel," The American Political Science Review, 73 (1979), 32-49.

499 _____. "Public Opinion and Voting Behavior," Handbook of Political Science 4, eds. F. Greenstein and N. Polsby. Reading, MA: Addison-Wesley, 1975.

500 Conway, M; Stevens, A.; and Smith, R. "The Relation between Media Use and Children's Civic Awareness," Journalism Quarterly, 52 (1975), 531-538.

501 Conway, M. Margaret. "Political Participation in Midterm Congressional Elections: Attitudinal and Social Characteristics during the 1970's," American Politics Quarterly, 9 (1981), 221-244.

502 _____; Ahern, David; and Wyckoff, Mikel L. "The Mass Media and Changes in Adolescents' Political Knowledge during an Election Cycle," Political Behavior, 3 (1981), 69-80.

503 _____; and Feigert, F. B. "Incentives and Task Performance among Party Precinct Workers," Western Political Quarterly, 27 (1974), 693-709.

504 _____; Wyckoff, Mikel L.; Feldbaum, E.; and Ahern, David. "The News Media in Children's Political Socialization," Public Opinion Quarterly, 45 (1981), 164-178.

Bibliography

505 Coombs, F. S.; Peters, J. G.; and Strom, G. S. "Bandwagon, Ballot Position, and Party Effects: An Experiment in Voting Choice," Experimental Study of Politics, 3 (1974), 31-57.

506 Coombs, Steven L. "Editorial Endorsements and Electoral Outcomes" (Ph.D. dissertation, The University of Michigan, 1978), Dissertation Abstracts International A, 39 (1979), 6309.

507 Cooper, E. H. "Political Generations and Recall of Public Events and Personalities" (Ph.D. dissertation, Claremont Graduate School, 1975), Dissertation Abstracts International B, 37 (1976), 520-521.

508 Cooper, S. L. "A Rhetorical Assessment of Lyndon Johnson's Presidential Press Conferences" (Ph.D. dissertation, Louisiana State University and Agricultural and Mechanical College, 1972), Dissertation Abstracts International B, 37 (1973), 7064.

509 Copeland, Gary W. "The Effects of Congressional Campaign Expenditures on Voting Behavior: A Behavioral and Policy Analysis" (Ph.D. dissertation, University of Iowa, 1979), Dissertation Abstracts International A, 40 (1980), 6403.

510 Copelin, Mary H. "An Analysis of the Logical and Ethical Foundations of the Rhetoric of Spiro T. Agnew in Attacking the Mass Media Through a Systematic Analysis of the Evidence" (Ph.D. dissertation, University of California, Los Angeles, 1974), Dissertation Abstracts International A, 35 (1974), 2425.

511 Corcoran, Paul E. Political Language and Rhetoric. Austin, TX: University of Texas Press, 1979.

512 Cornwell, Elmer E., Jr. "President and the Press: Phases in the Relationship," Annals of the American Academy of Political and Social Science, 427 (1976), 53-64.

513 _____. Presidential Leadership of Public Opinion. Westport, CT: Greenwood Press, 1979.

514 Corrigan, Dennis M. "Secrecy in Political Communication: Aspects of an Analytical Framework" (Ph.D. dissertation, University of Illinois at Urbana-Champaign, 1980), Journalism Abstracts, 18 (1980), 6-7.

515 Costantini, E.; and King, J. "Checkbook Democrats and their Copartisans: Campaign Contributors and California Political Leaders," American Politics Quarterly, 10 (1982), 65-92.

516 Costikyan, Edward N. How to Win Votes: The Politics of 1980. New York: Harcourt Brace Jovanovich, 1980.

517 Coughlin, Peter. "Incomplete Information, Noisy Signals and Uncertainty-Averse Voting in Political Elections: A Note," Public Choice, 28 (1976), 113-116.

518 Counts, T. M., Jr. "The Influence of Message and Source on Selection of Statements by Reporters," Journalism Quarterly, 52 (1975), 443-449.

519 Cover, A; and Brumberg, B. S. "Baby Books and Ballots: The Impact of Congressional Mail on Constituent Opinion," American Political Science Review, 76 (1982), 347-359.

520 "Covering the Political Campaign: Symposium," Journal of Communication, 28 (1978), 80-138.

521 Cox, H.; and Morgan, D. City Politics and the Press. New York: Cambridge University Press, 1973.

522 Cozby, P. C. "Student Reactions to Agnew's Resignation: Inconsistency Resolution in Another Natural-Occurring Event," Sociometry, 37 (1974), 450-457.

523 Cragen, John F.; and Shields, Donald C. Applied Communication Research: A Dramatistic Approach. Prospect Heights, IL: Waveland Press, Inc., 1981.

524 _____; and _____. "Foreign Policy Communication Dramas: How Mediated Rhetoric Played in Peoria in Campaign '76," Quarterly Journal of Speech, 63 (1977), 274-289.

525 Craig, Stephen C. "Citizen Demands and Political Reality: A Dynamic Model of Political Discontent" (Ph.D. dissertation, Northwestern University, 1979), Dissertation Abstracts International A, 40 (1979), 3503-3504.

526 _____. "Efficacy, Trust, and Political Behavior: An Attempt to Resolve a Lingering Conceptual Dilemma," American Politics Quarterly, 7 (1979), 225-239.

527 Crain, W. M.; and Deaton, T. H. "A Note on Political Participation as Consumption Behavior," Public Choice, 32 (1977), 131-136.

528 _____; and Tollison, R. D. "Campaign Expenditures and Political Competition," Journal of Law and Economics, 19 (1976), 177-188.

529 Crane, B. M. "The Silence Effect in Public Opinion" (Ph.D. dissertation, University of Wisconsin, Madison, 1979), Dissertation Abstracts International A, 40 (1980), 4284.

530 Cranston, A. "Is TV Fair to Politicians?" Television Quarterly, 13 (1976), 40-46.

531 Crater, Flora. Women Activist Guide for Women Candidates (rev. ed.). Falls Church, VA: Woman Activist, Inc., 1978.

532 _____. Woman Activist Guide to Precinct Politics (2nd ed.). Falls Church, VA: Woman Activist, Inc., 1979.

533 Crawford, Kenneth G. The Pressure Boys: The Inside Story of Lobbying in America. Salem, NH: Arno, 1974.

534 Crespi, I. "Attitude Measurement, Theory, and Prediction," Public Opinion Quarterly, 41 (1977), 285-294.

535 Crews, James M., Jr. "J.F.K. and the Mountaineers: John F. Kennedy's Rhetoric in the 1960 West Virginia Presidential Primary" (Ph.D. dissertation, Florida State University, 1980), Dissertation Abstracts International A, 41 (1981), 3778.

536 Crick, B. "Paying for the Parties: A Review," Political Quarterly, 46 (1975), 411-417.

537 _____. "Political Education, Elections and the Media," Political Quarterly, 49 (1978), 133-135.

538 Crittenden, John A. Parties and Elections in the United States. Englewood Cliffs, NJ: Prentice-Hall, 1982.

539 Crossman, R.H.S. "Financing Political Parties," Political Quarterly, 45 (1974), 333-334.

540 Crouse, Janice S. "The Carter-Ford Campaign Debates, 1976: The Images and Issues in Political Persuasion" (Ph.D. dissertation, State University of New York at Buffalo, 1979), Dissertation Abstracts International A, 40 (1979), 1733.

541 Crouse, Timothy. The Boys on the Bus. New York: Ballantine Books, 1974.

542 Culbertson, H.M.; and Somerick, N. "Variables Affect How Persons View Unnamed News Sources," Journalism Quarterly, 54 (1977), 58-69.

543 Cundy, D.T. "Affect, Cue-Giving and Political Attutude Formation: Survey Evidence in Support of a Social Conditioning Interpretation," Journal of Politics, 41 (1979), 75-105.

544 Cureton, Robert D. "A Methodological Comparison of Telephone and Face-to-Face Interviewing for Political Public Opinion Polling" (Ph. D. dissertation, Southern Illinois University, 1976), Dissertation Abstracts International A, 37 (1977), 5437.

545 Curtis, Alan M. "Political Speechwriting ('Ghostwriting') in the Nixon Administration, 1968-1972: Implications for Rhetorical Criticism" (Ph. D. dissertation, University of Southern California, 1973), Dissertation Abstracts International A, 35 (1974), 609-610.

546 Cushman, D. P.; and McPhee, R. D. (eds.). Message-Attitude-Behavior Relationships: Theory, Methodology, and Application. New York: Academic Press, 1980.

547 Czepiec, Helena. "The Impact of Television News and Party Identification on Candidate Image Adoption" (Ph. D. dissertation, Ohio State University, 1976), Dissertation Abstracts International A, 37 (1977), 5326.

548 Dabbs, James M., Jr. "Attitudes Toward Winner and Loser After an Election," Social Behavior and Personality, 3 (1975), 45-48.

549 Dacey, Raymond. "The Role of Ambiguity in Manipulating Voter Behavior," Theory and Decision, 10 (1979), 265-279.

550 Dagger, Richard K. "What is Political Obligation?" American Political Science Review, 71 (1977), 86-94.

551 Dahlgren, Peter C. "Network TV News and the Corporate State: The Subordinate Consciousness of the Viewer-Citizen" (Ph. D. dissertation, City University of New York, 1977), Dissertation Abstracts International A, 38 (1978), 4426.

552 _____; et al. "From Media Critique to the Pedagogy of Critical Discourse," The Nordicom Review of Nordic Mass Communication Research, 1 (1982), 5-7.

553 Dailey, A. R. "The Development of Adolescents' Political Attitudes" (Ph. D. dissertation, Johns Hopkins University, 1981), Dissertation Abstracts International A, 41 (1982), 4507.

554 Dailey, Joseph M. "The Eisenhower-Nixon Campaign Organization of 1952" (Ph. D. dissertation, University of Illinois at Urbana-Champaign, 1975), Dissertation Abstracts International A, 36 (1976), 5615.

555 Dalton, T. R. "Citizen Ignorance and Political Activity," Public Choice, 32, (1977), 85-89.

Bibliography

556 Danziger, J. N.; Dutton, W. H.; Kling, R.; and Kraemer, K. L. Computers and Politics: High Technology in American Local Government. New York: Columbia University Press, 1982.

557 Danziger, R. C. "Some Structural, Environmental, and Cognitive Determinants of Activism in the Local Political Party Organization" (Ph.D. dissertation, State University of New York at Buffalo, 1980), Dissertation Abstracts International A, 41 (1980), 382.

558 Darcy, R.; and Schramm, Sarah S. "When Women Run Against Men," Public Opinion Quarterly, 41 (1977), 1-12.

559 Dash, Samuel. Chief Counsel: Inside the Ervin Committee: The Untold Story of Watergate. New York: Random House, 1976.

560 Davidson, Dorothy K. "Candidate Evaluation: Rational Instrument or Affective Response" (Ph.D. dissertation, Florida State University, 1982), Dissertation Abstracts International A, 43 (1982), 2079.

561 Davis, Dennis K. "Assessing the Role of Mass Communication in the Social Processes: A Comment on 'Decline and Fall at the White House'," Communication Research, 4 (1977), 23-24.

562 _____. "Influence on Vote Decisions," The Great Debates: Carter vs. Ford 1976, ed. Sidney Kraus. Bloomington, IN: Indiana University Press, 1979.

563 _____; and Kraus, Sidney. "Public Communication and Televised Presidential Debates," Communication Yearbook 6, ed. Michael Burgoon. Beverly Hills, CA: Sage Publications, 1982.

564 Davis, Devra Lee. "Watergate: Government by Negation," Theory and Society, 1 (1974), 111-115.

565 Davis, Dwight F. "Issue Information and Connotation in Candidate Imagery: Evidence from a Laboratory," International Political Science Review, 2 (1981), 461-480.

_____; Kaid, Lynda Lee; and Singleton, Donald L. "Information Effects of Political Commentary," Experimental Study of Politics, 6 (1977), 45-68.

567 Davis, James W. National Conventions: Nominations Under the Big Top (rev. ed.). Woodbury, NY: Barron's Educational Series, Inc., 1973.

568 _____. Presidential Primaries: Road to the White House. Westport, CT: Greenwood Press, 1980.

569 Davis, Lanny J. The Emerging Democratic Majority: Lessons and Legacies from the New Politics. New York: Stein and Day, 1974.

570 Davis, Leslie K. "Camera Eye-Contact by the Candidates in the Presidential Debates of 1976," Journalism Quarterly, 55 (1978), 431-437, 455.

571 Davis, Mark H.; and Runge, Thomas E. "Beliefs and Attitudes in a Gubernatorial Primary: Some Limitations in the Fishbein Model," Journal of Applied Social Psychology, 11 (1981), 93-113.

572 Davis, Vincent (ed.). The Post-Imperial Presidency. New Brunswick, NJ: Transaction Books, 1980.

573 Davison, W. P. Mass Communication and Conflict Resolution. New York: Praeger, 1974.

574 _____; and Yu, T. C. F. Mass Communication Research: Major Issues and Future Directions. New York: Praeger Special Studies, 1974.

575 Dawson, P. A.; and Zinser, J. E. "Political Finance and Participation in Congressional Elections," Annals of the American Academy of Political and Social Science, 425 (1976), 59-73.

576 Dawson, R.; Prewitt, K.; and Dawson, K. Political Socialization. Boston, MA: Little, Brown, 1977.

577 Day, Edith H. "A Rhetorical and Content Analysis of Florida's Gubernatorial Inaugural Addresses, 1845 to 1971" (Ph.D. dissertation, Florida State University, 1973), Dissertation Abstracts International A, 34 (1974), 6782.

578 Deahl, Maureen, E. "The Independent Candidate--Campaign '80: A Content Analysis of the Coverage of John B. Anderson in Three News Magazines" (Master's thesis, North Texas State University, 1982), Masters Abstracts, 20 (1982), 368.

579 Dean, P. D., Jr.; and Vasquez, J. A. "From Power Politics to Issue Politics: Bipolarity and Multipolarity in Light of a New Paradigm," Western Political Quarterly, 29 (1976), 7-28.

580 deBock, Harold. "A Field Experiment on In-State Election Poll Reports and the Intensity of Prospective Voter Candidate Preference and Turnout Motivation in the 1972 Presidential Election Campaign" (Ph.D. dissertation, Indiana University, 1974), Dissertation Abstracts International A, 35 (1974), 2309-2310.

581 _____. "Influence of the Ford-Carter Debates on Dutch TV Viewers," Journalism Quarterly, 55 (1978), 583-585.

582 _____. "Influence of In-State Election Poll Reports on Candidate Preference in 1972," Journalism Quarterly, 53 (1976), 457-462.

583 Declercq, Eugene. "The Use of Polling in Congressional Campaigns," Public Opinion Quarterly, 42 (1978), 247-258.

584 Deegan, John, Jr.; and White, Kenneth J. "An Analysis of Non-partisan Election Media Expenditure Decisions Using Limited Dependent Variable Methods," Social Science Research, 5 (1976), 127-135.

585 De Fleur, Melvin; and Ball-Rokeach, Sandra. Theories of Mass Communication. New York: McKay, 1975.

586 DeGeorge, William F. "An Experimental Test of the Agenda-Setting Function" (Ph.D. dissertation, Syracuse University, 1981), Dissertation Abstracts International A, 42 (1982), 4633-4634.

587 DeMause, Lloyd. "Jimmy Carter and American Fantasy," Journal of Psychohistory, 5 (1977), 151-173.

588 _____; and Ebel, Henry (eds.). Jimmy Carter and American Fantasy: Psychohistorical Explorations. New York: Psychohistory Press, 1977.

589 De Mesquita, B. B. "Need for Achievement and Competitiveness as Determinants of Political Party Success in Elections and Coalitions," American Political Science Review, 68 (1974), 1207-1220.

590 Dempsey, J. R. "Independent Voters: The Characteristics and Significance of Non-Aligned Voters in American Politics" (Ph.D. dissertation, University of Massachusetts, 1975), Dissertation Abstracts International A, 36 (1975), 3977.

591 Dennis, E. E. "The Regeneration of Political Cartooning," Journalism Quarterly, 51 (1974), 664-669.

592 Dennis, E; Ismach, A.; and Gillmor, D. Enduring Issues in Mass Communication. St. Paul, MN: West Publishing Co., 1977.

593 Dennis, Jack. Political Socialization Research: A Bibliography. Beverly Hills, CA: Sage Publications, 1973.

594 _____. Socialization to Politics. New York: Wiley, 1973.

595 _____; and Chaffee, Steven H. "Legitimation in the 1976 U.S. Election Campaign," Communication Research, 5 (1978), 371-394.

596 _____; and Webster, Carol. "Children's Images of the President and of Government in 1962 and 1974," American Politics Quarterly, 3 (1975), 386-405.

597 Denton, Robert E., Jr. "The Rhetorical Functions of Slogans: Classifications and Characteristics," Communication Quarterly, 28 (1980), 10-18.

598 _____. The Symbolic Dimensions of the American Presidency. Prospect Heights, IL: Waveland Press, Inc., 1982.

599 Derman, Michael. The George Wallace Myth. New York: Bantam Books, Inc., 1976.

600 Desmond, Roger J.; and Donohue, Thomas R. "The Role of the 1976 Televised Presidential Debates in Political Socialization of Adolescents," Communication Quarterly, 29 (1981), 302-308.

601 de Sola Pool, Ithiel. "Government and the Media; Review Essay," American Political Science Review, 70 (1976), 1234-1241.

602 _____. "Newsmen and Statesman: Adversaries or Cronies?" Aspen Notebook of Government and the Media, eds. W. Rivers and M. J. Nyham. New York: Praeger, 1973.

603 DeStephen, Daniel E. "Tactics in Conflict: A Study of Tactic Usage in the Controversy Over the Impeachment of President Richard M. Nixon" (Ph.D. dissertation, University of Utah, 1977), Dissertation Abstracts International A, 38 (1977), 1735-1736.

604 Devlin, L. Patrick. "Analysis of Kennedy's Communication in the 1980 Campaign," Quarterly Journal of Speech, 68 (1982), 397-417.

605 _____. "Contrasts in Presidential Campaign Commercials of 1972," Journal of Broadcasting, 18 (1973-74), 17-26.

606 _____. "Contrasts in Presidential Campaign Commercials of 1976," Central States Speech Journal, 28 (1977), 238-249.

607 _____. "Contrasts in Presidential Campaign Commercials of 1980," Political Communication Review, 7 (1982), 1-38.

608 _____. "The Influences of Ghostwriting on Rhetorical Criticism," Today's Speech, 22 (1974), 7-12.

609 _____. "The McGovern Canvass: A Study in Interpersonal Campaigning," Central States Speech Journal, 24 (1973), 83-90.

610 _____. "Reagan's and Carter's Ad Men Review the 1980 Television Campaigns," Communication Quarterly, 30 (1981), 3-12.

611 De Voursney, Robert M. "Issues and Electoral Instability: A Test of Alternate Explanations for Voting Defection in the 1968 American Presidential Election" (Ph. D. dissertation, University of North Carolina at Chapel Hill, 1977), Dissertation Abstracts International A, 39 (1978), 441-442.

612 de Vree, J. K. "A Theory of Human Behavior and of the Political Process," Acta Politica, 11 (1976), 489-533.

613 Diamond, Edwin. "The New Campaign Journalism," Columbia Journalism Review, 14 (1976), 11-14.

614 _____. Sign-Off: The Last Days of Television. Cambridge, MA: The MIT Press, 1982.

615 _____. Tin Kazoo: Television, Politics, and the News. Cambridge, MA: The MIT Press, 1975.

616 Dick, Jane. Volunteers and the Making of Presidents. New York: Dodd, Mead and Co., 1980.

617 Dickson, A. D. R. "When Rejects Re-Run: A Study in Independency," Political Quarterly, 46 (1975), 271-279.

618 Dickson, Paul. The Electronic Battlefield. Bloomington, IN: Indiana University Press, 1976.

619 DiClerico, Robert. The American President. Englewood Cliffs, NJ: Prentice-Hall, Inc., 1979.

620 Dietz, Karen D. R. "An Attitudinal Approach to Voting Behavior" (Ph. D. dissertation, University of Texas at Austin, 1976), Dissertation Abstracts International A, 37 (1977), 7938.

621 Dimbleby, D. "Conference Television: Serving the Viewer or the Party?" The Listener, 104 (1980), 536.

622 Dimmick, J. W. "The Gatekeepers: Media Organizations as Political Coalitions," Communication Research, 6 (1979), 203-222.

623 _____; McCagin, T. A.; and Bolten, W. T. "Media Use and the Life Span," American Behavioral Scientist, 23 (1979), 7-31.

624 Doll, Howard D.; and Bradley, Bert E. "A Study of the Objectivity of Television News Reporting of the 1972 Presidential Campaign," Central States Speech Journal, 25 (1974), 254-263.

625 Dominick, Joseph R.; Wurtzel, Alan; and Lometti, Guy. "Television Journalism vs. Show Business: A Content Analysis of Eyewitness News," Journalism Quarterly, 52 (1975), 213-218.

626 Donaghy, Mary Lynn Anderson. "Who Were the People: An Analysis of Data Obtained from the Grass-Roots Workers in Eugene McCarthy's 1968 Presidential Campaign" (Master's thesis, American University, 1973), Masters Abstracts, 11 (1973), 493.

627 Donahue, B. F. "Political Use of Religious Symbols: A Case Study of the 1972 Presidential Campaign," Review of Politics, 37 (1975), 48-65.

628 Donohue, G. A.; Tichenor, P. J.; and Olien, C. N. "Mass Media and the Knowledge Gap: A Hypothesis Reconsidered," Communication Research, 2 (1975), 2-23.

629 Donohue, Thomas R. "Impact of Viewer Predispositions on Political T.V. Commercials," Journal of Broadcasting, 18 (1973-74), 3-15.

630 ———. "Viewer Perceptions of Color and Black-and-White Paid Political Advertising," Journalism Quarterly, 50 (1973), 660-665.

631 ———; and Meyer, T. P. "Perceptions and Misperceptions of Political Advertising," Journal of Business Communication, 10 (1973), 29-40.

632 Dougherty, R. Goodbye Mr. Christian: A Personal Account of McGovern's Rise and Fall. Garden City, NY: Doubleday and Co., 1973.

633 Douglas, J. D. "Watergate: Harbinger of the American Prince," Theory and Society, 1 (1974), 89-97.

634 Douglas, James. "Was Reagan's Victory a Watershed in American Politics?" Political Quarterly, 52 (1981), 171-183.

635 Douglas, Paul N. "Electronic Nominating Conventions," Public Relations Journal, 30 (1974), 26-28.

636 Dovring, K. Frontiers of Communication: The Americas in Search of Political Culture. North Quincy, MA: Christopher Publishing House, 1975.

637 Downes, Margaret M. "The Management and Manipulation of Presidential Reality" (Ph. D. dissertation, Claremont Graduate School, 1982), Dissertation Abstracts International A, 43 (1982), 912.

638 Downey, Joel. Winning Election to Public Office: The ABC's of Conducting a Local Political Campaign. Pittsburgh, PA: Downey, Joel, 1977.

639 Downie, Leonard, Jr. The New Muckrakers. Washington, D. C.: New Republic Books, 1976.

640 Drew, D. G.; and Reeves, B. B. "Children and Television News," Journalism Quarterly, 57 (1980), 44-54.

641 Drew, E. Portrait of an Election: The 1980 Presidential Campaign. New York: Simon & Schuster, 1981.

642 Dreyer, E. C.; and Rosenbaum, W. A. Political Opinion and Behavior: Essays and Studies. MA: Duxbury Press, 1976.

643 Druckman, D.; Rozelle, R. M.; and Baxter, J. D. Nonverbal Communication: Survey, Theory, and Research. Beverly Hills, CA: Sage Publications, 1982.

644 Drury, Becky S. "A Rhetorical Analysis and Comparison of the Speaking of William Jennings Bryan and George Corley Wallace within a Political Framework of Populism" (Ph. D. dissertation, Purdue University, 1976), Dissertation Abstracts International A, 37 (1977), 4695-4696.

645 Dunham, Roger G.; and Mauss, Armand L. "Waves from Watergate: Evidence Concerning the Impact of the Watergate Scandal Upon Political Legitimacy and Social Control," Pacific Sociological Review, 19 (1976), 469-490.

646 Dunn, D. D. "Policy Preferences of Party Contributors and Voters," Social Science Quarterly, 55 (1975), 983-990.

647 Dunsay, Marsha. "Editorial Reaction to Gerald R. Ford: The Effects of Watergate" (Master's thesis, California State University, Northridge, 1976), Journalism Abstracts, 14 (1976), 90-91.

648 Du Preez, P. "Application of Kelly's Personal Construct Theory to the Analysis of Political Debates," Journal of Social Psychology, 95 (1975), 267-270.

649 Durnad, R. M.; and Lambert, Z. V. "Dogmatism and Exposure to Political Candidates," Psychological Reports, 36 (1975), 423-429.

650 Dybvig, H. E. "Some Non-Print Resources on Political Campaign Communication," *Political Communication Review*, 1 (1975), 6-7.

651 Dye, Thomas; and Gray, Virginia (eds.). *The Determinants of Public Policy*. Lexington, MA: Lexington Books, 1980.

652 Dyson, James W.; and Brownstein, Charles N. "Campaign Information, Attitudinal Voting and the Electoral Context: An Experimental Investigation," *Experimental Study of Politics*, 7 (1979), 1-19.

653 _____; and Scioli, Frank P., Jr. "Communication and Candidate Selection: Relationships of Information and Personal Characteristics to Vote Choice," *Social Science Quarterly*, 55 (1974), 77-90.

654 Eagly, Alice H.; and Chaiken, Shelly. "Why Would Anyone Say That? Causal Attribution of Statements About the Watergate Scandal," *Sociometry*, 39 (1976), 236-243.

655 Ealy, Steven D. *Communication, Speech and Politics: Habermas and Political Analysis*. Lanham, MD: University Press of America, 1981.

656 Eatok, P. "A Small but Stinging Twig: Reflections of a Black Campaigner," *Politics*, 8 (1973), 152-154.

657 Edelman, Murray. *Political Language: Words that Succeed and Policies that Fail*. New York: Academic Press, 1977.

658 Edelstein, Alex. "Decision Making and Mass Communication," *New Models for Mass Communication Research*, ed. P. Clarke. Beverly Hills, CA: Sage Publications, 1973.

659 _____. *The Uses of Mass Communication in Decision Making*. New York: Praeger, 1974.

660 _____; and Tefft, Diane P. "Media Credibility and Respondent Credulity with Respect to Watergate," *Communication Research*, 1 (1974), 426-439.

661 Edgar, P. *The Politics of the Press*. Melbourne: Macmillan Company of Australia, 1979.

662 Edwards, G. "The Presidency, the Media, and the First Amendment," *Presidential Studies Quarterly*, 11 (1981), 42-47.

663 Edwards, Lee H. *You Can Make the Difference*. New York: Crown Publishers, 1980.

Bibliography 59

664 Edwardson, M.; Grooms, D.; and Proudlove, S. "Television News Information Gain from Interesting Video vs. Talking Heads," Journal of Broadcasting, 25 (1981), 15-24.

665 Eiland, Millard F. "Journalistic Criticism of Richard Nixon's Watergate Speaking of 1973" (Ph.D. dissertation, The Louisiana State University and Agricultural and Mechanical College, 1974), Dissertation Abstracts International A, 36 (1975), 27.

666 Einsiedel, Edna F. "Television Network Coverage of the Eagleton Affair: A Case Study," Journalism Quarterly, 52 (1975), 56-60.

667 _____; and Bibee, M. J. "News Magazines and Minority Candidates--Campaign '76," Journalism Quarterly, 56 (1979), 102-105.

668 Elebash, Camille; and Rosene, James. "Issues in Political Advertising in a Deep South Gubernatorial Race," Journalism Quarterly, 59 (1982), 420-423.

669 Elections '80: Timely Reports to Keep Journalists, Scholars, and the Public Abreast of Developing Issues, Events, and Trends. Washington, D.C.: Congressional Quarterly, Inc., 1980.

670 Elections, 1982. Washington, D.C.: Congressional Quarterly, Inc., 1982.

671 Elliott, Philip. "Press Performance as Political Ritual," Mass Communication Yearbook 3, eds. D. Charles Whitney, Ellen Wartella, and Sven Windahl. Beverly Hills, CA: Sage Publications, 1982, 583-620.

672 _____. "Uses and Gratifications Research: A Critique and a Sociological Alternative," The Uses of Mass Communication, eds. Jay G. Blumler and Elihu Katz. Beverly Hills/London: Sage Publications, 1974.

673 Elliott, William R.; and Schenck-Hamlin, William J. "Film, Politics and the Press: The Influence of 'All the President's Men,'" Journalism Quarterly, 56 (1979), 546-553.

674 Ellul, Jacques. Propaganda: The Formation of Men's Attitudes. New York: Random House, 1973.

675 Ellwood, John W. "The Growth and Development of the Wallace Organization of 1968: A Study of Third Party Formation" (Ph.D. dissertation, Johns Hopkins University, 1972), Dissertation Abstracts International A, 36 (1976), 6914.

676 _____; and Spitzer, Robert J. "The Democratic National Telethons: Their Successes and Failures," Journal of

Politics, 41 (1979), 828-864.

677 Elway, H. Stuart. "The Parties, the Media and Political Knowledge" (Master's thesis, University of Washington, 1975). Journalism Abstracts, 13 (1975), 69-70.

678 Emery, Edwin. "Changing Role of the Mass Media in American Politics," The Annals of the American Academy of Political and Social Science, 427 (1976), 84-94.

679 Ender, R. L. "The Floating Voter: Identifying Characteristics Which Differentiate Stable and Floating Voters" (Ph.D. dissertation, Syracuse University, 1977), Dissertation Abstracts International A, 38 (1978), 5021.

680 Enelow, James; and Hinich, Melvin J. "A New Approach to Voter Uncertainty in the Downsian Spatial Model," American Journal of Political Science, 25 (1981), 483-493.

681 _____; and _____. "Nonspatial Candidate Characteristics and Electoral Competition," Journal of Politics, 44 (1982), 115-130.

682 Ennis, M. J. "Bias in the Press," Political Science, 26 (1974), 68-70.

683 Entman, Robert M.; and Paletz, David L. "Media and the Conservative Myth," Journal of Communication, 30 (1980), 154-165.

684 Ephron, Nora. Scribble, Scribble: The Media According to Nora Ephron. New York: Alfred Knopf, 1978.

685 Epstein, Edward J. Between Fact and Fiction: The Problem of Journalism. New York: Random House, 1975.

686 _____. News from Nowhere. New York: Random House, 1973.

687 Epstein, Laurily K.; and Strom, Gerald. "Election Night Projections and West Coast Turnout," American Politics Quarterly, 9 (1981), 497-489.

688 Erbring, Lutz; Goldenberg, Edie N.; and Miller, Arthur H. "Front-page News and Real-World Cues: A New Look at Agenda-Setting by the Media," American Journal of Political Science, 24 (1980), 16-49.

689 Erickson, Keith V. "Jimmy Carter: The Rhetoric of Private and Civic Piety," Western Journal of Speech Communication, 44 (1980), 221-235.

690 _____; and Schmidt, Wallace V. "Presidential Political

Silence: Rhetoric and the Rose Garden Strategy," Southern Speech Communication Journal, 47 (1982), 402-421.

691 Erikson, Robert S.; Luttbeg, N.; and Tedin, K. American Public Opinion: Its Origins, Content, and Impact. New York: John Wiley, 1980.

692 _____; _____; and _____. "The Influence of Newspaper Endorsements in Presidential Elections: The Case of 1964," American Journal of Political Science, 20 (1976), 207-233.

693 Erlich, Howard S. "An Investigation of George Wallace's 1972 Campaign Rhetoric: Was It Populist" (Ph.D. dissertation, University of Massachusetts, 1975), Dissertation Abstracts International A, 36 (1975), 3210.

694 Erskine, H. "The Polls: Corruption in Government," Public Opinion Quarterly, 37 (1973-74), 628-644.

695 _____. "The Polls: Presidential Power," Public Opinion Quarterly, 37 (1973), 488-503.

696 Ettema, J.; and Kline, F. Gerald. "Deficits, Differences and Ceilings: Contingent Conditions for Understanding the Knowledge Gap," Communication Research, 4 (1977), 179-202.

697 _____; and Whitney, D. C. (eds.). Individuals in Mass Media Organizations: Creativity and Constraint. Beverly Hills, CA: Sage Publications, 1982.

698 Evans, Gary L. "Marvin Lionel Esch, A Republican Incumbent and his 1974 Congressional Campaign: A Case Study in Political Persuasive Communication" (Ph.D. dissertation, University of Michigan, 1977), Dissertation Abstracts International A, 38 (1977), 3138-3139.

699 Evans, Katherine W. "Jody Powell on the Press and the Presidency," Washington Journalism Review, 3 (1981), 34-37.

700 _____. "A Talk with Dave Gergen," Washington Journalism Review, 4 (1982), 41-45.

701 _____; and Karnowski, Steve. "Candidates and their Gurus Criticize Coverage," Washington Journalism Review, 2 (1980), 28-31.

702 Evans, Susan H. "The Broken Quill: Journalism in Congressional Campaigns" (Ph.D. dissertation, University of Michigan, 1981), Dissertation Abstracts International A, 42 (1981), 2346-2347.

703 Evarts, Dru. "A Content Analysis of Ohio's Eleven Largest Newspapers, Three National News Magazines, and Evening Newscasts of the Three Commercial Television Networks During the 1972 Presidential Campaigns" (Ph.D. dissertation, Ohio University, 1977), Dissertation Abstracts International A, 38 (1978), 4423.

704 _____; and Stemple, Guido H., III. "Coverage of the 1972 Campaign by T.V., News Magazines, and the Major Newspapers," Journalism Quarterly, 51 (1974), 645-648.

705 Everson, David H. Public Opinion and Interest Groups in American Politics. New York: Franklin Watts, Inc., 1982.

706 Ewen, Stuart; and Ewen, Elizabeth. Channels of Desire: Mass Images and the Shaping of American Consciousness. New York: McGraw-Hill, 1982.

707 Faber, Karl-Georg. "The Use of History in Political Debate," History and Theory, 17 (1978), 36-37.

708 Fadely, Lawrence D. "George Wallace: Agitator Rhetorician. A Rhetorical Criticism of George Corley Wallace's 1968 Presidential Campaign" (Ph.D. dissertation, University of Pittsburgh, 1974), Dissertation Abstracts International A, 35 (1975), 6270.

709 Falco, Maria J. Bigotry: Ethnic, Machine, and Sexual Politics in a Senatorial Election. Westport, CT: Greenwood Press, 1980.

710 Fant, Charles H. "National Politics on Commercial Network Television" (Master's thesis, University of Missouri, 1979), Journalism Abstracts, 18 (1980), 57-58.

711 _____. "Televising Presidential Conventions, 1952-1980," Journal of Communication, 30 (1980), 130-139.

712 Farrell, T. B. "Political Communication: Its Investigation and Praxis," Western Journal of Speech Communication, 40 (1976), 91-103.

713 Farrell, Thomas B. "Political Conventions as Legitimation Ritual," Communication Monographs, 45 (1978), 294-305.

714 Fedler, Fred. "The Media and Minority Groups: A Study of Adequacy of Access," Journalism Quarterly, 50 (1973), 109-117.

715 _____. " '100 Jobs' Dominate News During Florida Election," Journalism Quarterly, 58 (1981), 302-305.

716 _____; Meeske, M.; and Hall, J. "Time Magazine Revisited: Presidential Stereotypes Persist," Journalism Quarterly, 56 (1979), 353-359.

717 _____; and Taylor, Phillip. "Broadcasting's Impact on Selection of News Stories by Readers," Journalism Quarterly, 55 (1978), 301-305, 333.

718 Feigert, Frank B. "Illusions of Ticket-Splitting," American Politics Quarterly, 7 (1979), 470-488.

719 _____. "Political Competence and Mass Media Use," Public Opinion Quarterly, 40 (1976), 234-238.

720 Felkins, Patricia K. "Perceptions of J.F.K.: Image and Myth" (Ph.D. dissertation, University of Missouri-Columbia, 1975), Dissertation Abstracts International A, 37 (1976), 1870.

721 Felknor, Bruce L. Dirty Politics. Westport, CT: Greenwood Press, 1976.

722 Felson, Marcus; and Sudman, Seymour. "The Accuracy of Presidential-Preference Primary Polls," Public Opinion Quarterly, 39 (1975), 232-236.

723 Feltner, P.; and Goldie, L. "Impact of Socialization and Personality of the Female Voter: Speculations Tested with 1964 Presidential Data," Western Political Quarterly, 27 (1974), 680-692.

724 Fenno, Richard. Homestyle. Boston: Little, Brown, 1978.

725 Ferguson, T.; and Rogers, J. (eds.). The Hidden Election. New York: Pantheon Books, 1981.

726 Ferri, Anthony J. "Differences in Television Screen Attention, Coterminus Non-Viewing Behavior, and Program Recall-Comprehension Between Heavy and Casual College Viewers" (Ph.D. dissertation, Wayne State University, 1979).

727 Field, Mervin. "Presidential Election Polling: Are the States Righter?" Public Opinion, 4 (1981), 16-19.

728 _____. "Polls and Public Policy," Journal of Advertising Research, 19 (1979), 11-17.

729 Fields, J.; and Schuman, H. "Public Beliefs About the Beliefs of the Public," Public Opinion Quarterly, 40 (1976-77), 427-448.

730 Fig, Martin R. "Political Television Commercials: A Survey of Alachua County Residents' Expectations and Opinions"

(Master's thesis, University of Florida, 1980), Journalism Abstracts, 19 (1981), 41.

731   Filler, Louis. The Muckrakers. University Park, PA: Pennsylvania State University, 1976.

732   Finch, Gerald B. "Policy and Candidate Choice in the 1968 American Presidential Election" (Ph.D. dissertation, University of Minnesota, 1973), Dissertation Abstracts International A, 34 (1974), 4344-4345.

733   Fine, Gary A. "Recall of Information about Diffusion of a Major News Event," Journalism Quarterly, 52 (1975), 751-755.

734   Fink, Edward L.; and Noell, James J. "Interpersonal Communication Following the Wallace Shooting," Human Communication Research, 1 (1975), 159-167.

735   Finkelstein, Leo, Jr. "The Calendrical Rite of the Ascension to Power," Western Journal of Speech Communication, 45 (1981), 51-59.

736   _____. "The Calendrical Rite of the Ascension to Power: A Generic Inquiry into 20th-Century Presidential Inaugural Addresses" (Ph.D. dissertation, Rensselaer Polytechnic Institute, 1978), Dissertation Abstracts International A, 39 (1979), 4574.

737   Fiorina, Morris P. Retrospective Voting in American National Elections. New Haven, CT: Yale University Press, 1981.

738   _____. "The Voting Decision: Instrumental and Expressive Aspects," Journal of Politics, 38 (1976), 390-413.

739   Fischer, R. A. "Pinback Put-Downs: The Campaign Button as Political Satire," Journal of Popular Culture, 13 (1980), 645-653.

740   Fishbein, Martin; and Coombs, Fred S. "Basis for Decision: An Attitudinal Analysis of Voting Behavior," Journal of Applied Social Psychology, 4 (1974), 95-124.

741   Fishel, Jeff (ed.). Parties and Elections in an Anti-Party Age: American Politics and the Crisis of Confidence. Bloomington, IN: Indiana University Press, 1978.

742   _____. Party and Opposition: Congressional Challenger in American Politics. New York: McKay, 1973.

743   Fisher, Walter R. "Reaffirmation and Subversion of the American Dream," Quarterly Journal of Speech, 59 (1973), 160-167.

744 _____. "Rhetorical Fiction and the Presidency," Quarterly Journal of Speech, 66 (1980), 119-126.

745 _____. "Romantic Democracy, Ronald Reagan, and Presidential Heroes," Western Journal of Speech Communication, 46 (1982), 299-310.

746 Fishman, M. Manufacturing the News. Austin, TX: University of Texas Press, 1980.

747 Fiske, J.; and Hartley, J. Reading Television. London: Methuen, 1978.

748 Fiske, S. T.; and Kinder, D. R. "Involvement, Expertise, and Schema Use: Evidence From Political Cognition," Personality, Cognition, and Social Interaction, eds. N. Cantor and J. Kihlstrom. Hillsdale, NJ: L. Erlbaum Associates, 1981.

749 Fitzgerald, R. "The Images of Power in American Political Cartoons," Praxis, 1 (1976), 1-27.

750 Fixler, P. E., Jr. "A Content Analysis of American Presidential Rhetoric: An Exploratory Study of Misrepresentative and Deceptive Language in the Major Public Communications of Presidents Kennedy, Johnson, and Nixon" (Ph.D. dissertation, University of Southern California, 1979), Dissertation Abstracts International A, 39 (1979), 6733-6734.

751 Flanigan, William; and Zingale, Nancy. Political Behavior of the American Electorate. 4th ed. Newton, MA: Allyn and Bacon, Inc., 1979.

752 Flaningam, Carl D. "Complementary Images: The Off-Year Election Campaigns of Richard Nixon in 1954 and Spiro Agnew in 1970" (Ph.D. dissertation, Purdue University, 1973), Dissertation Abstracts International A, 35 (1974), 610.

753 Fleck, Robert A. "How Media Planners Process Information," Journal of Advertising Research, 13 (1973), 14-18.

754 Fletcher, James E. "Commercial versus Public Television Audiences: Public Activities and the Watergate Hearings," Communication Quarterly, 25 (1977), 13-16.

755 Flowers, George A., Jr. "The Role of Mass Media in the Watergate Affair" (Master's thesis, University of Florida, 1973), Journalism Abstracts, 12 (1974), 102.

756 Flynn, Elizabeth D. "Male/Female Political Socialization: An Exploratory Examination of the Male/Female Differences

in Political Socialization with Regard to Political Awareness, Political Participation, and Political Efficacy" (Master's thesis, University of Louisville, 1979), Masters Abstracts, 18 (1980), 121.

757 Fochs, Arnold. Advertising That Won Elections. Duluth, MN: A. J. Publishing Co., 1980.

758 Fogel, Norman J. "The Impact of Cognitive Dissonance on Electoral Behavior" (Ph.D. dissertation, Ohio State University, 1974), Dissertation Abstracts International A, 35 (1975), 7362-7363.

759 Foley, John; Britton, Dennis A.; Everett, Eugene B. (eds.). Nominating the President: The Process and the Press. New York: Praeger, 1980.

760 Foote, Joe S. "Coorientation in the Network Television News-processing System: Coverage of the United States House of Representatives" (Ph.D. dissertation, University of Texas at Austin, 1979).

761 Forgas, J. P.; Kagan, C.; and Frey, D. "The Cognitive Representation of Political Personalities: A Cross-Cultural Comparison," International Journal of Psychology, 12 (1977), 19-30.

762 Foss, Sonja K. "Abandonment of Genus: The Evolution of Political Rhetoric," Central States Speech Journal, 33 (1982), 367-378.

763 Foti, R. J.; Fraser, S. L.; and Lord, R. G. "Effects of Leadership Labels and Prototypes on Perceptions of Political Leaders," Journal of Applied Psychology, 67 (1972), 326-333.

764 Fowler, Gilbert L., Jr. "Predicting Political News Coverage by Newspaper Characteristics," Journalism Quarterly, 56 (1979), 172-175.

765 Fowler, J. S.; and Showalter, S. W. "Evening Network News Selection: A Confirmation of News Judgment," Journalism Quarterly, 51 (1974), 712-715.

766 Fowler, L. L. "Candidate Perceptions of Electoral Coalitions," American Politics Quarterly, 8 (1980), 483-494.

767 Fowlkes, D. L. "Real-Politics and Play-Politics: The Effects of Watergate and Political Gaming on Undergraduate Students' Political Interest and Political Trust," Simulation and Games, 8 (1977), 419-428.

768 _____. "The Relative Effects of the Family, the School,

Peer Groups, and the Mass Media on the Political Socialization of High School Seniors in the United States" (Ph. D. dissertation, Emory University, 1974), Dissertation Abstracts International A, 35 (1974), 3074.

769 Fox, William S.; and Williams, James D. "Political Orientation and Music Preferences Among College Students," Public Opinion Quarterly, 38 (1974), 352-371.

770 Frakes, K. L. "Effects of Communicative Process on Perceived Source Credibility and Attitude Change in a Political Setting" (Ph. D. dissertation, University of Northern Colorado, 1978), Dissertation Abstracts International A, 39 (1979), 7012-7013.

771 Francis, J. D.; and Busch, L. "What We Now Know About I Don't Knows (1960, 1964, and 1968 Presidential Election Studies)," Public Opinion Quarterly, 39 (1975), 207-218.

772 Frank, R. E.; and Greenberg, M. G. The Public's Use of Television. Beverly Hills, CA: Sage Publications, Inc., 1980.

773 Frank, Robert S. "The Grammar of Film on Television News," Journalism Quarterly, 51 (1974), 245-250.

774 _____. Message Dimensions of Television News. Lexington, MA: Lexington Books, 1973.

775 _____. "Nonverbal and Paralinguistic Analysis of Political Behavior: The First McGovern-Humphrey California Primary Debate," A Psychological Examination of Political Leaders, eds. Margaret G. Hermann and Thomas W. Milburn. New York: Free Press, 1977.

776 Frasure, William G. "Campaign Finance Reform: Problems of Implementation and Democratic Theory" (Ph. D. dissertation, Johns Hopkins University, 1977), Dissertation Abstracts International A, 37 (1977), 6721-6722.

777 Fredd, James B. "News Magazine Use of and Attitudes Toward Leaks in their Coverage of the Decline and Fall of Spiro T. Agnew" (Master's thesis, North Texas State University, 1977), Masters Abstracts, 16 (1978), 40.

778 Freedman, Anne E.; and Freedman, P. E. The Psychology of Political Control. New York: St. Martin's Press, 1975.

779 Freedman, Stanley R. "American Presidential Elections: Issues and Voter Motivation" (Ph. D. dissertation, Florida State University, 1975), Dissertation Abstracts International A, 36 (1975), 509-510.

780 Freejohn, J. A.; and Noll, R. G. "Uncertainty and the Formal Theory of Political Campaigns," American Political Science Review, 72 (1978), 492-505.

781 Freeman, Dorothy E. "A Critical Analysis of the Rhetorical Strategies Employed in the Political Speaking of George C. Wallace in the 1968 Presidential Campaign" (Ph. D. dissertation, Indiana University, 1981), Dissertation Abstracts International A, 42 (1982), 3806-3807.

782 Freeman, Douglas N. "Personal Construct Theory, Political Perception, and Mass Communication: The Judgmental Dimensions Employed in the Evaluation of Political Figures on Mass Media Messages" (Ph. D. dissertation, University of Illinois at Urbana-Champaign, 1976), Dissertation Abstracts International A, (1977), 24.

783 French, B. A. The Presidential Press Conference: Its History and Role in the American Political System. Lanham, MD: University Press of America, 1982.

784 Freshley, Dwight L. "Manipulating Public Expectations: Pre- and Postprimary Statements in the '76 Campaign," Southern Speech Communication Journal, 45 (1980), 223-239.

785 Friedman, Howard S.; DiMatteo, M. Robin; and Mertz, Timothy I. "Nonverbal Communication on Television News: The Facial Expressions of Broadcasters during Coverage of a Presidential Election Campaign," Personality and Social Psychology Bulletin, 6 (1980), 427-435.

786 _____; Mertz, Timothy I.; and DiMatteo, M. Robin. "Perceived Bias in the Facial Expressions of Television News Broadcasters," Journal of Communication, 30 (1980), 103-111.

787 Friendly, Fred W. "The Campaign to Politicize Broadcasting," Columbia Journalism Review, 11 (1973), 9-18.

788 _____. The Good Guys, The Bad Guys and the First Amendment: Free Speech vs. Fairness Broadcasting. New York: Random House, 1976.

789 Fritz, Sara. "Reagan's Honeymoon with the Press is Over," Washington Journalism Review, 4 (1982), 37-40.

790 Frohlich, N.; et al. "Test of Downsian Voter Rationality: 1964 Presidential Voting," American Political Science Review, 72 (1978), 178-197.

791 Frye, Jerry K. "American Newspapers vs. Agnew's 1970 Political Campaign," Journal of Applied Communication Research, 4 (1976), 25-39.

Bibliography

792 _____. "Press Mediation in the Dissemination of Vice President Spiro Agnew's Campaign Speeches of October 19, 1969 to November 3, 1970" (Ph. D. dissertation, University of Michigan, 1974), Dissertation Abstracts International A, 35 (1974), 3028-3029.

793 Fuertsch, David F. "Lyndon B. Johnson and Civil Rights: The Rhetorical Development of a Political Realist" (Ph. D. dissertation, University of Texas at Austin, 1974), Dissertation Abstracts International A, 35 (1975), 5558.

794 Fulero, Solomon M. "Perceived Influence of Endorsements on Voting," Journalism Quarterly, 54 (1977), 789-791.

795 _____; and Fischoff, Baruch. "Differential Media Evaluation and Satisfaction with Election Results: The Bearer of Good and Bad Tidings," Communication Research, 3 (1976), 22-36.

796 Fuller, Cheryl E. S. "A Weaverian Study of President Ford's Efforts to Sell His Energy Package" (Master's thesis, North Texas State University, 1975), Masters Abstracts, 14 (1976), 53.

797 Fullington, M. G. "Presidential Management and Executive Scandal," Presidential Studies Quarterly, 9 (1979), 192-201.

798 Funderburk, D. Presidents and Politics. Monterey, CA: Brooks/Cole, 1982.

799 Funkhouser, G. R. "The Issues of the Sixties: An Exploratory Study in the Dynamics of Public Opinion," Public Opinion Quarterly, 37 (1973), 62-75.

800 _____. "Trends in Media Coverage of the Issues of the Sixties," Journalism Quarterly, 50 (1973), 533-538.

801 Gaby, Daniel M. "Politics and Public Relations," Public Relations Journal, 36 (1980), 11-12.

802 _____; and Treusch, M. H. Election Campaign Handbook. Englewood Cliffs, NJ: Prentice-Hall, 1976.

803 Gadziala, Stephen M. "A Reexamination of the Agenda-Setting Function of the 1976 Debates" (Master's thesis, Ohio State University, 1981), Journalism Abstracts, 19 (1981), 44.

804 Gafke, Roger; and Leuthold, David. "Caveat on E & P Poll on Newspaper Endorsements," Journalism Quarterly, 56 (1979), 383-386.

805 _____; and _____. "The Effect on Voters of Misleading,

Confusing, and Difficult Ballot Titles," Public Opinion Quarterly, 43 (1979), 394-401.

806 Gale, Gary. "The Operation of a Political Press Office in a Mayoral Election in a Major American City: Cleveland, 1975" (Master's thesis, University of Missouri, 1976), Journalism Abstracts, 15 (1977), 62-63.

807 Gallup, George H. The Gallup Poll: Public Opinion, 1972-1977. Wilmington, DE: Scholarly Resources, 1978.

808 _____. The International Gallup Polls: Public Opinion 1978. Wilmington, DE: Scholarly Resources, 1980.

809 _____. Sophisticated Poll Watcher's Guide. Princeton, NJ: Princeton Opinion Press, 1976.

810 Galnoor, Itzhak. "Political Communication and the Study of Politics," Communication Yearbook 4, ed. Dan D. Nimmo. New Brunswick, NJ: Transaction Books, 1980.

811 Gandy, Oscar H., Jr. Beyond Agenda-Setting: Information Subsidies and Public Policy. Norwood, NJ: Ablex Publishing Co., 1982.

812 Ganley, Oswald H.; and Ganly, Gladys D. To Inform or To Control? The New Communications Networks. New York: McGraw-Hill, 1982.

813 Gans, Herbert J. "Debates: Lessons 1976 Can Offer 1980," Columbia Journalism Review, 15 (1977), 25+.

814 _____. Deciding What's News: A Study of CBS Evening News, NBC Nightly News, Newsweek, and Time. New York: Pantheon Books, 1979.

815 Garay, Ronald. "Congressional Television vs. the Congressional Record: What Congress Says and What Congress Means," Quarterly Journal of Speech, 67 (1981), 193-198.

816 _____. "Implementing Televised Coverage of Sessions of the U.S. Congress," Journalism Quarterly, 55 (1978), 527-539.

817 Gardner, C. Media, Politics and Culture: A Socialist View. Atlantic Highlands, NJ: Humanities Press, 1979.

818 Garrett, James B.; and Wallace, Benjamin. "Cognitive Consistency, Repression-Sensitization, and Level of Moral Judgment: Reactions of College Students to the Watergate Scandal," Journal of Social Psychology, 98 (1976), 69-76.

819 _____; and _____. "Effect of Communicator-Communicatee

Similarity in Political Affiliation upon Petition Signing Compliance," Journal of Psychology, 90 (1976), 95-98.

820 Garrison, Glenn D. "An Analysis of Media, Social, and Political Influences on Time of Voting Decisions in Presidential Elections" (Ph. D. dissertation, North Texas State University, 1981), Dissertation Abstracts International A, 42 (1982), 4918.

821 Gaziano, Joseph L. "The Role of Professional Media Consultants in Political Advertising Campaigns for State-Wide Candidates in the 1972 and 1973 General Elections" (Ph. D. dissertation, Northern Illinois University, 1975), Dissertation Abstracts International A, 36 (1976), 7604.

822 Geddes, R. "Finance of Political Parties," Political Quarterly, 45 (1974), 341-345.

823 Gelineau, Elaine P.; and Merenda, Peter F. "Student's Perceptions of Jimmy Carter, Ted Kennedy, and the Ideal President," Perceptual and Motor Skills, 51 (1980), 147-155.

824 _____; and _____. "Students' Pre-Election Perceptions of Jimmy Carter and Ronald Reagan," Perceptual and Motor Skills, 52 (1981), 491-498.

825 Genova, B.; and Greenberg, B. "Interest in News and the Knowledge Gap," Public Opinion Quarterly, 43 (1979), 79-91.

826 Gerbner, George. "Communication: Society Is the Message," Communications, 1 (1974), 57-64.

827 _____ (ed.). Mass Media Policies in Changing Cultures. New York: John Wiley, 1977.

828 _____; Gross, L.; Morgan, M.; and Signorielli, N. "Charting the Mainstream: Television's Contributions to Political Orientations," Journal of Communication, 32 (1982), 100-127.

829 Germond, Jack W.; and Witcover, Jules. Blue Smoke and Mirrors: How Reagan Won and Why Carter Lost the Election of 1980. New York: Viking Press, 1981.

830 _____; and _____. "Bert Lance, the Newshounds, and Dog Days in Washington," Columbia Journalism Review, 16 (1977), 27-31.

831 _____; and _____. "Presidential Debates: An Overview," The Past and Future of Presidential Debates, ed. Austin Ranney. Washington, D.C.: American Enterprise Institute, 1979.

832 Gerstle, Jacques. "The Study of Campaign Debating on Television: A Comparative Analysis of U.S. and French Approaches--A French Perspective," Political Communication Review, 4 (1979), 34-40.

833 Gibson, James W.; and Felkins, Patricia K. "A Nixon Lexicon," Western Speech, 38 (1974), 190-198.

834 Gibson, William. "Network News: Elements of a Theory," Social Text, 3 (1980), 88-111.

835 Giertz, J. F.; and Sullivan, D. H. "Campaign Expenditures and Election Outcomes: A Critical Note," Public Choice, 31 (1977), 157-162.

836 Giggelman, Linda J. C. "Kenneth Burke's Concept of Identification as Applied to Selected Speeches of Edmund Muskie" (Master's thesis, North Texas State University, 1974), Masters Abstracts, 13 (1975), 46.

837 Gilberg, S.; et al. "State of the Union Address and the Press Agenda," Journalism Quarterly, 57 (1980), 584-588.

838 Gilbert, R. E. "Television and Presidential Power," Journal of Social, Political and Economic Studies, 6 (1981), 75-93.

839 Gilmour, R. S.; and Lamb, R. B. Political Alienation in Contemporary America. New York: St. Martin's Press, 1976.

840 Gilson, Lawrence. Money and Secrecy: A Citizen's Guide to Reforming State and Federal Practices. New York: Praeger, 1973.

841 Ginsberg, B. "Elections and Public Policy," American Political Science Review, 70 (1976), 41-49.

842 _____; and Weissberg, R. "Elections and the Mobilization of Popular Support," American Journal of Political Science, 22 (1978), 31-55.

843 Ginsburg, D. H. Regulation of Broadcasting: Law and Policy Towards Radio, Television, and Cable Communication. St. Paul, MN: West Publishing, 1978.

844 Gitlin, Todd. "Making Democracy Safe for America," Columbia Journalism Review, 19 (1980), 53-58.

845 _____. "Spotlights and Shadows: Television and the Culture of Politics," College English, 38 (1977), 789-801.

846 Glantz, S. A.; et al. "Election Outcomes: Whose Money Matters," Journal of Politics, 38 (1976), 1033-1038.

Bibliography

847 Glashan, R. R. *American Governors and Gubernatorial Elections*. Westport, CT: Beckler Books, 1979.

848 Glassman, R. "Legitimacy and Manufactured Charisma," *Social Research*, 42 (1975), 615-636.

849 Glenn, Ethel R. C. "Rhetorical Strategies in the 1972 Democratic Nominating Process" (Ph.D. dissertation, University of Texas at Austin, 1973), *Dissertation Abstracts International A*, 34 (1974), 6152.

850 Glynn, Carroll J.; and McLeod, Jack M. "Public Opinion, Communication Processes, and Voting Decisions," *Communication Yearbook 6*, ed. Michael Burgoon. Beverly Hills, CA: Sage Publications, 1982.

851 Goehlert, B. *Political Behavior: A Bibliography*. Monticello, IL: Vance Bibliography, 1981.

852 Goff, David H. "Television Advertising of Political Candidates: Impact Dimensions for Urban and Non-Urban Voters" (Ph.D. dissertation, University of Massachusetts, 1975), *Dissertation Abstracts International A*, 36 (1976), 5615-5616.

853 Gold, Ellen Reid. "Political Apologia: The Ritual of Self-Defense," *Communication Monographs*, 45 (1978), 306-316.

854 Goldenberg, Edie N.; and Traugott, Michael W. "Congressional Campaign Effects on Candidate Recognition and Evaluation," *Political Behavior*, 2 (1980), 61-90.

855 Goldie, Grace W. *Facing the Nation: Television and Politics 1936-76*. Atlantic Highlands, NJ: Humanities Press, Inc., 1977.

856 Golding, P. "Media Role in National Development: Critique of a Theoretical Orthodoxy," *Journal of Communication*, 24 (1974), 39-53.

857 Goldman, Ralph M. *Contemporary Perspectives on Politics*. New Brunswick, NJ: Transaction Books, 1976.

858 Goldstein, Joel. "Candidate Popularity and Campaign Contributions in the Pre-Nomination Stage of the Presidential Selection Process: The Case of the 1976 Election," *Presidential Studies Quarterly*, 9 (1979), 329-333.

859 _____. "The Influence of Money on the Pre-Nomination Stage of the Presidential Selection Process: The Case of the 1976 Election," *Presidential Studies Quarterly*, 8 (1978), 164-179.

860 Goldstein, Waller (ed.). *Planning, Politics, and the Public*

Interest. New York: Columbia University Press, 1978.

861 Goldwin, Robert A. (ed.). Political Parties in the Eighties. Washington, D.C.: American Enterprise Institute for Public Policy Research, 1980.

862 Golembiewski, R. T.; et al. Dilemmas of Political Participation: Issues for Thought and Simulations for Action. Englewood Cliffs, NJ: Prentice-Hall, 1973.

863 Gollin, A. E. "Exploring the Liaison Between Polling and the Press," Public Opinion Quarterly, 44 (1980), 445-461.

864 _____ (ed.). "Polls and the News Media: A Symposium," Public Opinion Quarterly, 44 (1980), 445-597.

865 Gonchar, R. M.; and Hahn, D. F. "Political Rhetoric: A Reassessment of Critical Methodologies," Journal of Applied Communications Research, 6 (1978), 55-63.

866 _____; and _____. "Richard Nixon and Presidential Mythology," Journal of Applied Communications Research, 1 (1973), 25-48.

867 Good, Lawrence R. "Perceived Value of a Politician's Characteristics," Perceptual and Motor Skills, 44 (1977), 54.

868 Goodhardt, G. J.; Ehrenberg, A. S. C.; and Collins, M. A. The Television Audience: Patterns of Viewing. Lexington, MA: Saxon House, 1975.

869 Goodin, R. E. Manipulatory Politics. New Haven, CT: Yale University Press, 1980.

870 Goot, M. Langley, E.; and South, H. "The Concept of Preference in Voting Behavior," Politics, 10 (1975), 44-53.

871 Gopoian, J. David. "Issue Preferences and Candidate Choice in Presidential Primaries," American Journal of Political Science, 26 (1982), 523-546.

872 _____. "Issue-Voting in Presidential Primary Elections: A Comparative State Analysis of the 1976 Presidential Primaries" (Ph.D. dissertation, Indiana University, 1980), Dissertation Abstracts International A, 41 (1980), 2271-2272.

873 Gordon, A. C.; and Heinz, J. P. Public Access to Information. New Brunswick, NJ: Transaction Books, 1979.

874 Gordon, I.; and Whiteley, P. "Comment: Johnston on Campaign Expenditure and the Efficacy of Advertising," Political Studies, 28 (1980), 293-296.

Bibliography

875 Gordon, N. A. "Constitutional Right to Candidacy," Political Science Quarterly, 91 (1976), 471-487.

876 Gormezano, Keith. Name Identification: Its Effect on Voter Choice and Election Outcome. Iowa City, IA: Le Beacon Presse, 1980.

877 Gormley, William T., Jr. "Coverage of State Government in the Mass Media," State Government, 52 (1979), 46-51.

878 _____. "Newspaper Agendas and Political Elites," Journalism Quarterly, 52 (1975), 304-308.

879 _____. "Television Coverage of State Government," Public Opinion Quarterly, 42 (1978), 354-359.

880 Gosnell, H. F. Getting Out the Vote. New York: AMS Press, 1976.

881 _____; and Smolka, R. G. American Parties and Elections. Columbus, OH: Merrill, 1976.

882 Goudy, F. W. "American Political Behavior and the Election Process: A Bibliographic Essay," American Library Association, 19 (1980), 237-244.

883 Gouran, Dennis S. "Small Group Research and the Demystification of the Political Process," Political Communication Review, 2 (1977), 1-5.

884 _____. "The Watergate Coverup: Its Dynamics and Its Implications," Communication Monographs, 43 (1976), 176-186.

885 Graber, Doris A. "Effect of Incumbency on Coverage Patterns in the 1972 Presidential Campaign," Journalism Quarterly, 53 (1976), 499-508.

886 _____. "The Impact of Media Research on Public Opinion Studies," Mass Communication Review Yearbook 3, eds. D. Charles Whitney, Ellen Wartella, and Sven Windahl. Beverly Hills, CA: Sage Publications, 1982, 555-564.

887 _____. Mass Media and American Politics. Washington, D.C.: Congressional Quarterly, 1980.

888 _____. "Media Coverage and Voter Learning During the Presidential Primary Season," Georgia Journal of Political Science, 7 (1979), 19-48.

889 _____. "Political Languages," Handbook of Political Communication, eds. Dan D. Nimmo and Keith R. Sanders. Beverly Hills, CA: Sage Publications, 1981, 195-223.

890 _____ (ed.). The President and the Public. Philadelphia: Institute for the Study of Human Issues, 1982.

891 _____. "Press and Television as Opinion Resources in Presidential Campaigns," Public Opinion Quarterly, 40 (1976), 285-303.

892 _____. "Press Coverage and Voter Reaction in the 1968 Presidential Election," Political Science Quarterly, 89 (1974), 68-100.

893 _____. "Problems in Measuring Audience Effects," The Presidential Debates: Media, Electoral and Policy Perspectives, eds. George F. Bishop, Robert G. Meadow, and Marilyn Jackson-Beeck. New York: Praeger, 1978.

894 _____. Verbal Behavior and Politics. Champaign, IL: University of Illinois Press, 1976.

895 _____; and Kum, Young Yun. "Why John Q. Voter Did Not Learn Much from the 1976 Presidential Debates," Communication Yearbook 2, ed., Brent D. Ruben. New Brunswick, NJ: Transaction Books, 1978, 407-421.

896 Graeber, Max C. "A Rhetorical Analysis of the Campaign Speaking of Mills Godwin, Jr., for Governor of Virginia, 1965" (Ph.D. dissertation, Bowling Green State University 1973), Dissertation Abstracts International A, 34 (1974), 7365.

897 Granberg, Donald. "Social Judgment Theory," Communication Yearbook 6, ed. Michael Burgoon. Beverly Hills, CA: Sage Publications, 1982.

898 _____; and Brent, Edward E. "Dove-Hawk Placements in the 1968 Election: Application of Social Judgment and Balance Theories," Journal of Personality and Social Psychology, 29 (1974), 687-695.

899 _____; and _____. "Perceptions of Issue Positions of Presidential Candidates," American Scientist, 68 (1980), 617-646.

900 _____; Harris, Wayne; and King, Michael. "Assimilation But Little Contrast in the 1976 U.S. Presidential Election," Journal of Psychology, 108 (1981), 241-247.

901 _____; and Jenks, Richard. "Assimilation and Contrast Effects in the 1972 Election," Human Relations, 30 (1977) 623-640.

902 Gray, Lee L. How We Choose a President (5th ed.). New York: St. Martin's Press, 1980.

Bibliography

903 Great Presidential Campaigns as Reported in the New York Times: Program Guide. Sanford, NC: Microfilming Corporation of America, 1980.

904 Green, Earnestine. "A Rhetorical Evaluation of the 1976 Democratic Keynote Addresses" (Ph. D. dissertation, Ohio State University, 1978), Dissertation Abstracts International A, 39 (1979), 4591-4592.

905 Green, G. N. "McCarthyism in Texas: The 1954 Campaign," The Southern Quarterly, 16 (1978), 255-276.

906 Greenblatt, Milton. "The Effectiveness of Political Cartoons in Stimulating Literal Comprehension and Critical Thinking-Reading by High School Social Studies Students" (Ph. D. dissertation, University of Maryland, 1979), Dissertation Abstracts International A, 40 (1979), 2581-2582.

907 _____. "Psychopolitics," American Journal of Psychiatry, 131 (1974), 1197-1203.

908 _____. "Towards a Definition of Psychopolitics," Psychiatric Annals, 5 (1975), 6-11.

909 Greene, Bob. Running: A Nixon-McGovern Campaign Journal. Chicago, IL: Regnery, 1973.

910 Greenfield, Jeff. "Campaign Reporting: Advice from a Double Agent," Columbia Journalism Review, 14 (1975), 37-39.

911 _____. "A Charm Book for Candidates," Columbia Journalism Review, 19 (1980), 34-37.

912 _____. Playing to Win: An Insider's Guide to Politics. New York: Simon & Schuster, 1980.

913 _____. The Real Campaign: How the Media Missed the Story of the 1980 Campaign. New York: Summit Books, 1982.

914 Greenley, A. M. Building Coalitions: American Politics in the 1970s. New York: New Viewpoints, 1974.

915 Greenstein, Fred I. "The Benevolent Leader Revisited: Children's Images of Political Leaders in Three Democracies," American Political Science Review, 69 (1975), 1371-1398.

916 _____. "Eisenhower as an Activist President: A Look at New Evidence," Political Science Quarterly, 94 (1979), 575-600.

917 _____. Personality and Politics: Problems of Evidence, Inference and Conceptualization. New York: W. W. Norton, 1975.

918 _____; and Polsby, Nelson W. (eds.). Handbook of Political Science, Vols. 1-8. Reading, MA: Addison-Wesley, 1975.

919 Gregg, Richard B. "The Rhetoric of Political Newscasting," Central States Speech Journal, 28 (1977), 221-237.

920 Gribben, William J. "The 'Aspect' of Argument in the Ford-Carter Debates of 1976" (Master's thesis, University of West Florida, 1981), Masters Abstracts, 20 (1982), 233.

921 Grice, George L. " 'We are a People of Peace, But. . . ': A Rhetorical Study of President Lyndon B. Johnson's Statements on United States Military Involvement in Vietnam" (Ph.D. dissertation, University of Texas at Austin, 1976), Dissertation Abstracts International A, 37 (1976), 2496.

922 Griffin, Robert J. "An Information Processing Approach to Uses and Gratifications" (Ph.D. dissertation, University of Wisconsin, 1980), Journalism Abstracts, 18 (1980), 13.

923 Groennings, S.; and Hawley, J. P. To Be a Congressman: The Promise and the Power. Washington, D. C.: Acropolis Books, 1973.

924 Groff, D. D.; et al. "Horsefeathers: The Media, the Campaign, and the Economic Crisis," Columbia Journalism Review, 19 (1980), 4-6.

925 Gronbeck, Bruce E. "The Functions of Presidential Campaigning," Communication Monographs, 45 (1978), 268-280.

926 _____. "The Rhetoric of Political Corruption: Sociolinguistic, Dialectical, and Ceremonial Processes," Quarterly Journal of Speech, 64 (1978), 155-172.

927 Grooms, L. A. How Elections Are Stolen. Lincolnton, NC: Tally Press, 1976.

928 Gross, A. E.; et al. "Persuasion, Surveillance, and Voting Behavior," Journal of Experimental Social Psychology, 10 (1974), 451-460.

929 Gross, D. A. "Representative Styles and Legislative Behavior," Western Political Quarterly, 31 (1978), 359-371.

930 Grossman, Michael B.; and Kumar, Martha J. "Milton's Army: The White House Press Corps," Political Communication and Persuasion, 1 (1981), 145-208.

931 _____; and _____. Portraying the President: The White House and the News Media. Baltimore, MD: Johns Hopkins University Press, 1981.

Bibliography

932 _____; and _____. "The White House and the News Media: The Phases of their Relationship," Political Science Quarterly, 94 (1979), 37-54.

933 _____; and Rourke, F. E. "Media and the Presidency: An Exchange Analysis," Political Science Quarterly, 91 (1976), 455-470.

934 Grush, Joseph E. "Impact of Candidate Expenditures, Regionality, and Prior Outcomes on the 1976 Democratic Presidential Primaries," Journal of Personality and Social Psychology, 38 (1980), 337-347.

935 _____; McKeough, Kevin L.; and Ahlering, Robert F. "Extrapolating Laboratory Exposure Research to Actual Political Elections," Journal of Personality and Social Psychology, 36 (1978), 257-270.

936 Guerra, D. M. "Network Television News Policy and the Nixon Administration: A Comparison" (Ph.D. dissertation, New York University, 1974), Dissertation Abstracts International A, 35 (1974), 1136.

937 Gunter, Barrie. "Remembering Television News: Effects of Picture Content," Journal of General Psychology, 102 (1980), 127-133.

938 Gunter, J. F. "An Introduction to the Great Debate," Journal of Communication, 28 (1978), 142-156.

939 Gustafson, M. "The President's Mail (Is It Worthwhile to Write to the President?)," Presidential Studies Quarterly, 7 (1977), 36-44.

940 Guzzetta, S. J. 'Sal'. The Campaign Manual. Alexandria, VA: Campaign Publishing Co., Inc., 1981.

941 Gyory, B. N.; and Riley, T. E. "Presidential Leadership and the New Progressivism: The Anderson Candidacy," Presidential Studies Quarterly, 10 (1980), 492-496.

942 Haappanen, Lawrence W. "Value Congruence in Voter Preference" (Ph.D. dissertation, Washington State University, 1974), Dissertation Abstracts International A, 35 (1975), 6839-6840.

943 Hadley, Arthur T. The Empty Polling Booth. Englewood Cliffs, NJ: Prentice-Hall, 1978.

944 _____. The Invisible Primary. Englewood Cliffs, NJ: Prentice-Hall, Inc., 1976.

945 Hadley, Roger H. "Applications of Cognitive Style as a Predictor of Recall, Information Salience, and Attitudes Toward Television Commercials" (Ph.D. dissertation, University of Oklahoma, 1978).

946 Hager, D. R. "The Interpersonal Dimension of Political Communication: An Exploratory Study," Social Science Journal, 9 (1974), 56-67.

947 Hagner, P.; and Rieselback, L. "The Impact of the 1976 Presidential Debates: Conversion or Reinforcement?" The Presidential Debates, eds. George Bishop, Robert Meadow, and Marilyn Jackson-Beeck. New York: Praeger, 1978.

948 Hagner, Paul R. "Political Learning in the 1976 Campaign" (Ph.D. dissertation, Indiana University, 1981), Dissertation Abstracts International A, 42 (1981), 1297.

949 Hahn, D. F. "One's Reborn Every Minute: Carter's Religious Appeal in 1976," Communication Quarterly, 28 (1980), 56-62.

950 Haigh, Robert W; Gerbner, George; and Byrne, Richard (eds.). Communications in the Twenty-First Century. New York: Wiley-Interscience, 1981.

951 Haight, Timothy R. "The Mass Media and Presidential Popularity 1961-1976" (Ph.D. dissertation, Stanford University, 1979), Journalism Abstracts, 18 (1980), 14.

952 _____; and Brody, Richard A. "The Mass Media and Presidential Popularity: Presidential Broadcasting and News in the Nixon Administration," Communication Research, 4 (1977), 41-60.

953 Hain, Paul L. "How an Endorsement Affected a Non-Partisan Mayoral Vote," Journalism Quarterly, 52 (1975), 337-340.

954 Hake, Theodore L. Political Buttons, Book 2: 1920-1976. York, PA: Hake's Americana and Collectibles, 1977.

955 Halberstam, David. The Powers that Be. New York: Knopf, 1979.

956 _____. "Television and Politics/The Politics of Television," Media and Methods, 17 (1980), 16-18+.

957 Hale, Katherine D. "Measuring the Impact of a Televised Political Program: Combining Three Research Perspectives" (Ph.D. dissertation, University of Oklahoma, 1977), Dissertation Abstracts International A, 38 (1977), 1720.

958 Hall, S. "Deviancy, Politics, and the Media," Deviance and

Social Control, eds. P. Rock and M. McIntosh. London: Hutchinson Publishing, 1973.

959 _____. "Media Power: The Double Bind," Journal of Communication, 24 (1974), 19-26.

960 Hamilton, J. W. "Some Reflections on Richard Nixon in the Light of his Resignation and Farewell Speeches," Journal of Psychohistory, 4 (1977), 491-511.

961 Hanson, Colan T. "A Rhetorical Analysis of the 1974 U.S. Senate Campaign in North Dakota" (Ph.D. dissertation, Wayne State University, 1978), Dissertation Abstracts International A, 39 (1978), 1187.

962 Hanson, David J. "Authoritarianism and Candidate Preference in the 1980 Presidential Election," Psychological Reports, 49 (1981), 326.

963 _____. "Authoritarianism as a Variable in Political Research," Politico, 40 (1975), 700-705.

964 _____; and White, Bruce J. "Authoritarianism and Candidate Preference in the 1972 Presidential Election," Psychological Reports, 32 (1973), 1158.

965 Hantz, Alan M. "A Longitudinal Study of the Expectations and Gratifications Associated with the 1976 Presidential and Vice-Presidential Debates" (Ph.D. dissertation, Southern Illinois University at Carbondale, 1978), Dissertation Abstracts International A, 40 (1979), 1135.

966 Hardin, C. M. Presidential Power and Accountability. Chicago, IL: University of Chicago Press, 1975.

967 Hargrove, Erwin C. The Power of the Modern Presidency. Philadelphia, PA: Temple University Press, 1975.

968 Harrell, J.; Ware, B. L.; and Linkugel, W. A. "Failure of Apology in American Politics: Nixon on Watergate," Communication Monographs, 62 (1975), 245-261.

969 Harrell, K. F. The Role of Television in U.S. Politics and Government: A Bibliography, 1961-1981. New York: Vance Bibliographies, 1981.

970 Harrigan, L. F. "Individual Styles of Political Activism: Their Consequences for Local Party Organization" (Ph.D. dissertation, The American University, 1977), Dissertation Abstracts International A, 37 (1977), 7286-7287.

971 Harris, Irving D. "The Psychologies of Presidents," Journal of Psychohistory, 3 (1976), 337-350.

972 Harris, Kenneth F. "A Dramatistic Model of Political Mass Communications with Special Attention to the Fool-Making Process" (Master's thesis, California State University, Fullerton, 1982), Masters Abstracts, 20 (1982), 372.

973 Harrison, Gail C. "The Presidents and the Press: Their Moods, Manners and Methods Since 1952" (Master's thesis, East Texas State University, 1976), Journalism Abstracts, 15 (1977), 71.

974 Harrison, Robert D. "Heckling as Rhetoric" (Ph.D. dissertation, Pennsylvania State University, 1981), Dissertation Abstracts International A, 42 (1981), 1373-1374.

975 Hart, Gary W. Right from the Start: A Chronicle of the McGovern Campaign. New York: Quadrangle, 1973.

976 Hart, Roderick P. "Absolutism and Situation: Prolegomena to a Rhetorical Biography of Richard M. Nixon," Communication Monographs, 43 (1976), 204-228.

977 _____. "A Commentary on Popular Assumptions about Political Communication," Human Communications Research, 8 (1982), 366-389.

978 _____. The Political Pulpit. West Lafayette, IN: Purdue University Press, 1977.

979 Hartman, John S. "Carter and the Utopian Group-Fantasy," Journal of Psychohistory, 5 (1977), 239-258.

980 Hartshorn, Elinor C. "The Quiet Campaigner: Edward W. Brooke in Massachusetts" (Ph.D. dissertation, University of Massachusetts, 1973), Dissertation Abstracts International A, 34 (1974), 6715.

981 Harward, D. W. Crisis in Confidence: The Impact of Watergate. Boston, MA: Little, Brown, 1974.

982 Haselswerdt, Michael V. "Campaign Behavior of Political Parties: Campaigns in Mid-Michigan" (Ph.D. dissertation, Michigan State University, 1974), Dissertation Abstracts International A, 35 (1975), 6208.

983 Hawkins, Robert P.; and Pingree, Suzanne. "Using Television to Construct Social Reality," Journal of Broadcasting, 25 (1981), 347-364.

984 _____; _____; and Roberts, Donald F. "Watergate and Political Socialization: The Inescapable Event," American Politics Quarterly, 3 (1975), 406-422.

985 _____; _____; Smith, K.; and Bechtolt, W. "Adolescents'

Responses to Issues and Images," The Great Debates: Carter vs. Ford, 1976, ed. Sidney Kraus. Bloomington, IN: Indiana University Press, 1979.

986 Hays, Robert E., II. "Television-Newspaper Credibility: An Experimental Study" (Ed. D. dissertation, East Texas State University, 1979).

987 Heath, Robert L. "Common Cause and Nonpartisan Influence in Political Campaigns: A Case Study," Central States Speech Journal, 25 (1974), 182-189.

988 Hecht, Marie B. Beyond the Presidency: The Residues of Power. New York: Macmillan, 1976.

989 Heclo, Hugh. A Government of Strangers: Executive Politics in Washington. Washington, D.C.: Brookings Institute, 1977.

990 _____. Studying the Presidency. New York: Ford Foundation, 1977.

991 Hedman, L. "Mass Media, Opinion-Makers, and Public Opinion on Development Issues," Communications, 5 (1980), 107-134.

992 Heighton, Elizabeth J.; and Cunningham, Don R. Advertising in the Broadcast Media. Belmont, CA: Wadsworth, 1976.

993 Heitzmann, W. R. "The Political Cartoon as a Teaching Device," Teaching Political Science," 6 (1979), 166-184.

994 Hellweg, Susan. "An Examination of Voter Conceptualization of the Ideal Political Candidate," Southern Speech Communication Journal, 44 (1979), 373-385.

995 _____. "Perception of a Communication Source: An Examination of the Ideal Political Candidate as a Function of Selected Voter Characteristics" (Ph.D. dissertation, University of Southern California, 1977), Dissertation Abstracts International A, 38 (1978), 6397.

996 _____; and Phillips, S. L. "Verbal and Visual Analysis of the 1980 Houston Republican Presidential Primary Debate," Southern Speech Communication Journal, 47 (1981), 23-38.

997 Henderson, Bill. "An Evaluation of the October, 1972, Rhetorical Strategy of the White House Which Chose to Attack the Washington Post Coverage of Watergate: A Fantasy Theme Analysis of the Rhetorical Situation" (Ph.D. dissertation, University of Minnesota, 1975), Dissertation Abstracts International A, 37 (1976), 32-33.

998 Hepburn, Mary A. Making Your Vote Count: Registration, Campaigns, and Elections in Georgia. Athens, GA: University of Georgia, Institute of Government, 1976.

999 Herbers, John. No Thank You, Mr. President. New York: W. W. Norton, 1976.

1000 Hermann, Margaret G.; and Milburn, Thomas W. (eds.). A Psychological Examination of Political Leaders. New York: Free Press, 1977.

1001 Hermet, Guy, et al. (eds.). Elections Without Choice. New York: Halsted Press, 1978.

1002 Herschensohn, Bruce. The Gods of Antenna. New Rochelle, NY: Arlington House, 1976.

1003 Hershey, Marjorie R. The Making of Campaign Strategy. Lexington, MA: D. C. Health and Company, 1974.

1004 _____; and Hill, David B. "Watergate and Preadults' Attitudes Toward the Presidency," American Journal of Political Science, 19 (1975), 703-726.

1005 Hertzog, Robert L. "The Effects of News Commentary on the Image of Political Debaters: An Experimental Study" (Master's thesis, North Texas State University, 1977), Masters Abstracts, 16 (1978), 109.

1006 Herzik, Eric B.; and Dodson, Mary L. "Public Expectations and the Presidency: Barber's 'Climate of Expectations' Examined," Presidential Studies Quarterly, 12 (1982), 485-490.

1007 Herzon, Frederick. "Intensity of Opinion and the Organization of Political Attitudes," Western Political Quarterly, 28 (1975), 72-84.

1008 Hess, Richard C. "The 1970 Senatorial Campaign in Indiana: A Rhetorical Case Study of Political Communication" (Ph. D. dissertation, Ohio State University, 1973), Dissertation Abstracts International A, 34 (1974), 7365.

1009 Hess, Stephen. Organizing the Presidency. Washington, D. C.: Brookings Institution, 1976.

1010 _____. The Presidential Campaign: The Leadership Selection Process After Watergate. Washington, D. C.: Brookings Institution, 1974.

1011 _____. The Washington Reporters. Washington, D. C.: The Brookings Institution, 1981.

1012 Hesse, Michael B. "Coorientation Study of Wisconsin State Senators and their Constituencies," Journalism Quarterly, 53 (1976), 626-633+.

1013 _____. "A Coorientational Study of Wisconsin State Senators: Their Role in the Communication Process" (Ph.D. dissertation, University of Wisconsin-Madison, 1975), Dissertation Abstracts International A, 36 (1975), 1143-1144.

1014 _____. "Strategies of the Political Communication Process," Public Relations Review, 7 (1981), 32-47.

1015 Hickman, Jacqueline D. "Initiation to Politics: Child and Family" (Master's thesis, California State University, Fullerton, 1975), Masters Abstracts, 13 (1975), 165-166.

1016 Hicks, J. M. "Conservative Voting and Personality," Social Behavior and Personality, 2 (1974), 43-49.

1017 Hiebert, Ray, et al. (eds.). The Political Image Merchants: Strategies for the Seventies. 2nd ed. Washington, D.C.: Acropolis Books Ltd., 1975.

1018 Hikel, G. K. Beyond the Polls: Political Ideology and Its Correlates. Indianapolis, IN: Heath, 1973.

1019 Hilderbrand, R. C. Power and the People. Chapel Hill, NC: University of North Carolina Press, 1981.

1020 Hill, A. P. "The Effect of Party Organization Election Expenses and the 1970 Election," Political Studies, 22 (1974), 215-217.

1021 Hill, David B.; and Luttbeg, Norman R. Trends in American Electoral Behavior. Itasca, IL: F.E. Peacock, Publishers, 1980.

1022 Hill, K. Q. "Taxpayer Support for the Presidential Election Campaign Fund," Social Science Quarterly, 62 (1981), 767-771.

1023 _____; and Hurley, P. A. "Mass Participation, Electoral Competitiveness, and Issue-Attitude Agreement Between Congressmen and Their Constituents," British Journal of Political Science, 9 (1979), 507-511.

1024 Hillbruner, Anthony. "Archetype and Signature: Nixon and the 1973 Inaugural," Central States Speech Journal, 25 (1974), 169-181.

1025 Hillenberg, George M. "Free Expression Implications of the New Federal Elections Law," Journalism Quarterly, 50 (1973), 527-532.

1026 Hillert, Margaret E. "Press Coverage by Four Selected Newspapers of the 1964, 1968 and 1972 George Wallace Presidential Campaigns" (Master's thesis, Purdue University, 1977), Journalism Abstracts, 17 (1979), 72-73.

1027 Himelstein, Jerry. "Rhetorical Continuities in the Politics of Race: The Closed Society Revisited," Southern Speech Communication Journal, 48 (1983), 153-166.

1028 Himmelweit, Hilde T.; Biberian, M. J.; and Stockdale, J. "Memory for Past Vote: Implications of a Study of Bias in Recall," British Journal of Political Science, 8 (1978), 365-374.

1029 _____; et al. How Voters Decide: A Longitudinal Study of Political Attitudes and Voting Extending Over Fifteen Years. New York: Academic Press, 1981.

1030 Hinckley, Barbara. "The American Voter in Congressional Elections," American Political Science Review, 74 (1980), 641-650.

1031 _____. Congressional Elections. Washington, D.C.: Congressional Quarterly, 1981.

1032 _____. "House Re-Elections and Senate Defeats: The Role of the Challenger," British Journal of Political Science, 10 (1980), 441-460.

1033 _____. "The Initially Strongest Player; Coalition Games and Presidential Nominations," American Behavioral Scientist, 18 (1975), 497-512.

1034 _____. "Issues, Information Costs, and Congressional Elections," American Politics Quarterly, 4 (1976), 131-152.

1035 _____; et al. "Information and the Vote: A Comparative Election Study," American Politics Quarterly, 2 (1974), 131-158.

1036 Hindman, A. P. "The Interaction of Political Values and Viewing Aggression on Anger and Aggression" (Ph.D. dissertation, University of Massachusetts, 1973), Dissertation Abstracts International B, 34 (1973), 2933-2934.

1037 Hippely, John F., Jr. "An Analysis of the Elements of Tragedy in a Poetic Vision: The Eagleton Affair" (Ph.D. dissertation, Washington State University, 1979), Dissertation Abstracts International A, 40 (1979), 26.

1038 Hirsch, Paul; Miller, Peter V.; and Kline, F. Gerald. Strategies for Communication Research. Beverly Hills, CA: Sage Publications, 1978.

1039 Hirschfield, Robert S. (ed.). Selection-Election: A Forum on the American Presidency. Hawthorne, NY: Aldine Publishing Co., 1982.

1040 Hitlin, R. A.; and Jackson, J. S., III. "On Amateur and Professional Politicians," Journal of Politics, 39 (1977), 786-793.

1041 Hodson, Timothy A. "The Impact of Campaign Finance Reforms on the Nature and Functions of Political Campaigns" (Ph.D. dissertation, University of California, Santa Barbara, 1977), Dissertation Abstracts International A, 38 (1977), 2322.

1042 Hoeh, David C. "The Biography of a Campaign Strategy, Management, Result; McCarthy in New Hampshire 1968" (Ph.D. dissertation, University of Massachusetts, 1978), Dissertation Abstracts International A, 39 (1979), 5123.

1043 Hoffer, T. W.; and Nelson, R. A. "Docudrama on American Television," Journal of the University Film Association, 30 (1978), 21-27.

1044 Hoffman, N. V. Make-Believe Presidents: Illusions of Power from McKinley to Carter. New York: Pantheon Books, 1978.

1045 Hofstetter, C. Richard. Bias in the News: Network Television Coverage of the 1972 Election Campaign. Columbus, OH: Ohio State University Press, 1976.

1046 _____. "Content Analysis," Handbook of Political Communication, eds. Dan D. Nimmo and Keith R. Sanders. Beverly Hills, CA: Sage Publications, 1981, 529-560.

1047 _____. "News Bias in the 1972 Campaign: Across-Media Comparison," Journalism Monographs, 58 (1978), 1-30.

1048 _____. "Perceptions of News Bias in the 1972 Presidential Campaign," Journalism Quarterly, 56 (1979), 370-374.

1049 _____; and Buss, Terry F. "Bias in Television News Coverage of Political Events: A Methodological Analysis," Journal of Broadcasting, 22 (1978), 517-530.

1050 _____; and _____. "Politics and Last-Minute Political Television," Western Political Quarterly, 33 (1980), 24-37.

1051 _____; and Moore, David W. "Television News Coverage of Presidential Primaries," Journalism Quarterly, 59 (1982), 651-654.

1052 _____; and _____. "Watching TV News and Supporting the Military: A Surprising Impact of the News Media," Armed Forces and Society, 5 (1979), 261-269.

1053 _____; and Zukin, Cliff. "TV Network News and Advertising in the Nixon and McGovern Campaigns," Journalism Quarterly, 56 (1979), 106-115, 152.

1054 _____; _____; and Buss, Terry F. "Political Imagery and Information in an Age of Television," Journalism Quarterly, 55 (1978), 562-569.

1055 Hogan, Bill. "Ronald Reagan's Close Encounters with the Fourth Estate," Washington Journalism Review, 3 (1981), 32-35.

1056 Hollander, S., Jr. "On the Strength of a Newspaper Endorsement," Public Opinion Quarterly, 43 (1979), 405-407.

1057 Hollenback, James Barry. "The Political Speaking of Roscoe Conkling of New York" (Ph.D. dissertation, Ohio University, 1973), Dissertation Abstracts International A, 34 (1974), 7912.

1058 Holloway, Harry; and George, John. Public Opinion: Coalitions, Elites, and Masses. New York: St. Martin's Press, 1979.

1059 Holm, John; Kraus, Sidney; and Bockner, A. P. "Communication and Opinion Formation: Issues Generated by the Watergate Hearings," Communication Research, 1 (1974), 368-390.

1060 Holt, Virginia M. "The Mediating Role of Political Expectations Between Mass Media Agendas and Perceptions of a Political Campaign" (Master's thesis, University of Maryland, 1976), Journalism Abstracts, 15 (1977), 75.

1061 Homet, R. S., Jr. Politics, Cultures and Communication: European vs. American Approaches to Communications Policymaking. New York: Aspen Institute for Communication Studies, 1979.

1062 Hoopes, Roy. Political Campaigning. New York: Franklin Watts, Inc., 1979.

1063 Hormik, Robert C. "Mass Media Use and the 'Revolution of Rising Frustrations': A Reconsideration of the Theory," Communication Research, 4 (1977), 387-413.

1064 Houlberg, Charles F. "Television Newscasters and News: The Perception and Selection of Local Newscasters and Stations" (Ph.D. dissertation, Ohio State University, 1982), Dissertation Abstracts International A, 43 (1982), 2482.

1065 House, J. S.; and Mason, W. M. "Political Alienation in America, 1952-1968," American Sociological Review, 40 (1975), 123-147.

1066 How to Organize and Implement a Successful Non-Partisan Voter Participation Campaign. Washington, D. C.: Joint Center for Political Studies, 1980.

1067 Howard, Anthony. "The Parties, Elections and Television" Sight and Sound, 47 (1978), 206-209.

1068 Howell, Michael J. "Theodore H. White as a Speech Critic: An Analysis of His Treatment of Speechmaking in Three Presidential Campaigns, 1960-1968" (Master's thesis, State University of New York, Geneseo, 1972), Masters Abstracts, 11 (1973), 349.

1069 Howell, Susan E. "Local Election Campaigns: The Effects of Office Level on Campaign Style," Journal of Politics, 42 (1980), 1135-1145.

1070 _____. "Political Information: The Effects of System and Individual Characteristics," Comparative Political Studies, 8 (1976), 413-435.

1071 _____; and Oiler, William S. "Campaign Activities and Local Election Outcomes," Social Science Quarterly, 62 (1981), 151-160.

1072 Howell, Susan R. "American Political Parties in a Presidential Campaign: A Study of the 1972 Local Campaign Activists" (Ph.D. dissertation, Ohio State University, 1976), Dissertation Abstracts International A, 37 (1976), 3153-3154.

1073 Howitt, Dennis. The Mass Media and Social Problems. Oxford and New York: Pergamon Press, 1982.

1074 Hudson, K. The Language of Modern Politics. London, England: Macmillan, 1980.

1075 Hudson, W. Gail. "The Role of Humor in John F. Kennedy's 1960 Presidential Campaign" (Ph.D. dissertation, Southern Illinois University at Carbondale, 1979), Dissertation Abstracts International A, 40 (1979), 2984.

1076 Hughes, A. Psychology and the Political Experience. London, England: Cambridge University Press, 1975.

1077 Hughes, Emmet J. The Living Presidency; The Resources and Dilemmas of the American Presidential Office. New York: Coward, McCann and Geoghegan, 1973.

1078 Hulbary, W. E. "Adolescent Political Self-Images and Political Involvement: The Relative Effects of High School Black Studies Courses and Prior Socialization" (Ph. D. dissertation, University of Iowa, 1972), Dissertation Abstracts International A, 33 (1973), 6980.

1079 Hull, B. C. "A Legal Study of the Political Activities of Public School Employees: Their Candidacy for Public Offices and Their Campaigning for Other Political Candidates and Issues" (Ph. D. dissertation, University of Georgia, 1980), Dissertation Abstracts International A, 41 (1980), 1866-1867.

1080 Hulteng, John L. The Messenger's Motives: Ethical Problems of the News Media. Englewood Cliffs, NJ: Prentice-Hall, 1976.

1081 Humke, Ronald G.; Schmitt, Raymond L.; and Grupp, Stanley E. "Candidates, Issues and Party in Newspaper Political Advertisements," Journalism Quarterly, 52 (1975), 499-504.

1082 Hunt, T. "Beyond the Journalistic Event: The Changing Concept of News," Mass Comm Review, 1 (1974), 23-32.

1083 Hunter, Deborah. "The Aftermath of Carl Stokes: An Analysis of Political Drama in the 1971 Cleveland Mayoral Campaign," Journal of Black Studies, 8 (1978), 337-354.

1084 _____. "Arnold R. Pinkney and the 1971 Cleveland Mayoral Campaign: The Case for the Strategy of Flexible Responses" (Ph. D. dissertation, State University of New York at Buffalo, 1979), Dissertation Abstracts International A, 40 (1980), 4799.

1085 Hurley, Patricia A. "The Electoral Basis of Congressional Performance" (Ph. D. dissertation, Rice University, 1976), Dissertation Abstracts International A, 37 (1976), 2397.

1086 _____; and Hill K. Q. "The Prospects for Issue Voting in Contemporary Congressional Elections," American Politics Quarterly, 8 (1980), 425-448.

1087 Hutcheson, J. D.; and Shevin, J. Citizen Groups in Local Politics: A Bibliographic Review. Santa Barbara, CA: ABC-Clio, 1976.

1088 Hvistendahl, J. K. Effect of Placement of Biasing Information," Journalism Quarterly, 56 (1979), 863-865.

1089 Hy, Ronn. "Mass Media in Election Campaigns," Public Administration Survey, 20 (1973), 1-6.

1090 Hyde, Michael J. (ed.). Communication Philosophy and the Technological Age. University, AL: University of Alabama Press, 1982.

1091 Hyman, E. J. "The Politics of Manipulation: Social Psychological Factors Associated with Political Behavior and Social Manipulation" (Ph.D. dissertation, University of California, Berkeley, 1975), Dissertation Abstracts International B, 37 (1976), 526-527.

1092 Hyman, H. H. "Surveys in the Study of Political Psychology," Handbook of Political Psychology, ed. J. N. Knutson. San Francisco, CA: Jossey-Bass, 1973.

1093 Hynes, Thomas J., Jr. "'McGovern, Come Down': An Analysis of Senator George McGovern's Confrontation with Demostrators, Doral Beach Hotel, July 12, 1972," Southern Speech Communication Journal, 39 (1974), 269-278.

1094 Inglehart, Ronald. The Silent Revolution: Changing Values and Political Styles Among Western Publics. Princeton, NJ: Princeton University Press, 1977.

1095 Inglish, John M. "The Relationship of Newspaper Editorial Endorsements of Certain County and District Candidates, Newspaper Partisanship, and Vote Share in Rural Missouri Counties During the 1968, 1970, 1972, and 1974 General Elections" (Master's thesis, Central Missouri State University, 1975), Journalism Abstracts, 14 (1976), 117-118.

1096 Ions, Edmund. "The American Primary Elections and Conventions of 1976," Parliamentary Affairs, 30 (1977), 59-68.

1097 Ippolito, D. S.; et al. Public Opinion and Responsible Democracy. Englewood Cliffs, NJ: Prentice-Hall, 1976.

1098 Isaacs, S. "Were Polls Overemphasized?" Columbia Journalism Review, 11 (1973), 9-30.

1099 Israel, Michael L. "The Lost Cause Candidate: The Myth of Competition in Uncompetitive American Congressional Elections" (Ph.D. dissertation, Rutgers University, The State University of New Jersey, 1974), Dissertation Abstracts International A, 35 (1974), 535-536.

1100 Iyengar, Shanto. "Television News and Issue Salience: A Reexamination of the Agenda-Setting Hypothesis," American Politics Quarterly, 7 (1979), 385-416.

1101 _____; Peters, Mark D.; and Kinder, Donald R. "Experimental Demonstrations of the 'Not-So-Minimal' Consequences of Television News Programs," American Political Science Review, 76 (1982), 848-858.

1102 Jablonski, Carol J. "Richard Nixon's Irish Wake: A Case of Generic Transference," Central States Speech Journal, 30 (1979), 164-173.

1103 Jaccard, James; Knox, Richard; and Brinberg, David. "Designing Political Campaigns to Elect a Candidate: Toward a Social Psychological Theory of Voting Behavior," Journal of Applied Social Psychology, 10 (1980), 367-383.

1104 _____; _____; and _____. "Prediction of Behavior from Beliefs: An Extension and Test of a Subjective Probability Model," Journal of Personality and Social Psychology, 37 (1979), 1239-1248.

1105 Jackman, M. R. "The Relation Between Verbal Attitude and Overt Behavior: A Public Opinion Application," Social Forces, 55 (1976), 1-15.

1106 Jackson, John. Constituencies and Leaders in Congress: Their Effects on Senate Voting Behavior. Cambridge, MA: Harvard University Press, 1974.

1107 _____. "Issues, Party Choice and Presidential Votes," American Journal of Political Science, 19 (1975), 161-186.

1108 Jackson-Beeck, Marilyn. "Interpersonal and Mass Communication in Children's Political Socialization," Journalism Quarterly, 56 (1979), 48-53.

1109 _____. "Mass Media Exposure and Individual Political Activity" (Ph.D. dissertation, University of Pennsylvania, 1979), Dissertation Abstracts International A, 40 (1979), 1136.

1110 _____; and Kraus, Sidney. "Political Communication Theory and Research: An Overview 1978-79," Communication Yearbook 4, ed. Dan D. Nimmo. New Brunswick, NJ: Transaction Books, 1980, 449-465.

1111 _____; and Meadow, Robert G. "Content Analysis of Televised Communication Events: The Presidential Debates," Communication Research, 6 (1979), 321-344.

1112 _____; and _____. "The Triple Agenda of Presidential Debates," Public Opinion Quarterly, 43 (1979), 173-180.

1113 Jacobson, Gary C. "The Effect of Campaign Spending in Congressional Elections," American Political Science Review, 72 (1978), 469-491.

1114 _____. "The Impact of Broadcast Campaigning on Electoral Outcomes," Journal of Politics, 37 (1975), 769-793.

1115 _____. "Incumbents' Advantages in the 1978 U.S. Congressional Elections," Legislative Studies Quarterly, 6 (1981), 183-200.

1116 _____. Money in Congressional Elections. New Haven, CT: Yale University Press, 1980.

1117 _____. "Practical Consequences of Campaign Finance Reform: An Incumbent Protection Act?" Public Policy, 24 (1976), 1-32.

1118 _____. "Presidential Coattails in 1972," Public Opinion Quarterly, 40 (1976), 194-200.

1119 _____; and Kernell, S. Strategy and Choice in Congressional Elections. New Haven, CT: Yale University Press, 1981.

1120 James, J. L.; and James, D. B. "Lessons of Watergate: The Nixon Campaigns: 1968 and 1972," Current History, 67 (1974), 30-33.

1121 Jameson, M. M. "Political Style Among Party Activists in Texas: A Study of Delegates to the 1972 Democratic and Republican State Conventions" (Ph.D. dissertation, University of Houston, 1974), Dissertation Abstracts International A, 35 (1975), 7365.

1122 Jamieson, K. H.; and Campbell, K. K. "Rhetorical Hybrids: Fusions of Genetic Elements," Quarterly Journal of Speech, 68 (1982), 146-157.

1123 Jenkins, S. "The Press as Politician in Local Planning," Political Quarterly, 44 (1973), 47-57.

1124 Jennings, M. Kent. "Another Look at the Life Cycle and Political Participation," American Journal of Political Science, 23 (1979), 755-771.

1125 _____; and Niemi, Richard G. Generations and Politics. Princeton, NJ: Princeton University Press, 1981.

1126 _____; and _____. The Political Character of Adolescence. Princeton, NJ: Princeton University Press, 1974.

1127 Jensen, R. "Armies, Admen and Crusaders: Strategies to Win Elections," Public Opinion, 3 (1980), 44-49.

1128 Jewell, Malcolm E.; and Olson, David M. American State Political Parties and Elections. Homewood, IL: Dorsey Press, 1982.

1129 Johannes, John R.; and McAdams, John C. "The Congressional Incumbency Effect: Is It Casework, Policy Compatibility, or Something Else? An Examination of the 1978 Election," American Journal of Political Science, 25 (1981), 512-542.

1130 Johnson, Charles A.; Shaefer, Roger C.; and McKnight, R. Neal. "The Salience of Judicial Candidates and Elections," Social Science Quarterly, 59 (1978), 371-378.

1131 Johnson, G. W. (ed.). The Johnson Presidential Press Conferences. New York: Earl M. Coleman Enterprises, 1978.

1132 Johnson, Joel T.; and Taylor, Shelley E. "The Effect of Metaphor on Political Attitudes," Basic and Applied Social Psychology, 2 (1981), 305-316.

1133 Johnson, Keith R.; and Powell, Thomas R. "Levels of Response to Stimulus Letters," Psychological Reports, 37 (1975), 378.

1134 Johnson, Morris R. "Television and Politicization: A Test of Competing Models," Journalism Quarterly, 50 (1973), 447-455.

1135 Johnson, R. T. Managing the White House. New York: Harper and Row, 1974.

1136 Johnson, Willie S. "The Bumpers-Fulbright Senate Race: A Rhetorical Analysis" (Ph.D. dissertation, University of Illinois at Urbana-Champaign, 1981), Dissertation Abstracts International A, 42 (1981), 2365.

1137 Johnston, R. J. "Campaign Expenditure and the Efficacy of Advertising: A Response," Political Studies, 29 (1981), 113-114.

1138 _____. "Local Effects in Voting at a Local Election," Association of American Geographers Annals, 64 (1974), 418-429.

1139 _____. "Resource Allocation and Political Campaigns: Notes Toward a Methodology," Policy and Politics, 5 (1976), 181-200.

1140 Johnstone, Christopher L. "Electing Ourselves in 1976: Jimmy Carter and the American Faith," Journal of Western Speech Communication, 42 (1978), 241-249.

1141 Jones, B. D. "Candidate Perceptions by Detroit-Area Actives: Some Evidence Concerning Stokes' 'Axiom of Common Reference,'" Michigan Academician, 6 (1973), 137-148.

1142 _____. "Competitiveness, Role Orientations, and Legislative Responsiveness," Journal of Politics, 35 (1973), 924-947.

1143 Jones, Billy V. "Attitude Change Toward the Candidates of the 1980 Presidential Election," Journal of Social Psychology, 116 (1982), 297-298.

1144 _____. "Attitude Change Toward the Winner and the Loser of the 1976 Presidential Election," Journal of Psychology, 96 (1977), 213-215.

1145 Jones, Cliff A.; and Kaid, Lynda Lee. "Political Campaign Regulation and the Constitution: Oklahoma's Campaign Contributions and Expenditures Act," Oklahoma Law Review, 29 (1976), 684-711.

1146 Jones, J. S. "Political Socialization in Picture Books 1972-1976" (Ph.D. dissertation, University of Akron, 1979), Dissertation Abstracts International A, 39 (1979), 6108.

1147 Jones, James M. "Dogmatism and Political Preferences," Psychological Reports, 33 (1973), 640.

1148 Jones, M. E. "Issues, Issue Publics, and Electoral Behavior" (Ph.D. dissertation, University of Oklahoma, 1974), Dissertation Abstracts International A, 34 (1974), 5266-5267.

1149 Jones, R. S. "State Public Campaign Finance: Implications for Partisan Politics," American Journal of Political Science, 25 (1981), 342-361.

1150 Jones, Warren H. "Political Information and Constraint: Methodological and Theoretical Implications, (Ph.D. dissertation, Oklahoma State University, 1974), Dissertation Abstracts International B, 35 (1975), 5084.

1151 Joslyn, Richard A. "The Content of Political Spot Ads," Journalism Quarterly, 57 (1980), 92-98.

1152 _____. "The Impact of Campaign Spot Advertising on Voting Defections," Human Communication Research, 7 (1981), 347-360.

1153 _____. "The Impact of Television on Partisan Politics" (Ph.D. dissertation, Cornell University, 1977), Dissertation Abstracts International A, 38 (1978), 5684-5685.

1154 _____. "Manifestations of Elazar's Political Subcultures: State Public Opinion and the Content of Political Campaign Advertising," Publius, 10 (1980), 37-58.

1155 _____; and Galderisa, Peter F. "The Impact of Adolescent Perceptions of the Presidency: A Test of the 'Spillover' Hypothesis," Youth and Society, 9 (1977), 151-170.

1156 Julian, Faye D. "Nonverbal Determinants of a Television Newscaster's Credibility: An Experimental Study" (Ph.D. dissertation, University of Tennessee, 1977), Dissertation Abstracts International A, 38 (1978), 3786.

1157 Jung, Hwa Y. The Crisis of Political Understanding: A Phenomenological Perspective in the Conduct of Political Inquiry. West Brookfield, MA: Duquesne University Press, 1979.

1158 Just, M. R. "Political Polling and Political Television," Current History, 67 (1974), 79-82.

1159 Kahle, Lynn R.; and Berman, John J. "Attitudes Cause Behaviors: A Cross-Lagged Panel Analysis," Journal of Personality and Social Psychology, 37 (1979), 315-321.

1160 Kaid, Lynda Lee. "An Analysis of Studies of the 1976 Presidential Debates," Political Communication Review, 3 (1978), 1-2.

1161 _____. "Guide to the Literature (of Political Communication)," Handbook of Political Communication, ed. Dan D. Nimmo and Keith R. Sanders. Beverly Hills, CA: Sage Publications, 1981, 693-701.

1162 _____. "The Impact of Political Television Commercials," Proceedings of the Speech Communication Association Summer Conference on Mass Communication in Education and Society, ed. Robert Davis. Falls Church, VA: Speech Communication Association, 1978.

1163 _____. "The Impact of Political Television Commercials: An Experimental Study of Type, Length, and Partisan Evaluation" (Ph.D. dissertation, Southern Illinois University, 1975), Dissertation Abstracts International A, 36 (1976), 4829-4830.

1164 _____. "Measures of Political Advertising," Journal of Advertising Research, 16 (1976), 49-53.

1165 _____. "The Neglected Candidate: Interpersonal Communication in Political Campaigns," Journal of Western Speech Communication, 41 (1977), 245-252.

Bibliography 97

1166 _____. "Newspaper Treatment of a Candidate's News Releases," Journalism Quarterly. 53 (1976), 135-137.

1167 _____. "Non-Print Materials in Presidential Libraries," Political Communication Review, 1 (1975), 8-9.

1168 _____. "Paid Television Advertising and Candidate Name Identification," Campaigns and Elections: The Journal of Political Action, 3 (1982), 34-36.

1169 _____. "Political Advertising," Handbook of Political Communication, eds. Dan D. Nimmo and Keith R. Sanders. Beverly Hills, CA: Sage Publications, Inc., 1981, 249-271.

1170 _____. "Studies of the 1980 Elections," Political Communication Review, 5 (1980), 1-15.

1171 _____. "Teaching Political Communication as a Skill," News for Teachers of Political Science, 33 (1982), 2-3.

1172 _____; Corgan, Craig; and Clampitt, Phil. "Perceptions of a Political Campaign Event: Media vs. Personal Viewing," Journal of Broadcasting, 20 (1976), 303-312.

1173 _____; Fahey, James; and Hale, Katherine. "Political Uses of Cable Television," State Government, 51 (1978), 212-214.

1174 _____; Hale, Kathy; and Williams, Jo Ann. "Media Agenda Setting of a Specific Political Event," Journalism Quarterly, 54 (1977), 584-587.

1175 _____; and Hirsch, Robert O. "Selective Exposure and Candidate Image: A Field Study Over Time," Central States Speech Journal, 24 (1973), 48-51.

1176 _____; and Sanders, Keith R. Communication and Politics: A Selected, Annotated Bibliography. Annandale, VA: Speech Communication Association, 1980.

1177 _____; and _____. "The Evolution of Jimmy Carter's Image," Cahiers de la Communication, 1 (1981), 185-204.

1178 _____; and _____. "Political Television Commercials: An Experimental Study of Type and Length," Communication Research, 5 (1978), 57-70.

1179 _____; _____; and Hirsch, Robert O. Political Campaign Communication: A Bibliography and Guide to the Literature. Metuchen, NJ: Scarecrow Press, Inc., 1974.

1180 _____; Singleton, Donald L.; and Davis, Dwight. "Instant Analysis of Televised Political Addresses: The Speaker vs. the Commentator," Communication Yearbook 1, ed. Brent Ruben. New Brunswick, NJ: Transaction Books, 1977, 452-464.

1181 _____; Towers, Wayne M.; and Myers, Sandra L. "Television Docudrama and Political Cynicism: A Study of 'Washington Behind Closed Doors'," Social Science Quarterly, 62 (1981), 161-168.

1182 Kallina, Edmund F. "The State's Attorney and the President; The Inside Story of the 1960 Presidential Election in Illinois," Journal of American Studies, 12 (1978), 147-160.

1183 Kampelman, M. M. "Congress, the Media, and the Presidency," Academy of Political Science Proceedings 32, 1 (1975), 85-97.

1184 Kane, L. L. "The Contemporary Presidency: A Synthesis-Psychohistory, Election Theory, and Role Analysis" (Ph.D. dissertation, Boston University Graduate School, 1977), Dissertation Abstracts International A, 38 (1977), 2323-2324.

1185 Karabenick, Stuart A.; Lerner, Richard M.; and Beecher, Michael D. "Relation of Political Affiliation to Helping Behavior on Election Day, November 7, 1982," Journal of Social Psychology, 91 (1973), 223-227.

1186 Karam, Thomas J. "Political Imagemaking: An Analysis of the Television Commercials Aired During Louis Lambert's 1979 Gubernatorial Campaign" (Ph.D. dissertation, The Louisiana State University and Agricultural and Mechanical College, 1982), Dissertation Abstracts International A, 43 (1982), 586.

1187 Karayn, J. "The Case for Permanent Presidential Debates," The Past and Future of Presidential Debates, ed. Austin Ranney. Washington, D.C.: American Enterprise Institute, 1979.

1188 Karnig, A. K.; and Walter, B. O. "Registration and Voting: Putting First Things Second," Social Science Quarterly, 55 (1974), 159-166.

1189 Karp, Walter. "Subliminal Politics in the Evening News," Channels, 2 (1982), 23-56.

1190 Karpman, Stephen B. "Who's Zoo on Election Day?" Transactional Analysis, 5 (1975), 396-397.

1191 Kassebaum, N. L. "The Essence of Leadership," Presidential Studies Quarterly, 9 (1979), 239-242.

1192 Katan, Joseph. "Community Work and Political Parties During Electoral Campaigns," Community Development Journal, 9 (1974), 125-132.

1193 Katoch, John P.; and Traugott, Michael W. "Costs and Values in the Calculus of Voting," American Journal of Political Science, 26 (1982), 361-376.

1194 Katulu, R. A. "Apology of Richard M. Nixon," Today's Speech, 23 (1975), 1-5.

1195 Katz, Elihu (ed.). Mass Media and Social Change. Beverly Hills, CA: Sage Publications, Inc., 1981.

1196 _____. "On Conceptualizing Media Effects," Studies in Communications, ed. Elihu Katz. Greenwood, CT: JAI Press, 1980, 119-141.

1197 _____. "The Uses of Becker, Blumler, and Swanson," Communication Research, 6 (1979), 74-83.

1198 _____; Adoni, Hanna; and Parness, P. "Remembering the News: What the Picture Adds to Recall," Journalism Quarterly, 54 (1977), 231-239.

1199 _____; Blumler, Jay G.; and Gurevitch, Michael. "Utilization of Mass Communication by the Individual," The Uses of Mass Communications, eds. Jay G. Blumler and Elihu Katz. Beverly Hills, CA: Sage Publications, 1974.

1200 _____; Gurevitch, Michael; and Haas, H. "On the Use of Mass Media for Important Things," American Sociological Review, 38 (1973), 164-181.

1201 Katz, Richard S. A Theory of Parties and Electoral Systems. Baltimore, MD: Johns Hopkins University Press, 1981.

1202 Kau, James B.; and Rubin, Paul H. Congressmen, Constituents, and Contributors: An Analysis of Determinants of Roll-Call Voting in the House of Representatives. Hingham, MA: Kluwer-Nijhoff Publishing, 1981.

1203 Kaufer, David S. "The Ironist and Hypocrite as Presidential Symbols: A Nixon-Kennedy Analog," Communication Quarterly, 27 (1979), 20-26.

1204 Kawar, A. "Political Trust and Participation, 1968-1976: A Critical Investigation" (Ph.D. dissertation, University of Utah, 1979), Dissertation Abstracts International A, 39 (1979), 6939.

1205 Kay, Beatrice. Victory in the Voting Booth. Sedona, AZ: Education and Training Consultants Co., 1981.

1206 Kay, Jack. "Agenda Setting Applied to Detroit News Coverage of the 1976 Ford-Carter Campaign," Michigan Speech Association Journal, 12 (1977), 47-56.

1207 _____. "A Synthesis of Methodologies Used in the Study of Political Communication Applied to the 1976 Presidential Election Campaign" (Ph.D. dissertation, Wayne State University, 1979), Dissertation Abstracts International A, 40 (1980), 5646.

1208 Kayden, Xandra. Campaign Organization. Lexington, MA: D.C. Heath and Co., College Dept., 1978.

1209 _____. "The Political Campaign as an Organization," Public Policy, 21 (1973), 263-290.

1210 Kazee, Thomas A. "Congressional Elections and the Rerun Phenomenon: A Study of Candidate Recruitment and Incumbency Advantage" (Ph.D. dissertation, Ohio State University, 1978), Dissertation Abstracts International A, 39 (1979), 6311.

1211 _____. "Television Exposure and Attitude Change: The Impact of Political Interest," Public Opinion Quarterly, 45 (1981), 507-518.

1212 Kearney, E. (ed.). Dimensions of the Modern Presidency. St. Louis: Forum Press, 1981.

1213 Keating, John P.; and Latane, Bibb. "Politicians on TV: The Image is the Message," Journal of Social Issues, 32 (1976), 116-132.

1214 Keele, Gary D. "An Examination of a Concept of Image in Presidential Campaigning: The Humphrey-Nixon Campaign of 1968" (Ph.D. dissertation, University of Southern California, 1977), Dissertation Abstracts International A, 38 (1978), 4446-4447.

1215 Keeter, Charles S. "Television, Newspapers, and the Bases of Choice in American Presidential Elections" (Ph.D. dissertation, University of North Carolina at Chapel Hill, 1979), Dissertation Abstracts International A, 40 (1979), 2859-2860.

1216 Kellerman, B. "Campaigning Since Kennedy: The Family as Surrogate," Presidential Studies Quarterly, 10 (1980), 244-254.

1217 _____. "The Political Function of the Presidential Family," Presidential Studies Quarterly, 8 (1978), 303-318.

1218 Kelly, Walt. Pogo Re-Runs: Some Reflections on Elections. New York: Simon & Schuster, 1974.

Bibliography 101

1219 Kendrick, R. Strategies for Political Participation. Cambridge, MA: Winthrop Publishers, 1974.

1220 Kennamer, James David. "The Parent-Adolescent Dyad in the Formation of Political Attitudes and Perceptions: Political Discussion, Political Information and Public Affairs Mass Media Use" (Ph.D. dissertation, University of Wisconsin-Madison, 1982), Dissertation Abstracts International A, 43 (1982), 1335.

1221 _____; and Chaffee, Steven H. "Communication of Political Information During Early Presidential Primaries: Cognitions, Affect, and Uncertainty," Communication Yearbook 5, ed. Michael Burgoon. New Brunswick, NJ: Transaction Books, 1982, 627-650.

1222 Kennedy, J. F. The Kennedy Presidential Press Conferences. New York: Earl M. Coleman Enterprises, Inc., 1978.

1223 Kent, F. R. The Great Game of Politics: An Effort to Present the Elementary Human Facts about Politics, Politicians, and Political Machines. New York: Arno Press, 1974.

1224 Kent, K. E., and Rush, Ramona R. "How Communication Behavior of Older Persons Affects Their Public Affairs Knowledge," Journalism Quarterly, 53 (1975), 40-46.

1225 Kern, Montague. "The Presidency and the Press: John F. Kennedy's Foreign Policy Crises and the Politics of Newspaper Coverage" (Ph.D. dissertation, Johns Hopkins University, 1979), Dissertation Abstracts International A, 40 (1980), 5168-5169.

1226 Kernell, Samuel H. "Explaining Presidential Popularity: How Ad Hoc Theorizing, Misplaced Emphasis, and Insufficient Care in Measuring One's Variables Refuted Common Sense and Led Conventional Wisdom Down the Path of Anomalies," American Political Science Review, 72 (1978), 506-522.

1227 _____. "Presidential Popularity and Electoral Preference: A Model of Short-Term Political Change" (Ph.D. dissertation, University of California, Berkeley, 1975), Dissertation Abstracts International A, 37 (1976), 567-568.

1228 _____. "Presidential Popularity and Negative Voting: An Alternative Explanation of the Midterm Congressional Decline of the President's Party," American Political Science Review, 71 (1977), 44-66.

1229 Kessel, John H. "The Parameters of Presidential Politics," Social Science Quarterly, 55 (1974), 8-24.

1230 _____. Presidential Campaign Politics: Coalition Strategies and Citizen Response. Homewood, IL: Dorsey Press, 1980.

1231 _____. "The Seasons of Presidential Politics," Social Science Quarterly, 58 (1977), 418-435.

1232 Kessler, F. P. The Dilemmas of Presidential Leadership: Of Caretakers and Kings. Englewood Cliffs, NJ: Prentice-Hall, 1982.

1233 Kessler, M. S. "Role of Surrogate Speakers in the 1980 Presidential Campaign," Quarterly Journal of Speech, 67 (1981), 146-156.

1234 Khun, R. "Government and Broadcasting in the 1980s: A Cross-Channel Perspective," Political Quarterly, 53 (1982), 443-448.

1235 Kim, Chong Lim; and Racheter, Donald P. "Candidates' Perception of Voter Competence: A Comparison of Winning and Losing Candidates," American Political Science Review, 67 (1973), 906-913.

1236 Kimball, P. "Who Needs Gavel-to-Gavel Convention Coverage?" Columbia Journalism Review, 15 (1976), 28-30.

1237 Kimsey, William D. "A Path Analytic Study of Antecedents and Consequences of Exposure to Political Campaign Information in the 1976 Presidential Election" (Ph.D. dissertation, Southern Illinois University, 1977), Dissertation Abstracts International A, 38 (1977), 1414.

1238 _____; and Atwood, L. Erwin. "A Path Model of Political Cognitions and Attitudes, Communication and Voting Behavior in a Congressional Election," Communication Monographs, 46 (1979), 219-230.

1239 _____; and Hantz, Alan M. "Decisional Agenda of Decided and Undecided Voters," Journal of Applied Communication Research, 6 (1978), 65-72.

1240 Kinder, Donald R. "Balance Theory and Political Person Perception: Asymmetry in Beliefs About Political Leaders" (Ph.D. dissertation, University of California, Los Angeles, 1975), Dissertation Abstracts International B, 36 (1976), 5868-5869.

1241 _____. "Political Person Perception: The Asymmetrical Influence of Sentiment and Choice on Perceptions of Presidential Candidates," Journal of Personality and Social Psychology, 36 (1978), 859-871.

Bibliography 103

1242 _____. "Presidents, Prosperity, and Public Opinion," Public Opinion Quarterly, 45 (1981), 1-21.

1243 _____; et al. "Presidential Prototypes," Political Behavior, 2 (1980), 315-337.

1244 King, Michael. "Assimilation and Contrast of Presidential Candidates' Issue Positions, 1972," Public Opinion Quarterly, 41 (1977-78), 515-522.

1245 King, S. B.; and Peabody, R. L. "Control of Presidential Campaign Financing," Academy of Political Science Proceedings, 32 (1975), 180-195.

1246 Kingdon, John W. Congressmen's Voting Decisions, 2nd ed. New York: Harper and Row Publishers, 1980.

1247 Kirkpatrick, Jeane. The New Presidential Elite: Men and Women in National Politics. New York: Russell Sage Foundation, 1976.

1248 _____. Political Woman. New York: Basic Books, 1974.

1249 Kirkpatrick, Samuel A. (ed.). American Electoral Behavior: Change and Stability. Beverly Hills, CA: Sage Publications, 1976.

1250 _____; Bernick, E. Lee; Thompson, Robert J.; and Rycroft, Robert W. "Risks in Political Decision-Making: An Experimental Analysis of Choice Shifts," Experimental Study of Politics, 4 (February, 1975), 55-92.

1251 _____; et al. "Candidates, Parties, and Issues in the American Electorate: Two Decades of Change," American Politics Quarterly, 3 (1975), 247-283.

1252 Kitchens, James T. "An Experimental Study of Campaign Issues and Candidates' Personality Traits as Influencing Variables on Voting Behavior" (Ph.D. dissertation, University of Florida, 1974), Dissertation Abstracts International A, 36 (1975), 1168.

1253 Klein, Herbert G. Making It Perfectly Clear: An Inside Account of Nixon's Love-Hate Relationship with the Media. Garden City, NY: Doubleday, 1980.

1254 Klein, R. "The Powers of the Press," Political Quarterly, 44 (1973), 33-46.

1255 Klein, T.; and Danzig, F. How to be Heard: Making the Media Work for You. New York: Macmillan, 1974.

1256 Kleinau, Marvin D. "The Role of Rhetoric in the Political

Resurrection of Richard M. Nixon: 1963-1968" (Ph. D. dissertation, Southern Illinois University at Carbondale, 1978), Dissertation Abstracts International A, 39 (1978), 538.

1257 Kleppner, Paul; and Burnham, Walter D. The Evolution of American Electoral Systems. Westport, CT: Greenwood Press, 1982.

1258 Klorman, R. "Chronopolitics: What Time Do People Vote?" Public Opinion Quarterly, 40 (1976), 182-193.

1259 Klumpp, James F.; and Lukehart, Jeffrey K. "The Pardoning of Richard Nixon: A Failure in Motivational Strategy," Journal of Western Speech Communication, 42 (1978), 116-123.

1260 Knappman, Edward W. (ed.). Government and the Media in Conflict: 1970-1974. New York: Facts on File, 1975.

1261 Knutson, Jeanne N. (ed.). Handbook of Political Psychology. San Francisco: Jossey Bass, 1973.

1262 _____. "Personality Correlates of Political Behavior: A Longitudinal Analysis" (Ph. D. dissertation, University of California, Los Angeles, 1973), Dissertation Abstracts International B, 34 (1974), 3468.

1263 Kohler, Vincent D. "The Editorial Attitude of the Washington Post in Three Presidential Elections, with Emphasis on the Watergate Affair" (Master's thesis, Iowa State University, 1975), Journalism Abstracts, 13 (1975), 93-94.

1264 Kokkeler, Larry A. "Communication Variables, Candidate Image and Voting Behavior: A Study of Influence in the 1972 Presidential and Gubernatorial Elections" (Ph. D. dissertation, Southern Illinois University, 1973), Dissertation Abstracts International A, 34 (1974), 6014.

1265 Koltun, David. "Motivational Factors Affecting a Person's Intention to Vote" (Ph. D. dissertation, University of Illinois at Urbana-Champaign, 1975), Dissertation Abstracts International A, 36 (1976), 6280-6281.

1266 Kosich, Dorothy Y. "The Effect of News Endorsements in Nevada Assembly Races" (Master's thesis, University of Nevada, Reno, 1981), Masters Abstracts, 20 (1982), 290.

1267 Kotler, P.; and Kotler, N. "Business Marketing for Political Candidates," Campaigns and Elections, 2 (1981), 24-33.

1268 Kotz, Nick, et al. "Horsefeathers: The Media, the Campaign and the Economic Crisis," Columbia Journalism Review, 19 (1980), 41-46.

1269 Kovenock, D. "Influence in the U.S. House of Representatives: A Statistical Analysis of Communication," American Politics Quarterly, 1 (1973), 402-464.

1270 Kowalski, J. P. S. Voter Behavior and Campaign Strategies in School Finance Elections. Arlington, VA: Educational Research Service, Inc., 1977.

1271 Krasnow, E.; and Longley, L. The Politics of Broadcast Regulation. New York: St. Martin's, 1978.

1272 Kraus, Sidney (ed.). The Great Debates: Carter vs. Ford, 1976. Bloomington, IN: Indiana University Press, 1979.

1273 _____ (ed.). The Great Debates: Kennedy vs. Nixon, 1960. Bloomington, IN: Indiana University Press, 1977.

1274 _____. "Mass Communication and the Election Process: A Re-assessment of Two Decades of Research," Speech Monographs, 41 (1974), 427-435.

1275 _____. "Mass Communication and Political Socialization: A Re-assessment of Two Decades of Research," Quarterly Journal of Speech, 59 (1973), 390-400.

1276 _____; and Davis, Dennis. "Construction of Political Reality in Society," The Effects of Mass Communication on Political Behavior, eds. Sidney Kraus and Dennis Davis. University Park, PA: Pennsylvania State University Press, 1976.

1277 _____; and _____. The Effects of Mass Communication on Political Behavior. University Park, PA: Pennsylvania State University Press, 1976.

1278 _____; and _____. "Political Debates," Handbook of Political Communication, eds. Dan D. Nimmo and Keith R. Sanders. Beverly Hills, CA: Sage Publications, Inc., 1981, 273-296.

1279 _____; Meyer, Timothy; and Shelby, Maurice, Jr. "Sixteen Months After Chappaquiddick: Effects of the Kennedy Broadcast," Journalism Quarterly, 51 (1974), 431-440.

1280 Kraut, Robert E.; and McConahay, John B. "How Being Interviewed Affects Voting: An Experiment," Public Opinion Quarterly, 37 (1973), 398-406.

1281 Kreger, D. S. "Press Opinion in the Eagleton Affair," Journalism Monographs, 35 (1974), 1-51.

1282 Krieghbaum, Hillier. "President Carter's Inauguration as an Image-Making Machine," Mass Comm Review, 4 (1976-77), 2-6.

1283 Kritzer, Herbert M.; and Erbank, Robert E. "Presidential Coattails Revisited: Partisan and Incumbency Effects," American Journal of Political Science, 23 (1979), 615-626.

1284 Krukones, Michael G. "Presidential Campaigns as Predictors of Performance in Office: 1912-1972" (Ph.D. dissertation, Miami University, 1979), Dissertation Abstracts International A, 40 (1979), 1667.

1285 Kruse, N. W. "The Scope of Apologetic Discourse: Establishing Generic Parameters," Southern Speech Communication Journal, 46 (1981), 278-291.

1286 Kuklinski, J. H.; and Elling, R. C. "Representational Role, Constituency Opinion, and Legislative Roll-Call Behavior," American Journal of Political Science, 21 (1977), 135-147.

1287 Kurland, Gerald. The Convention and the Crisis: Chicago 1968. Charlotteville, NY: SamHar Press, 1973.

1288 _____. The Political Machine: What It Is, How It Works. Charlotteville, NY: SamHar Press, 1974.

1289 Kushner, Harvey W.; and Urken, Arnold B. "VOTEPOW: A Computer Program for the Measurement of Voting Power Using Roll Call Data," Behavior Research Methods and Instrumentation, 6 (1974), 363-364.

1290 Ladd, Everett C., Jr. "Brittle Mandate: Electoral Dealignment and the 1980 Presidential Election," Political Science Quarterly, 96 (1981), 1-25.

1291 _____. "Opinion Roundup: Left, Right or Center--Which Way Are We Going," Public Opinion, 1 (1978), 33.

1292 _____. "Opinion Roundup: A Nation's Trust," Public Opinion, 2 (1979), 27.

1293 _____. "The Polls: The Question of Confidence," Public Opinion Quarterly, 40 (1976), 544-552.

1294 _____. Where Have all the Voters Gone? The Fracturing of America's Political Parties. New York: W. W. Norton, 1978.

1295 _____; and Ferree, G. D. "Were the Pollsters Really Wrong?" Public Opinion, 3 (1981), 13-17+.

1296 _____; and Lipset, Seymour, M. Academics, Politics and the 1972 Election. Washington, D. C.: The American Enterprise Institute, 1973.

1297 Laing, Robert B. "Public Opinion Perspective on Mass Communication and Agenda-Setting" (Ph. D. dissertation, University of Washington, 1975), Dissertation Abstracts International A, 37 (1976), 674-675.

1298 _____. "Public Opinion Trends in the Last Days of the Nixon Administration," Journalism Quarterly, 53 (1976), 294-302.

1299 Lamb, K. As Orange Goes: Twelve California Families and the Future of American Politics. New York: Norton, 1975.

1300 Lamm, H.; and Trommdorff, G. "Group Influences on Probability Judgments Concerning Social and Political Change," Psychological Reports, 35 (1974), 987-996.

1301 Lammers, William W. Presidential Politics: Patterns and Prospects. New York: Harper and Row, 1977.

1302 _____. "Presidential Press Conference Schedules: Who Hides, and When?" Political Science Quarterly, 96 (1981), 261-278.

1303 Lampert, Shlomo I. "A New Approach to Pre-Election Polling," Public Opinion Quarterly, 42 (1978), 259-264.

1304 Lang, Gladys Engel; and Lang, Kurt. "The First Debate and the Coverage Gap," Journal of Communication, 28 (1978), 93-98.

1305 _____; and _____. "The Formation of Public Opinion: Direct and Mediated Effects of the First Debate," The Presidential Debates, eds. George Bishop, Robert Meadow, and Marilyn Jackson-Beeck. New York: Praeger, 1978.

1306 _____; and _____. "Immediate and Delayed Responses to a Carter-Ford Debate: Assessing Public Opinion," Public Opinion Quarterly, 42 (1978), 322-341.

1307 _____; and _____. "Polling on Watergate: The Battle for Public Opinion," Public Opinion Quarterly, 44 (1980). 530-547.

1308 _____; and _____. "Watergate: An Exploration of the Agenda-Building Process," Mass Communication Review Yearbook 2, eds. G. C. Wilhoit and H. deBock. Beverly Hills, CA: Sage Publications, 1981, 447-468.

1309 Lang, Kurt; and Lang, Gladys Engel. "Televised Hearings: The Impact Out There," Columbia Journalism Review, 11 (1973), 52-57.

1310 Langenbucher, W. R. "The Responsibility of the Mass Media in a Changing Political Environment," Communication, 5 (1980), 333-338.

1311 Lanigan, Richard L. "A Critical Theory Approach," Handbook of Political Communication, eds. Dan D. Nimmo and Keith R. Sanders. Beverly Hills, CA: Sage Publications, 1981, 141-167.

1312 Lapomarda, Vincent A. "A Jesuit Runs for Congress: The Rev. Robert F. Drinan, S. J., and His 1970 Campaign," Journal of Church and State, 15 (1973), 205-222.

1313 Larson, Barbara A. "Criticism and the Campaign Concept of Persuasion: A Case Study Analysis of Method," Central States Speech Journal, 24 (1973), 52-59.

1314 Larson, Charles U. "A Content Analysis of Media Reporting of the Watergate Hearings," Communication Research, 1 (1974), 440-448.

1315 _____. "Media Metaphors: Two Models for Rhetorically Criticizing the Political Television Spot Advertisement," Central States Speech Journal, 33 (1982), 533-546.

1316 _____; and Weigele, T. C. "Political Communication Theory and Research: An Overview," Communication Yearbook 3, ed. Dan D. Nimmo. New Brunswick, NJ: Transaction Books, 1979, 457-473.

1317 Larson, James F. "International Affairs Coverage on U. S. Network Television," Journal of Communication, 29 (1979), 136-147.

1318 Lashner, Marilyn A. "The Chilling Effect of a White House Anti-Media Assault on Political Commentary in Network Television News Programs: Comparison of Newspaper and Television Vigorousness During the Nixon Administration" (Ph. D. dissertation, Temple University, 1979), Journalism Abstracts, 17 (1979), 17-18.

1319 Latimer, Harry D. "The Press Secretaries of Lyndon Johnson" (Ph. D. dissertation, Brown University, 1973), Dissertation Abstracts International A, 34 (1974), 6717.

1320 Lau, R. R. "Negativity in Person Perception with Applications to Political Behavior" (Ph. D. dissertation, University of California, Los Angeles, 1979), Dissertation Abstracts International B, 40 (1979), 2899-2900.

1321 Lau, Richard R.; Sears, David O.; and Center, Richard. "The Positivity Bias in Evaluations of Public Figures: Evidence Against Instrument Artifacts," Public Opinion Quarterly, 43 (1979), 347-358.

1322 Laudon, Kenneth C. Communications Technology and Democratic Participation. New York: Praeger Publishers, 1977.

1323 Laver, Michael. "How to be Sophisticated, Lie, Cheat, Bluff and Win at Politics," Political Theory, 26 (1978), 462-473.

1324 Lawrence, J. S.; and Timberg, B. "News and Mythic Selectivity: Mayaguez, Entebbe, Moyadishu," Journal of American Culture, 2 (1979), 321-330.

1325 Lea, James F. Political Consciousness and American Democracy. Jackson, MS: University Press of Mississippi, 1982.

1326 League of Women Voters of California. Face the Public: A Manual on Televised Political Debates. San Francisco: League of Women Voters of California, 1981.

1327 Leary, M. R. "Hindsight Distortion and the 1980 Presidential Election," Personality and Social Psychology Bulletin, 8 (1982), 257-263.

1328 Leary, Mary E. "California 1974: The Browning of Campaign Coverage," Columbia Journalism Review, 15 (1976), 18-21.

1329 _____. Phantom Politics: Campaigning in California. Washington, D. C.: Public Affairs Press, 1977.

1330 LeBlanc, H. L.; and Merrin, M. B. "Parties, Issues, and Candidates: Another Look at Responsible Parties," Western Political Quarterly, 31 (1978), 523-534.

1331 Lecavalier, G. R. "The Impact of Television on a Politician's and Party's Image: A Study of Propaganda in a Non-Electoral Period" (Ph.D. dissertation, Johns Hopkins University, 1975), Dissertation Abstracts International A, 36 (1976), 6975.

1332 Ledbetter, C., Jr. "State Legislators and the Electing of Presidents," State Government, 48 (1975), 138-141.

1333 _____; and Doyle, W. "Presidential Primaries," State Government, 48 (1975), 138-144.

1334 Lee, D. G.; Johnson, W. C.; and Beld, J. M. "The Rhetorical Challenge of the Carter Transition: To Build a

Governing Majority," Communication Yearbook 3, ed. Dan D. Nimmo. New Brunswick, NJ: Transaction Books, 1979.

1335 Lee, Michael R. "Predictors of Mass Media Exposure in the 1972 Presidential Campaign Environment" (Ph.D. dissertation, University of Denver, 1976), Dissertation Abstracts International A, 37 (1977), 6124.

1336 Lee, R. S. H. "Credibility of Newspaper and TV News," Journalism Quarterly, 55 (1978), 282-287.

1337 Lee, Ronald E. "The Rhetoric of the 'New Politics:' A Case Study of Robert F. Kennedy's 1968 Presidential Primary Campaign" (Ph.D. dissertation, University of Iowa, 1981), Dissertation Abstracts International A, 42 (1982), 2932.

1338 Lee, Seong Hyong. "A Factor Analytic Study of the Credibility of Newspaper and TV News" (Ph.D. dissertation, Kent State University, 1976), Dissertation Abstracts International A, 37 (1977), 4677-4678.

1339 Leeds, Patricia G. "The Conditions for Issue Voting: A Comparison of Presidential and Congressional Elections" (Ph.D. dissertation, University of Wisconsin-Madison, 1977), Dissertation Abstracts International A, 38 (1978), 6290-6291.

1340 Lehnen, Robert G. The American Citizen: Public Opinion and Political Participation. New York, Holt, Rinehart and Winston, Inc., 1976.

1341 Lemert, James B. Does Mass Communication Change Public Opinion After All? A New Approach to Effects Analysis. Chicago: Nelson-Hall, 1981.

1342 Lenchner, Paul. "Partisan Conflict in the Senate and the Realignment Process," Journal of Politics, 41 (1979), 680-686.

1343 Lengle, J. I.; and Shafer, B. E. Presidential Politics: Readings on Nominations and Elections. New York: St. Martin's Press, 1980.

1344 LeRoy, David J.; and Smith, F. Leslie. "Perceived Ethicality of Some TV News Production Techniques by a Sample of Florida Legislators," Speech Monographs, 40 (1973), 326-329.

1345 _____; Wotring, C. E.; and Lyle, J. "The Public Television Viewer and the Watergate Hearings," Communication Research, 1 (1974), 406-425.

Bibliography

1346 _____; _____; and _____. "Today in the Legislature: The Florida Story," Journal of Communication, 24 (1974), 92-98.

1347 Lesher, Stephan. Media Unbound: The Impact of Television Journalism on the Public. Boston, MA: Houghton Mifflin, 1982.

1348 Leubsdorf, C. P. "The Reporter and the Presidential Candidate," Annals of the American Academy of Political and Social Science, 427 (1976), 1-11.

1349 Levantrosser, W. F. "Financing Presidential Campaigns: The Impact of Reform Finance Laws on the Democratic Presidential Nomination of 1976," Presidential Studies Quarterly, 11 (1981), 280-287.

1350 Levesque, Terrence J. "Presidential Campaign Time Allocation" (Ph.D. dissertation, Carnegie-Mellon University, 1981), Dissertation Abstracts International A, 42 (1981), 1299.

1351 Levine, Stephen. "The Role of Fantasy in Political Behaviour," Political Science, 32 (1980), 85-100.

1352 Levy, Mark R. "The Audience Experience with Television News," Journalism Monographs, 55 (1978), 1-27.

1353 _____. "The Audience for Television News Interview Programs," Journal of Broadcasting, 22 (1978), 339-347.

1354 _____. "Opinion Leadership and Television News Use," Public Opinion Quarterly, 42 (1978), 402-406.

1355 _____. "The Uses-and-Gratifications of Television News" (Ph.D. dissertation, Columbia University, 1977), Dissertation Abstracts International A, 38 (1977), 532-533.

1356 Levy, Sheldon G. "Authoritarianism and Information Processing," Bulletin of the Psychonomic Society, 13 (1979), 240-242.

1357 _____. "Dogmatism, Locus of Control of Reinforcement, Importance of Issues, and Relationships to Political Activity," Journal of Applied Social Psychology, 3 (1973), 119-131.

1358 Lewellen, J. "Mass Media and Political Participation," Social Education, 40 (1976), 457-461.

1359 Lewels, Francisco Jose, Jr. "Uses of the News Media by the Chicano Movement: A Study in Minority Access" (Ph.D. dissertation, University of Missouri-Columbia,

1973), Dissertation Abstracts International A, 35 (1974), 1136.

1360 Lewis-Beck, Michael S.; and Rice, Tom W. "Presidential Popularity and Presidential Vote," Public Opinion Quarterly, 46 (1982), 534-537.

1361 Lichtenstein, A. "Differences in Impact of Local and National Televised Political Candidates' Debates," Western Journal of Speech Communication, 46 (1982), 291-298.

1362 Liebert, Robert M.; and Schwortzberg, Neala S. "Effects of Mass Media," Annual Review of Psychology, 28 (1977), 141-173.

1363 Lincoln, P. "All the Candidates' Men: Who's Whose," Politics Today, (March 1980), 32-37.

1364 Linkugel, William A.; and Cody, Dixie Lee. "Nixon, McGovern, and the Female Electorate," Today's Speech, 21 (1973), 25-32.

1365 Linton, David S. "Media Preferences and their Relationships to Mental Imagery and Abstract Reasoning Ability" (Ph.D. dissertation, New York University, 1982), Dissertation Abstracts International A, 43 (1982), 298.

1366 Lipset, Seymour M. "The Academic Mind at the Top: The Political Behavior and Values of Faculty Elites," Public Opinion Quarterly, 46 (1982), 143-168.

1367 _____. "Different Polls, Different Results in 1980 Politics," Public Opinion, August/September, 1981, 19-20.

1368 _____. Party Coalitions in the 1980's. San Francisco: ICS Press, 1981.

1369 _____. Political Man. Baltimore, MD: Johns Hopkins University Press, 1981.

1370 _____. "The Wavering Polls," The Public Interest, 43 (1976), 70-89.

1371 Littlewood, T. B. "Serving up News - With a Twist," Columbia Journalism Review, 13 (1974), 47-48.

1372 Locander, Robert. "Carter and the Press: The First Two Years," Presidential Studies Quarterly, 10 (1980), 106-120.

1373 _____. "The President, the Press, and the Public: Friends and Enemies of Democracy," Presidential Studies Quarterly, 8 (1978), 140-150.

Bibliography

1374 _____. "Presidential Communications" (Ph. D. dissertation, The University of New Mexico, 1976), Dissertation Abstracts International A, 38 (1977), 1000.

1375 Locke, Larry W. "A Study of Richard M. Nixon's Public 1968 Campaign Promises and their Fulfillment during his First Term in Office" (Ph. D. dissertation, Kent State University, 1978), Dissertation Abstracts International A, 39 (1978), 2619.

1376 Lodge, Henry Cabot. As It Was: An Inside View of Politics and Power in the '50s and '60s. New York: W. W. Norton, 1976.

1377 Logan, Larry. "A Guide to Campaign Media Consultants and Press Secretaries," Washington Journalism Review, 2 (1980), 46-47.

1378 Logue, Cal M.; and Patton, John M. "From Ambiguity to Dogma: The Rhetorical Symbols of Lyndon B. Johnson on Vietnam," Southern Speech Communication Journal, 47 (1982), 310-329.

1379 Lometh, Guy E.; Reeves, Byron; and Bybee, Carl R. "Investigating the Assumptions of Uses and Gratifications Research," Communication Research, 4 (1977), 321-338.

1380 Long, S. "Personality and Political Alienation Among White and Black Youth: A Test of the Social Deprivation Model," Journal of Politics, 40 (1978), 433-459.

1381 _____. "Political Alienation Among Black and White Adolescents: A Test of the Social Deprivation and Political Reality Models," American Politics Quarterly, 4 (1976), 267-304.

1382 _____. "Political Alienation: Reality and Reactance," Journal of Social Psychology, 104 (1978), 115-121.

1383 _____. "Political Hopelessness: A New Dimension of Systemic Disaffection," Journal of Social Psychology, 105 (1978), 205-211.

1384 Lonie, J. "Electioneering 1974 and Labor in Government," Politics, 10 (1975), 103-106.

1385 Loomis, B. A. "Resources into Results? Congressional Campaigns in Marginal Districts" (Ph. D. dissertation, University of Wisconsin, 1974), Dissertation Abstracts International A, 35 (1975), 4639-4640.

1386 Lord, Robert W. Running Conventions, Conferences and Meetings. New York: American Management Association, Inc., 1981.

1387 Lorenz, J. D. *Jerry Brown: The Man on the White Horse.* Boston, MA: Houghton Mifflin, 1978.

1388 Lotsof, E. J.; and Grot, J. S. "Interpersonal Trust, Internal-External Control and the Walker Report on the Democratic Convention Disorders," *Psychological Reports,* 32 (1973), 747-752.

1389 Lott, D. N. *Jimmy Carter and How He Won.* Los Angeles, CA: Petersen Publishing Company, 1977.

1390 Lovenduski, Joni; and Hills, Jill (eds.). *The Politics of the Second Electorate: Women and Public Participation: Britain, USA, Canada, Australia, France, Spain, West Germany, Italy, Sweden, Finland, Eastern Europe, U.S.S.R., Japan.* Boston, MA: Routledge and Kegan Paul, Ltd., 1981.

1391 Lowenstein, Douglas. "Covering the Primaries," *Washington Journalism Review,* 2 (1980), 38-42.

1392 Lower, E. "Primer for an Election Year," *Television Quarterly,* 13 (1976), 5-14.

1393 Lowi, T. J. "Interest Groups and the Consent to Govern: Getting the People Out, For What?" *Annals of the American Academy of Political and Social Science,* 413 (1974), 86-100.

1394 Lowry, Dennis T. "Measures of Network News Bias in the 1972 Presidential Campaign," *Journal of Broadcasting,* 18 (1974), 387-402.

1395 _____. "Subject Selection Bias in Communication Studies," *Journalism Quarterly,* 55 (1978), 577-578.

1396 Lubalin, Eve. "Presidential Ambition and Senatorial Behavior: The Impact of Ambition on the Behavior of Incumbent Politicians" (Ph.D. dissertation, Johns Hopkins University, 1982), *Dissertation Abstracts International A,* 43 (1982), 254-255.

1397 Lubell, Samuel. *The Future While It Happened.* New York: W. W. Norton, 1973.

1398 Lucas, William A.; and Adams, William C. "Talking, Television, and Voter Indecision," *Journal of Communication,* 28 (1978), 120-131.

1399 Lucy, William H. "Polls, Primaries, and Presidential Nominations," *Journal of Politics,* 35 (1973), 830-848.

1400 Lukas, A. *Nightmare: The Underside of the Nixon Years.* New York: Viking Press, 1976.

1401 Lupfer, Michael; and Kenny, Charles. "'Watergate is Just a Bunch of Honky Jive': The Impact of Watergate in Black and White Youths' View of the Presidency," Personality and Social Psychology Bulletin, 1 (1974), 163-165.

1402 _____; and Wald, Kenneth. "An Experimental Study of the First Carter-Ford Debate," Experimental Study of Politics, 7 (1979), 20-40.

1403 Lurie, Leonard. Party Politics: Why We Have Poor Presidents. Briarcliff Manor, NY: Stein and Day, 1980.

1404 Lutes, T. Political Campaign Management, Strategy and Technique. Monticello, IL: Vance Bibliography, 1981.

1405 Luttbeg, Norman R. (ed.). Public Opinion and Public Policy. Itasca, IL: F. E. Peacock Publishers, Inc., 1981.

1406 _____. Public Opinion and Public Policy: Models of Political Linkage. Homewood, IL: Dorsey Press, 1974.

1407 Lydenberg, S. D.; and Young, S. "Business Bankrolls for Local Ballots," Business and Society Review, 33 (1980), 51-55.

1408 Macaluso, Theodore F. "Parameters of 'Rational' Voting: Vote Switching in the 1968 Election," Journal of Politics, 37 (1975), 187-201.

1409 _____. "Parameters of Responsible Voting: Issues and the American Electorate, 1952-1968" (Ph.D. dissertation, Johns Hopkins University, 1975), Dissertation Abstracts International A, 39 (1978), 3116.

1410 _____. "Political Information, Party Identification and Voting Defection," Public Opinion Quarterly, 41 (1977), 255-260.

1411 MacDonald, A. P.; and Majumder, Ranjit K. "On the Resolution and Tolerance of Cognitive Inconsistency in Another Naturally Occurring Event: Attitudes and Beliefs Following the Senator Eagleton Incident," Journal of Applied Social Psychology, 3 (1973), 132-143.

1412 MacDougall, M. "Barkers and Snake Oil Politics (Presidential Candidates and Television Advertising)," Politics Today, 7 (1980), 34-37.

1413 MacDougall, Malcolm D. We Almost Made It. New York: Crown Publishers, 1977.

1414 Mackelprang, A. J.; Grofman, B.; and Triling, R. J. "Party Image and Electoral Behavior," American Politics Quarterly, 3 (1975), 284-314.

1415 MacKuen, Michael B.; and Coombs, Steven L. More Than News: Media Power in Public Affairs. Beverly Hills, CA: Sage Publications, Inc., 1981.

1416 MacManus, S. A. "City Council Election Procedures and Minority Representation: Are They Related?" Social Science Quarterly, 59 (1978), 153-162.

1417 _____. "City's First Female Officeholder: Coattails for Future Female Officeseekers?" Western Political Quarterly, 34 (1981), 88-99.

1418 Maddox, W. F.; and Handberg, R. "Presidential Affect and Chauvinism Among Children," American Journal of Political Science, 23 (1979), 426-433.

1419 Maddox, William S. "Candidate Images Among Voters and Non-Voters in 1976," American Politics Quarterly, 8 (1980), 209-220.

1420 _____; and Nimmo, Dan D. "In Search of the Ticket Splitter," Social Science Quarterly, 62 (1981), 401-408.

1421 _____; and Robins, Robert. "How People Magazine Covers Political Figures," Journalism Quarterly, 58 (1981), 113-115.

1422 Magiotto, Michael A.; and Piereson, James E. "Issue Public and Voter Choice," American Politics Quarterly, 6 (1978), 407-428.

1423 _____; and _____. "Partisan Identification and Electoral Choice: The Hostility Hypothesis," American Journal of Political Science, 21 (1977), 745-767.

1424 Maisel, Louis (ed.). Changing Campaign Techniques: Elections and Values in Contemporary Democracies. Beverly Hills, CA: Sage Publications, Inc., 1976.

1425 _____. "Congressional Elections in 1978: The Road to Nomination, the Road to Election," American Politics Quarterly, 9 (1981), 23-47.

1426 _____. From Obscurity to Oblivion: Running in the Congressional Primary. Knoxville, TN: University of Tennessee Press, 1982.

1427 _____; and Cooper, Joseph (eds.). The Impact of the Electoral Process. Beverly Hills, CA: Sage Publications, 1977.

1428 Makielski, S. J. Pressure Politics in America. Washington, D. C.: University Press of America, 1980.

Bibliography

1429 Malaney, Gary D.; and Buss, Terry F. "AP Wire Reports vs. CBS TV News Coverage of a Presidential Campaign," Journalism Quarterly, 56 (1979), 602-610.

1430 _____; and _____. "Information, Interest, and Attitude Change: Carter and the 1976 Post-Convention Campaign," Central States Speech Journal, 31 (1980), 63-73.

1431 Malbin, Michael J. "Campaign Financing and the Special Interests," Public Interest, 56 (1979), 21-42.

1432 _____ (ed.). Parties, Interest Groups and Campaign Finance Laws. Washington, D.C.: American Enterprise Institute for Public Policy Research, 1980.

1433 _____. Unelected Representatives. New York: Basic Books, 1979.

1434 Mandel, Ruth B. In the Running: The New Woman Candidate. New Haven, CT: Ticknor and Fields, 1981.

1435 Mander, Jerry. Four Arguments for the Elimination of Television. New York: William Morrow, 1978.

1436 Manheim, Jarol B. "Can Democracy Survive Television," Journal of Communication, 26 (1976), 84-90.

1437 _____. "The Honeymoon's Over: The News Conference and the Development of Presidential Style," Journal of Politics, 41 (1979), 55-74.

1438 _____. Politics Within: A Primer in Political Attitudes and Behavior. Englewood Cliffs, NJ: Prentice-Hall, 1975.

1439 _____. "Urbanization and Differential Press Coverage of the Congressional Campaign," Journalism Quarterly, 51 (1974), 649-653+.

1440 _____; and Lammers, William W. "The News Conference and Presidential Leadership of Public Opinion: Does the Tail Wag the Dog?" Presidential Studies Quarterly, 11 (1981), 177-188.

1441 Mankiewicz, Frank; and Swerdlow, Joel. Remote Control: Television and the Manipulation of American Life. New York: Time Books, 1978.

1442 Manley, J. F. "Presidential Power and White House Lobbying," Political Science Quarterly, 93 (1978-79), 255-276.

1443 Mann, Thomas E. "Candidate Saliency and Congressional Elections" (Ph.D. dissertation, the University of Michigan,

1977), *Dissertation Abstracts International A*, 38 (1978), 6912.

1444 _____. *Unsafe at Any Margin*. Washington, D. C.: American Enterprise Institute, 1978.

1445 _____; and Ornstein, N. "1982 Election: What Will It Mean?" *Public Opinion Quarterly*, 4 (1981), 48-50.

1446 _____; and Wolfinger, Raymond E. "Candidates and Parties in Congressional Elections," *American Political Science Review*, 74 (1980), 617-632.

1447 Mansfield, H. C., Jr. "The Media World and Democratic Representation," *Government and Opposition*, 14 (1979), 318-334.

1448 Mansfield, Michael W. "The Professional Campaigner: Perspectives and Perceptions" (Ph.D. dissertation, University of Missouri-Columbia, 1973), *Dissertation Abstracts International A*, 38 (1978), 5024-5025.

1449 _____; and Weaver, Ruth Ann. "Political Communication Theory and Research: An Overview," *Communication Yearbook 5*, ed. Michael Burgoon. New Brunswick, NJ: Transaction Books, 1982, 605-625.

1450 Margolis, Michael. "From Confusion to Confusion: Issues and the American Voter (1956-1972)," *American Political Science Review*, 71 (1977), 31-43.

1451 Marks, J. S. "Split Ticket Voting in 1964: Explanations from Four Theoretical Perspectives" (Ph.D. dissertation, Syracuse University, 1975), *Dissertation Abstracts International A*, 36 (1976), 6920-6921.

1452 Markus, Gregory B. "Political Attitudes During an Election Year: A Report on the 1980 NES Panel Study," *American Political Science Review*, 76 (1982), 538-560.

1453 _____. "The Political Environment and the Dynamics of Public Attitudes: A Panel Study," *American Journal of Political Science*, 23 (1979), 338-359.

1454 Marr, Theodore J. "Q and R Analyses of Panel Data on Political Candidate Image and Voter Communication," *Speech Monographs*, 40 (1973), 56-65.

1455 Marshall, T. "Participating in Politics: Do Political Parties Matter?" *Social Science*, 52 (1977), 221-225.

1456 Marshall, Thomas R. "The Benevolent Bureaucrat: Political Authority in Children's Literature and Television," *Western Political Quarterly*, 34 (1981), 389-398.

1457 _____. "Caucuses and Primaries: Measuring Reform in the Presidential Nomination Process," American Politics Quarterly, 7 (1979), 155-174.

1458 _____. "Party Responsibility Revisited: A Case of Policy Discussion at the Grass Roots," Western Political Quarterly, 32 (1979), 70-78.

1459 _____. "Turnout and Representation: Caucuses versus Primaries," American Journal of Political Science, 22 (1978), 169-182.

1460 Martin, D. R. "The Rhetorical Monitoring Patterns of Selected Political Communicators" (Ph.D. dissertation, University of Texas at Austin, 1980), Dissertation Abstracts International A, 41 (1981), 2829.

1461 Martin, D. S. "Person Perception and Real-life Electoral Behaviour," Australian Journal of Psychology, 30 (1978), 255-262.

1462 Martin, Guy Emerson. "Turnout and Preference Effects of Labor Intensive Campaign Contact: A Panel Analysis" (Ph.D. dissertation, Syracuse University, 1975), Dissertation Abstracts International A, 36 (1976), 6922.

1463 Martin, J. "Presidential Elections and Administration Support Among Congressmen," American Journal of Political Science, 20 (1976), 483-489.

1464 Martin, L. John. "Government and the News Media," Handbook of Political Communication, eds. Dan D. Nimmo and Keith R. Sanders. Beverly Hills, CA: Sage Publications, Inc., 1981, 445-465.

1465 _____. "Recent Theory on Mass Media Potential in Political Campaigns," Annals of the American Academy of Political and Social Science, 427 (1976), 125-133.

1466 _____ (ed.). "Role of the Mass Media in American Politics," Annals of the American Academy of Political and Social Science, 427 (1976), 1-33.

1467 Martin, Richard; and Taylor, Richard W. "Political Obligation: An Experimental Approach," Operant Subjectivity, 1 (1978), 61-69.

1468 Martin, William P.; and Singletary, Michael W. "Newspaper Treatment of State Government Releases," Journalism Quarterly, 58 (1981), 93-96.

1469 Martinson, David L. "Coverage of La Follette Offers Insights for 1972 Campaign," Journalism Quarterly, 52 (1975), 539-542.

1470 _____. "News Images of Presidential Candidates, 1920-1924: A Survey of Three Major Newspapers" (Ph.D. dissertation, University of Minnesota, 1974), Dissertation Abstracts International A, 35 (1975), 7935.

1471 Martoccia, C. T. "Authoritarianism and Party Switching in 1972," Perceptual and Motor Skills, 37 (1973), 694.

1472 Martz, J. D.; and Baloyra, E. A. Electoral Mobilization and Public Opinion. Chapel Hill, NC: University of North Carolina at Chapel Hill Press, 1976.

1473 Mashkin, K. S.; and Volgy, T. "Socio-Political Attitudes and Musical Preferences," Social Science Quarterly, 21 (1975), 450-459.

1474 Mason, W. "The Impact of Endorsements on Voting," Sociological Research Methods, 1 (1973), 463-495.

1475 Mass Media and American Politics. Washington, D. C.: Congressional Quarterly, 1980.

1476 Massing, Michael. "Reshuffling the White House Press Pack," Columbia Journalism Review, 20 (1981), 36-40.

1477 Matthews, Donald R. (ed.). Perspectives on Presidential Selection. Washington, D. C.: Brookings Institution, 1973.

1478 _____. "Presidential Nominations: Process and Outcomes," Choosing the President, ed. James D. Barber. Englewood Cliffs, NJ: Prentice-Hall, 1974.

1479 Maurer, David J. U. S. Politics and Elections: A Guide to Information Sources. Detroit, MI: Gale Research Co., 1978.

1480 Mauser, Gary A. "Positioning Political Candidates: An Application of Concept Evaluation Techniques," Journal of the Market Research Society, 22 (1980), 181-191.

1481 May, Ernest R.; and Fraser, Janet (eds.). Campaign '72: The Managers Speak. Cambridge, MA: Harvard University Press, 1973.

1482 May, T. "Paying for Party Politics," Political Quarterly, 48 (1977), 83-87.

1483 _____. "Paying for Politics--Hansard's Halfway House," Political Quarterly, 53 (1982), 77-81.

1484 Mayhew, David R. Congress: The Electoral Connection. New Haven, CT: Yale University Press, 1974.

Bibliography

1485 Mazlish, Bruce. In Search of Nixon: A Psycho-historical Inquiry. Baltimore, MD: Penguin, 1973.

1486 Mazmanian, Daniel A. Third Parties in Presidential Elections. Washington, D. C.: Brookings Institution, 1974.

1487 McArver, Patricia P. "Television Political Advertising and Its Impact on the Voter: A Comparison of the Images of Young and Old Candidates" (Master's thesis, University of North Carolina, 1973), Journalism Abstracts, 11 (1973), 161.

1488 McCain, Thomas A.; Chilberg, Joseph; and Wakshlag, Jacob. "The Effect of Camera Angle on Source Credibility and Attraction," Journal of Broadcasting, 21 (1977), 35-46.

1489 McCarthy, Eugene, et al. Regulation of Political Campaigns: How Successful? Washington, D. C.: American Enterprise Institute for Public Policy Research, 1977.

1490 McCleneghan, Jack Sean. "Effect of Endorsements in Texas Local Elections," Journalism Quarterly, 50 (1973), 360-366.

1491 _____. "Effect of Endorsements on News Space in Texas Papers," Journalism Quarterly, 55 (1978), 792-793.

1492 _____. "The Effects of Media Interaction and Other Campaign Variables in Mayoral Elections in Twenty-three Texas Metro Areas" (Ph.D. dissertation, University of Texas at Austin, 1979), Journalism Abstracts, 17 (1979), 22.

1493 _____. "Media and Non-Media Effects in Texas Mayoral Elections," Journalism Quarterly, 57 (1980), 129-134, 201.

1494 McClure, Robert D.; and Patterson, Thomas E. "Setting the Political Agenda: Print vs. Network News," Journal of Communication, 26 (1976), 23-28.

1495 _____; and _____. "Television News and Political Advertising," Communication Research, 1 (1974), 3-31.

1496 McCombs, Maxwell E. "The Agenda-Setting Approach," Handbook of Political Communication, eds. Dan D. Nimmo and Keith R. Sanders. Beverly Hills, CA: Sage Publications, 1981, 121-140.

1497 _____. "Agenda-Setting Function of Mass Media," Public Relations Review, 3 (1977), 89-95.

1498 _____. "Agenda-Setting Research: A Bibliographic Essay," Political Communication Review, 1 (1976), 1-7.

1499 _____. Elaborating the Agenda-Setting Influence of Mass Communication. Tokyo, Japan: Bulletin of the Institution for Communication Research, Keio University, 1976.

1500 _____. "Newspapers Versus Television: Mass Communication Effects Across Time," The Emergence of American Political Issues, eds. D. L. Shaw and M. E. McCombs. St. Paul, MN: West, 1977.

1501 _____. "Public Response to the Daily News," Women and the News, ed. L. K. Epstein. New York: Hastings House, 1978.

1502 _____; and Masel-Walter, L. "Agenda Setting: A New Perspective on Mass Communication," Mass Comm Review, 3 (1976), 3-7.

1503 _____; and Mullins, L. E. "Consequences of Education: Media Exposure, Political Interest and Information-Seeking Orientations," Mass Comm Review, 1 (1973), 27-31.

1504 _____; and Shaw, D. L. "The Agenda-Setting Function of the Press," The Emergence of American Political Issues, eds. D. L. Shaw and M. E. McCombs. St. Paul, MN: West, 1977.

1505 _____; and Weaver, D. N. Voters and the Mass Media: Information Seeking, Political Interest, and Issue Agendas. Buck Hill Falls, PA: American Association for Public Opinion Research, 1977.

1506 McCormick, James M.; and Coveyou, Michael R. "Mass Political Imagery and the Salience of International Affairs," American Politics Quarterly, 6 (1978), 498-509.

1507 McCormick, Richard P. The Presidential Game: The Origins of American Presidential Politics. New York: Oxford University Press, Inc., 1982.

1508 McCormick, Thelma, (ed.). The Decade of Dissent: Impact of the Sixties on Studies in Communication. Greenwich, CT: JAI Books, 1980.

1509 McCrone, Donald J.; and Kuklinski, James H. "The Delegate Theory of Representation," American Journal of Political Science, 23 (1979), 278-300.

1510 McDevitt, Roland D. "Congressional Campaign Finance and the Consequences of its Regulation" (Ph.D. dissertation, University of California, 1978), Dissertation Abstracts International A, 39 (1979), 5699-5700.

Bibliography

1511 McEwen, William J.; and Hamper, Donald J. "How Information Needs and Efforts Affect Channel Choice," Journalism Quarterly, 54 (1977), 149-153.

1512 McGaughey, R. H., III. "A Content Analysis of the Coverage Given the 1972 Democratic Primary for President in Twenty Selected Ohio Daily Newspapers" (Ph. D. dissertation, Ohio University, 1972), Dissertation Abstracts International A, 33 (1973), 6385.

1513 McGovern, George. An American Journey: The Presidential Campaign Speeches of George McGovern. New York: Random House, 1974.

1514 _____. Grassroots: The Autobiography of George McGovern. New York: Random House, 1978.

1515 McGuire, W. J. "Persuasion, Resistance, and Attitude Change," Handbook of Communication, eds. Ithiel de Sola Pool, et al. Chicago, IL: Rand McNally, 1973.

1516 McGuire, William J. "Psychological Motives and Communication Gratification Measures Through Political Effects Analysis," The Uses of Mass Communication, eds. Jay G. Blumler and Elihu Katz. Beverly Hills, CA: Sage Publications, 1974.

1517 McKay, David H. "The United States in Crisis: A Review of the American Political Literature," Government and Opposition, 14 (1979), 373-385.

1518 McKinney, Michael W. "Political Attitude and Opinion Structures among Mass Publics: An Empirical Analysis" (Ph. D. dissertation, University of Maryland, 1973), Dissertation Abstracts International A, 34 (1974), 7840-7841.

1519 McLean, S.; and Brennan, P. "Press Advertising Strategies and Democracy," Politics, 8 (1973), 205-211.

1520 McLeod, Jack M.; and Becker, Lee B. "Testing the Validity of Gratification Measures Through Political Effects Analysis," The Uses of Mass Communication, eds. Jay G. Blumler and Elihu Katz. Beverly Hills, CA: Sage Publications, 1974.

1521 _____; and _____. "The Uses and Gratifications Approach," Handbook of Political Communication, eds. Dan D. Nimmo and Keith R. Sanders. Beverly Hills, CA: Sage Publications, 1981, 67-99.

1522 _____; _____; and Byrnes, James E. "Another Look at the Agenda-Setting Function of the Press," Communication Research, 1 (1974), 131-166.

1523 _____ ; Brown, Jane D.; and Becker, Lee B. "Watergate and the 1974 Congressional Elections," Public Opinion Quarterly, 41 (1977), 181-195.

1524 _____ ; _____ ; _____ ; and Ziemke, Dean. "Decline and Fall at the White House: A Longitudinal Analysis of Communication Effects," Communication Research, 4 (1977), 3-22.

1525 _____ ; _____ ; _____ ; and _____. "Decline and Fall at the White House: A Rejoinder to Professor Davis," Communication Research, 4 (1977), 35-39.

1526 _____ ; Bybee, Carl R.; and Durall, Jean A. "Equivalence of Informed Political Participation: The 1976 Presidential Debates as a Source of Influence," Communication Research, 6 (1979), 463-487.

1527 _____ ; _____ ; and _____. "Evaluating Media Performance by Gratifications Sought and Received," Journalism Quarterly, 59 (1982), 3-12+.

1528 _____ ; Durall, J.; Ziemke, D.; and Bybee, C. "Reactions of Young and Older Voters: Expanding the Context of Debate Effects," The Great Debates: Ford vs. Carter, 1976, ed. Sidney Kraus. Bloomington, IN: Indiana University Press, 1979.

1529 McMurray, LaDonna L. "The Equal Time Law and the Free Flow of Communication: A Critical Study of the Humphrey-McGovern Debates" (Ph.D. dissertation, University of Southern California, 1975), Dissertation Abstracts International A, 36 (1976), 7047.

1530 McNitt, A. D. "Effect of Preprimary Endorsement on Competition for Nominations: An Examination of Different Nominating Systems," Journal of Politics, 42 (1980), 257-266.

1531 _____. "The Impact of State Legislation on Political Campaigns," State Government, 53 (1980), 135-139.

1532 McPeek, Robert W.; and Gross, Alan E. "Evaluations of Presidential Campaign Speakers as a Function of Similarity and Expectancy Information," Journal of Applied Social Psychology, 5 (1975), 75-85.

1533 McPhee, William N.; and Glaser, William A. (eds.). Public Opinion and Congressional Elections. Westport, CT: Greenwood Press, 1981.

1534 McPherson, J. Miller; Welch, Susan; and Clark, Cal. "The Stability and Reliability of Political Efficacy: Using Path

Analysis to Test Alternative Models," *American Political Science Review*, 71 (1977), 509-521.

1535 McQuail, Denis; and Gurevitch, Michael. "Explaining Audience Behavior: Three Approaches Considered," *The Uses of Mass Communication*, eds. Jay G. Blumler and Elihu Katz. Beverly Hills, CA: Sage Publications, 1974.

1536 _____; and Windahl, Sven. *Communication Models for the Study of Mass Communications*. New York: Longman, 1982.

1537 Meadow, Robert G. "Cross-Media Comparison of Coverage of the 1972 Presidential Campaign," *Journalism Quarterly*, 50 (1973), 482-488.

1538 _____. "Information and Maturation in the Political Socialization Process" (Ph.D. dissertation, University of Pennsylvania, 1976), *Dissertation Abstracts International A*, 37 (1977), 4590.

1539 _____. "Issue Emphasis and Public Opinion: The Media During the 1972 Presidential Campaign," *American Politics Quarterly*, 4 (1976), 177-192.

1540 _____. "Political Dimensions of Nonproduct Advertising," *Journal of Communication*, 31 (1981), 69-82.

1541 _____. *Politics as Communication*. Norwood, NJ: Ablex Publishing Co., 1980.

1542 _____; and Jackson-Beeck, Marilyn. "Candidate Political Philosophy: Revelations in the 1960 and 1976 Debates," *Presidential Studies Quarterly*, 10 (1980), 234-243.

1543 _____; and _____. "A Comparative Perspective on Presidential Debates: Issue Evolution in 1960 and 1976," *The Presidential Debates*, eds. George F. Bishop, Robert G. Meadow, and Marilyn Jackson-Beeck. New York: Praeger, 1978.

1544 _____; and _____. "Issue Evolution: A New Perspective on Presidential Debates," *Journal of Communication*, 28 (1978), 84-92.

1545 _____; and Sigelman, Lee. "Some Effects and Noneffects of Campaign Commercials: An Experimental Study," *Political Behavior*, 4 (1982), 163-175.

1546 Mears, W. R. "Debates; A View from the Inside," *Columbia Journalism Review*, 15 (1977), 21-25.

1547 Mebane, R. "The Great Game of Politics: A Study of Metaphor in the Mass Media" (Master's thesis, Annenberg

School of Communications, University of Pennsylvania, 1977).

1548 Medhurst, Martin J. "McGovern at Wheaton: A Quest for Redemption," Communication Quarterly, 25 (1977), 32-39.

1549 _____. "American Cosmology and the Rhetoric of Inaugural Prayer," Central States Speech Journal, 28 (1977), 272-282.

1550 _____. "'God Bless the President': The Rhetoric of Inaugural Prayer" (Ph.D. dissertation, Pennsylvania State University, 1980), Dissertation Abstracts International A, 41 (1981), 3779.

1551 _____; and DeSousa, Michael A. "Political Cartoons Rhetorical Form: A Taxonomy of Graphic Discourse," Communication Monographs, 48 (1981), 197-236.

1552 _____; and Dreibelbis, Gary C. "The Ghost of McGovern," Communication Quarterly, 26 (1978), 37-43.

1553 "Media Politics: Myths and Realities" (Symposium), Journal of Communication, 30 (1980), 102-180.

1554 Meehl, Paul E. "The Selfish Voter Paradox and the Throw-Away Vote Argument," American Political Science Review, 71 (1977), 11-30.

1555 "Meeting the Press," Public Opinion, 4 (1982), 10-12, 57.

1556 Meier, Kenneth J. "Party Identification and Vote Choice: The Causal Relationship," Western Political Quarterly, 28 (1975), 496-505.

1557 _____; and Campbell, James E. "Issue Voting: An Empirical Examination of Individually Necessary and Jointly Sufficient Conditions," American Politics Quarterly, 7 (1979), 21-50.

1558 Meisler, Stanley. "The Press/Political Frost North of the Border," Washington Journalism Review, 2 (1980), 50-51.

1559 Meltsner, Arnold J. (ed.). Politics and the Oval Office: Towards Presidential Governance. San Francisco, CA: Institute for Contemporary Studies, 1981.

1560 Meltzer, A. H.; and Vellrath, M. "Effects of Economic Policies on Votes for the Presidency: Some Evidence from Recent Elections," Journal of Law and Economics, 18 (1975), 781-805.

1561 Mendelsohn, Harold. "Some Reasons Why Information Campaigns Can Succeed," Public Opinion Quarterly, 37 (1973-74), 50-61.

1562 _____; and O'Keefe, Garrett J. The People Choose a President: Influences on Voter Decision-Making. New York: Praeger, 1976.

1563 Meno, Michael R.; Bell, Tony; and Bath, Lawrence. "Dynamics of Attitude Formation Regarding Women in Politics," Experimental Study of Politics, 5 (August, 1976), 25-39.

1564 Merenda, Peter F.; Shapurian, Reza; and Clarke, Walter V. "Pre-Election Public Image of Nixon and McGovern Given by English Students," Perceptual and Motor Skills, 38 (1974), 575-578.

1565 Merrill, J. C.; and Lowenstein, R. L. Media, Messages, and Men. New York: Longman, 1979.

1566 Merrin, Mary Beth. "The Issues in Issue Voting: An Analysis of the 1972 Election" (Ph.D. dissertation, George Washington University, 1976), Dissertation Abstracts International A, 37 (1976), 3157-3158.

1567 _____; and LeBlanc, Hugh L. "Parties and Candidates in 1972: Objects of Issue Voting," Western Political Quarterly, 32 (1979), 59-69.

1568 Merritt, Sharyne Ann. "Winners and Losers: Sex Differences in Municipal Elections," American Journal of Political Science, 21 (1977), 731-743.

1569 Mervin, David. "Personality and Ticket Splitting in U.S. Federal and Gubernatorial Elections," Political Studies, 21 (1973), 306-310.

1570 Messaris, Paul; Eckman, Bruce; and Gumpert, Gary. "Editing Structure in the Televised Versions of the 1976 Presidential Debates," Journal of Broadcasting, 23 (1969), 359-369.

1571 Messner, E. "Observation of Elected Public Officials by High School Students: An Example of Primary Prevention," Comprehensive Psychiatry, 18 (1977), 277-282.

1572 Meyer, Phillip. "Polls: Learning to Live with the Numbers," Columbia Journalism Review, 15 (1977), 29+.

1573 _____ (ed.). Precision Journalism: A Reporter's Introduction to Social Science Methods. 2nd ed. Bloomington, IN: Indiana University Press, 1978.

1574 Meyer, T. P., and Donohue, T. P. "Perceptions and Misperceptions of Political Advertising," Journal of Business Communication, 10 (1973), 29-40.

1575 Meyers, Manny. "Issues and Images: The Political Consultant and the Changing American Electoral Process" (Ph. D. dissertation, New York University, 1974), Dissertation Abstracts International A, 35 (1974), 1184-1185.

1576 Meyers, Renee A.; Newhouse, Thomas L.; and Garrett, Dennis E. "Political Momentum: Television News Treatment," Communication Monographs, 45 (1978), 382-388.

1577 Mezey, S. G. "Does Sex Make a Difference? A Case Study of Women in Politics," Western Political Quarterly, 31 (1978), 492-501.

1578 Mickelson, S. "Candidate in the Living Room," Annals of the American Academy of Political and Social Science, 427 (1976), 23-32.

1579 Mihevc, Nancy T. "Information, Valence, and Cognitive Complexity in the Political Domain," Journal of Psychology, 99 (1978), 163-177.

1580 Mikan, Frank G. "An Evaluation of the Campaign Finance Reform Recommendations of the Senate Watergate Committee" (Master's thesis, Duquesne University, 1975), Masters Abstracts, 13 (1975), 152.

1581 Milbrath, Lester W.; and Goel, M. I. Political Participation: How and Why Do People Get Involved in Politics? Washington, D. C.: University Press of America, 1982.

1582 Mileur, J. M.; and Sulzner, G. T. Campaigning for the Massachusetts Senate. Amherst, MA: University of Massachusetts Press, 1974.

1583 Miller, Arthur H. "Political Issues and Trust in Government," American Political Science Review, 68 (1974), 951-1001.

1584 _____; Erbring, Lutz; and Goldenberg, Edie. "Front Page News and Real-World Cues: Another Look at Agenda-Setting by the Media," American Journal of Political Science, 24 (1980), 16-24.

1585 _____; Goldenberg, Edie; and Erbring, Lutz. "Type-Set Politics: Impact of Newspapers on Public Confidence," American Political Science Review, 73 (1979), 67-84.

1586 _____; and MacKuen, Michael. "Informing the Electorate: A National Study," The Great Debates: Carter vs. Ford, 1976, ed. Sidney Kraus. Bloomington, IN: Indiana University Press, 1979.

Bibliography

1587 _____ ; and _____. "Learning About the Candidates: The 1976 Presidential Debates," Public Opinion Quarterly, 43 (1979), 326-346.

1588 _____ ; and Miller, W. E. "Issues, Candidates and Partisan Divisions in the 1972 American Presidential Election," British Journal of Political Science, 5 (1975), 393-434.

1589 _____ ; and Wattenberg, Martin. "Politics from the Pulpit: Religiosity and the 1980 Elections," Economic Outlook USA, 9 (1982), 61-64.

1590 Miller, D. F. "Metaphor and Political Knowledge," American Political Science Review, 73 (1979), 155-170.

1591 Miller, L. W.; and Sigelman, L. "Is the Audience the Message? A Note on LBJ's Vietnam Statements," Public Opinion Quarterly, 42 (1978), 71-80.

1592 Miller, M. Mark; and Reese, Stephen D. "Media Dependency as Interaction: Effects of Exposure and Reliance on Political Activity and Efficacy," Communication Research, 9 (1982), 227-248.

1593 Miller, Richard L. "Mere Exposure, Psychological Reactance and Attitude Change," Public Opinion Quarterly, 40 (1976), 229-233.

1594 Miller, Roy E. "Experimental Studies," Handbook of Political Communication, eds. Dan D. Nimmo and Keith R. Sanders. Beverly Hills, CA: Sage Publications, 1981, 561-589.

1595 _____ ; and Richey, W. L. "The Effects of a Campaign Brochure Drop in a County-Level Race for State's Attorney," Communication Yearbook 4, ed. Dan D. Nimmo. New Brunswick, NJ: Transaction Books, 1980.

1596 _____ ; and Robyn, Dorothy L. "A Field Experimental Study of Direct Mail in a Congressional Primary Campaign: What Effects Last Until Election Day?" Experimental Study of Politics, 4 (1975), 1-37.

1597 Miller, S. S. Presidential Power in a Nutshell. St. Paul, MN: West Publishing Company, 1977.

1598 Miller, Susan H. "Congress and the News Media: Coverage, Collaboration and Agenda-Setting" (Ph. D. dissertation, Stanford University, 1976), Dissertation Abstracts International A, 37 (1976), 2466.

1599 _____. "News Coverage of Congress: The Search for the Ultimate Spokesman," Journalism Quarterly, 54 (1977), 459-465.

1600 _____. "Reporters and Congressmen: Living in Symbiosis," Journalism Monographs, 53 (1978), 1-25.

1601 Miller, W. L. Electoral Dynamics. New York: St. Martin's Press, 1978.

1602 Miller, W. L. Yankee from Georgia: The Emergence of Jimmy Carter. New York: New York Times Books, 1978.

1603 Milne, Robert S., Jr. "Voter Attitude Organization and Change in the 1972 Presidential Election Campaign: A Test of Congruity Theory" (Ph.D. dissertation, Syracuse University, 1975), Dissertation Abstracts International A, 36 (1976), 6923.

1604 Minow, Newton N.; Martin, John Barlow; and Mitchell, Lee M. Presidential Television. New York: Basic Books, 1973.

1605 _____; and Mitchell, Lee M. "Incumbent Television: A Case of Indecent Exposure," Annals of the American Academy of Political and Social Science, 425 (1976), 74-87.

1606 Miroff, Bruce. Pragmatic Illusions: The Presidential Politics of John F. Kennedy. New York: David McKay Co., 1976.

1607 Mirsky, Isabel J. "The Effect of Attitude, Ego-Involvement, and Message Consistency on the Learning and Recall of Quantitative Information" (Ph.D. dissertation, Columbia University, 1976), Dissertation Abstracts International A, 38 (1977), 2416.

1608 Misiewicz, Joseph P. "TV Network News Coverage of Announced Presidential Candidates during the 1972 State Presidential Primaries" (Ph.D. dissertation, University of Michigan, 1974), Dissertation Abstracts International A, 35 (1975), 7336-7337.

1609 Mitchell, L. M. "Government as Broadcaster, Solution or Threat? Diversity in Broadcasting," Journal of Communication, 28 (1978), 69-76.

1610 Mitchell, Malcolm G. Propaganda, Polls and Public Opinion: Are People Manipulated? Englewood Cliffs, NJ: Prentice-Hall, 1977.

1611 Mitofsky, Warren J. (ed.). Campaign '78: A Comprehensive Political Handbook. New York: Arno Press, 1980.

1612 Mladenka, K. R.; and Hill, K. Q. "The Development of Political Orientations: A Partial Test of a Cognitive Development Hypothesis," Youth and Society, 2 (1975), 130-147.

Bibliography 131

1613 Mohrmann, G. P. "An Essay on Fantasy Theme Criticism," Quarterly Journal of Speech, 68 (1982), 109-133.

1614 Monroe, Kristen, R. "Economic Influences on Presidential Popularity," Public Opinion Quarterly, 42 (1978), 360-369.

1615 Montjoy, R. S. "Election Laws, Voting Decision, and Political Linkage: An Empirically Based Computer Simulation" (Ph. D. dissertation, Indiana University, 1977), Dissertation Abstracts International A, 38 (1977), 2327.

1616 Moodie, G. C. "On Political Scandals and Corruption," Government and Opposition, 15 (1980), 208-222.

1617 Moore, James P. "A Survey Study of Political and Communication Behaviors of College Undergraduate Students as Voters in a Presidential Election" (Ph. D. dissertation, University of Denver, 1974), Dissertation Abstracts International A, 35 (1974), 3078-3079.

1618 Moore, Jonathan (ed.). The Campaign for President: 1980 in Retrospect. Cambridge, MA: Ballinger Publishing Co., 1981.

1619 _____; and Fraser, J. Campaign for President. The Managers Look at '76. Cambridge, MA: Ballinger Publishing Company, 1977.

1620 _____; and Pierce, A. C. Voters, Primaries, and Parties. Cambridge, MA: Harvard University Press, 1976.

1621 Moreland, W. B. "Angels, Pinpoints, and Voters: The Pattern for a Coattail," American Journal of Political Science, 17 (1973), 170-176.

1622 Moreno, F. J. "The Myth of Political Rationality," International Journal of Social Psychiatry, 21 (1974-75), 21-26.

1623 Morgan, David. "Newspapers and Politics: Regional Newspapers in the U. S. and the U. K.," Journalism Quarterly, 54 (1977), 765-772.

1624 _____. "Political Linkage and Public Policy: Attitudinal Congruence Between Citizens and Officials," Western Political Quarterly, 26 (1973), 209-223.

1625 Morris, R. "Foreign-Policy Reporting: Quarantined for the Campaign," Columbia Journalism Review, 15 (1976), 19-22.

1626 _____. "This Is the First and Last Article CJR Will Run About Press Coverage of Foreign Policy During the

Presidential Campaign," Columbia Journalism Review, 18 (1980), 51.

1627 Morrison, James; and Blue, Richard. Political Change: A Film Guide. Minneapolis, MN: University of Minnesota Audio Visual Library Service, 1975;

1628 Morrow, Gary R. "Changes in Perceptions of Ford and Carter Following the First Presidential Debate," Perceptual and Motor Skills, 45 (1977), 423-429.

1629 _____; Clarke, Walter V.; Merenda, Peter F. "Perception of Role of the President: A Nine-Year Follow Up," Perceptual and Motor Skills, 38 (1974), 1259-1262.

1630 Mosier, N. R.; and Ahlgren, A. "Credibility of Precision Journalism," Journalism Quarterly, 58 (1981), 375-381.

1631 Mosley, P. "Images of the 'Floating Voter': Or, The 'Political Business Cycle' Revisited," Political Studies, 26 (1978), 375-394.

1632 Moss, Geoffrey. The Art and Politics of Geoffrey Moss. New York: Hawthorn, 1977.

1633 Muchnik, M. M. "Free Expression and Political Broadcasting on Public Radio and Television" (Ph.D. dissertation, University of Denver, 1973), Dissertation Abstracts International A, 34 (1974), 4304-4305.

1634 Muchow, David. The Vanishing Congress: Where Has All the Power Gone? Washington, D.C.: North American International, 1976.

1635 Mudd, Samuel; and Pohlman, Alan. "Sensitivity of Image Profile and Image Clarity Measures to Change: Nixon Through Watergate," Journal of Applied Psychology, 61 (1976), 223-228.

1636 Mueller, Claus. The Politics of Communication: A Study in the Political Sociology of Language, Socialization, and Legitimation. New York: Oxford University Press, 1973.

1637 Mueller, D. C. Public Choice. New York: Cambridge University Press, 1979.

1638 Mulcahy, Kevin V.; and Katz, Richard S. America Votes: What You Should Know About Elections Today. Englewood Cliffs, NJ: Prentice-Hall, Inc., 1976.

1639 Mulder, Ronald. "The Effects of Televised Political Ads in the 1975 Chicago Mayoral Election," Journalism Quarterly, 56 (1979), 336-340.

1640 _____. "The Effects of Televised Political Advertising: The 1975 Chicago Mayoral Election" (Ph. D. dissertation, University of Chicago, 1975), Dissertation Abstracts International A, 36 (1976), 7716.

1641 _____. "Log-Linear Analysis of Media Credibility," Journalism Quarterly, 58 (1981), 635-638.

1642 _____. "Media Credibility: A Use-Gratifications Approach," Journalism Quarterly, 57 (1980), 474-477.

1643 _____. "The Political Effects of the Carter-Ford Debate: An Experimental Analysis," Sociological Focus, 11 (1978), 33-45.

1644 Mullen, W. F. Presidential Power and Politics. New York: St. Martin's Press, 1976.

1645 Muller, Edward N. Aggressive Political Participation. Princeton, NJ: Princeton University Press, 1979.

1646 _____. "Behavioral Correlates of Political Support," American Political Science Review, 71 (1977), 454-467.

1647 _____. "Mass Politics: Focus on Participation," American Behavioral Scientist, 21 (1977), 63-83.

1648 _____; and Williams, C. J. "Dynamics of Political Support-Alienation," Comparative Political Studies, 13 (1980), 33-59.

1649 Muller, N. J. "Political Advertising in National Magazines," Practical Politics, 2 (1978), 16-20, 28.

1650 Mullins, Leslie E. "Agenda-Setting and the Young Voter," The Emergence of American Political Issues: The Agenda-Setting Function of the Press, eds. Donald L. Shaw and Maxwell E. McCombs. St. Paul, MN: West Publishing Co., 1977.

1651 _____. "Mass Communication on the Campus: A Descriptive and Causal Analysis of Information-Seeking and Political Behavior During the 1972 Presidential Campaign" (Ph. D. dissertation, University of North Carolina at Chapel Hill, 1974), Journalism Abstracts, 12 (1974), 27.

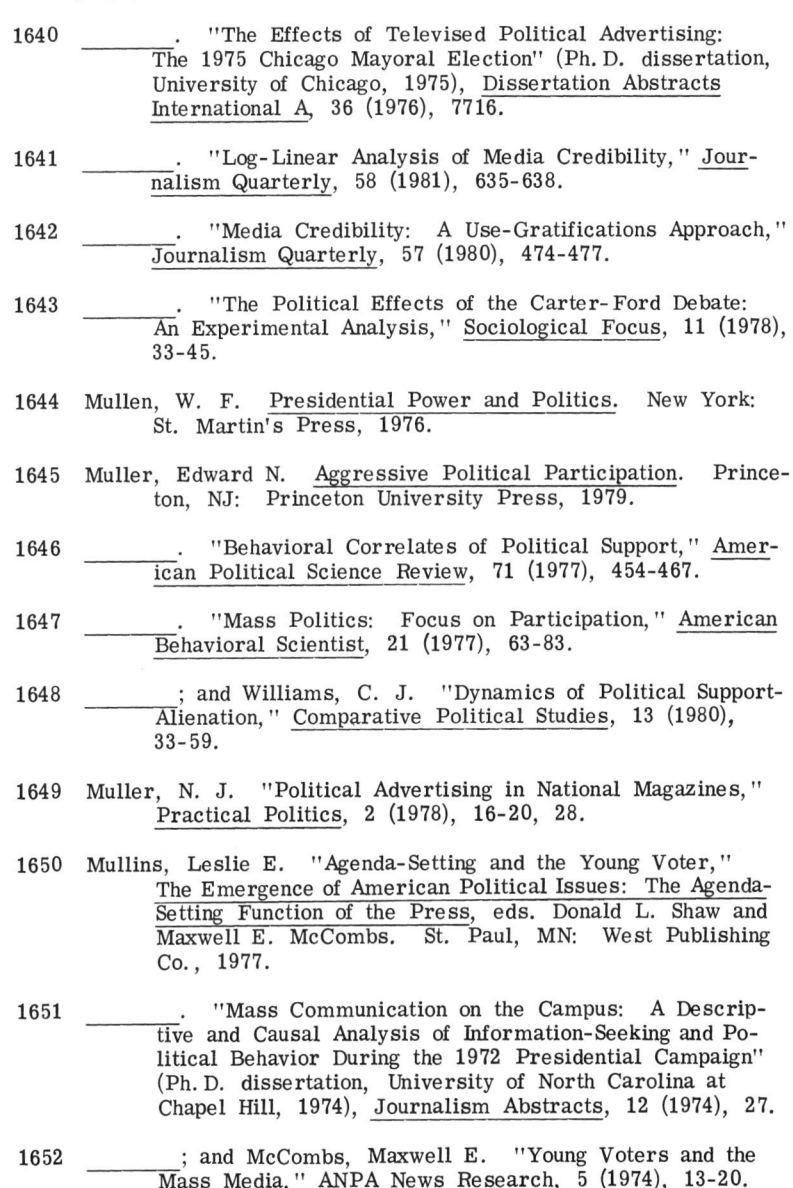

1652 _____; and McCombs, Maxwell E. "Young Voters and the Mass Media," ANPA News Research, 5 (1974), 13-20.

1653 Murphy, W. T. Voter Power: How to Work for the Person You Want Elected. Garden City, NY: Anchor Press, 1974.

1654 Murphy, William T., Jr. "Youth and Politics: A Study of Involvement in the 1970 Congressional Election" (Ph.D. dissertation, Princeton University, 1974), Dissertation Abstracts International A, 35 (1975), 6776-6777.

1655 Murray, Michael D. "Wallace and the Media: The 1972 Florida Primary," Southern Speech Communication Journal, 40 (1975), 429-440.

1656 Mussen, P.; Sullivan, L. B.; and Eisenberg-Berg, N. "Changes in Political-Economic Attitudes During Adolescence," Journal of Genetic Psychology, 130 (1977), 69-76.

1657 Myers, David S. "Editorials on the Economy in the 1980 Presidential Campaign," Journalism Quarterly, 59 (1982), 414-419.

1658 _____. "Editorials and the Economy in the 1976 Presidential Campaign," Journalism Quarterly, 55 (1978), 755-760.

1659 _____. "Editorials and Foreign Affairs in Recent Presidential Campaigns," Journalism Quarterly, 59 (1982), 540-547.

1660 _____. "Editorials and Foreign Affairs in the 1976 Presidential Campaign," Journalism Quarterly, 55 (1978), 92-99.

1661 _____. "Editorials and Foreign Affairs in the 1972 Presidential Campaign," Journalism Quarterly, 51 (1974), 251-257.

1662 Myers, Stacy C. "Howard Baker: A Rhetoric of Leadership," (Ph.D. dissertation, Southern Illinois University, 1973), Dissertation Abstracts International A, 34 (1974), 6156.

1663 Myerson, Michael. Watergate: Crime in the Suites. International Publishers, 1973.

1664 Nakanishi, Masao; Cooper, Lee G.; and Kassarkian, Harold H. "Voting for a Political Candidate Under Conditions of Minimal Information," Journal of Consumer Research, 1 (1974), 36-43.

1665 Nanda, K. "An Experiment in Voting Choice: Who Gets the 'Blind' Vote?" Experimental Study of Politics, 4 (1975), 20-35.

1666 Napolitan, J. "Media Costs and Effects in Political Campaigns," Annals of the American Academy of Political and Social Science, 427 (1976), 114-124.

Bibliography

1667 Narain, R. "Political Psychology: A New Field," Indian Educational Review, 12 (1977), 91-97.

1668 National Association of Broadcasters. Political Broadcast Catechism. 8th ed. Washington, D. C.: National Association of Broadcasters, 1976.

1669 National News Council. In the Public Interest: A Report, 1973-1975. New York: National News Council, 1975.

1670 Nelson, C. J. "The Effect of Incumbency on Voting in Congressional Elections, 1964-1974," Political Science Quarterly, 93 (1978-79), 665-678.

1671 Nelson, P. "Political Information," Journal of Law and Economics, 19 (1976), 315-346.

1672 Nelson, William E., Jr.; and Meranto, Philip J. Electing Black Mayors: Political Action in the Black Community. Columbus, OH: Ohio State University Press, 1977.

1673 Neuborne, Burt. The Rights of Candidates and Voters. New York: Avon Books, 1976.

1674 Neuman, W. Russell (ed.). The Social Impact of Television: A Research Agenda for the 1980s. Queenstown, MD: Aspen Institute for Humanistic Studies, 1981.

1675 _____. "Television and American Culture: The Mass Medium and the Pluralist Audience," Public Opinion Quarterly, 46 (1982), 471-487.

1676 Neustadt, Richard E. "The Constraining of the President: The Presidency after Watergate," British Journal of Political Science, 4 (1974), 383-398.

1677 _____. Presidential Power. New York: Wiley, 1976.

1678 _____. "Staffing the Presidency: Premature Notes on the New Administration," Political Science Quarterly, 93 (1978), 1-9, 12-14.

1679 Newell, S. A.; and King, T. R. "The Keynote Address of the Democratic National Convention, 1972: The Evolution of a Speech," Southern Speech Communication Journal, 39 (1974), 346-358.

1680 Nichols, Bill. Ideology and the Image: Social Representation in the Cinema and Other Media. Bloomington, IN: Indiana University Press, 1981.

1681 Nie, Norman H.; Verba, S.; and Petrocik, J. R. The Changing American Voter. Cambridge, MA: Harvard University Press, 1979.

1682　Niemi, Richard G. "The Costs of Voting and Nonvoting," Public Choice, 27 (1976), 115-119.

1683　_____; Hedges, R.; and Jennings, M. Kent. "The Similarity of Husbands' and Wives' Political Views," American Politics Quarterly, 5 (1977), 133-148.

1684　_____; and Weisberg, Herbert F. Controversies in American Voting Behavior. San Francisco, CA: W. H. Freeman, 1976.

1685　Nimmo, Dan D. "Alternative Approaches to the Study of Political Communication," Revue Francaise de Communication, 2 (1979), 9-22.

1686　_____. "Ethical Issues in Political Communication," Communication, 6 (no.2, 1981), 193-212.

1687　_____. "Mass Communication and Politics," Handbook of Political Behavior, Vol. 4, ed. S. Long. New York: Plenum Publishers, 1981.

1688　_____. Political Communication and Public Opinion in America. Santa Monica, CA: Goodyear Publishing, 1978.

1689　_____. "Political Communication Theory and Research: An Overview," Communication Yearbook 1, ed. Brent Ruben. New Brunswick, NJ: Transaction Books, 1977, 441-452.

1690　_____. "Political Image Makers and the Mass Media," The Annals of the American Academy of Political and Social Science, 427 (1976), 33-44.

1691　_____. Popular Images of Politics. Englewood Cliffs, NJ: Prentice-Hall, 1974.

1692　_____. "The Present in Light of a Future Now Past," Political Communication Review, 6 (1981), 51-59.

1693　_____. "A Response to Hart's Commentary," Human Communication Research, 8 (1982), 382-385.

1694　_____; and Combs, James E. "Fantasies and Melodrama in Television Network News: The Case of Three Mile Island," Western Journal of Speech Communication, 46 (1982), 45-55.

1695　_____; and _____. Subliminal Politics: Myths and Myth Makers in America. Englewood Cliffs, NJ: Prentice-Hall, 1980.

1696　_____; and Mansfield, Michael W. "Effects of Victory or Defeat Upon the Images of Political Candidates," Experimental Study of Politics, 3 (1974), 1-30.

Bibliography

1697 _____; and _____. Government and the News Media: Comparative Dimensions. Waco, TX: Baylor University Press, 1982.

1698 _____; and Rivers, W. L. (eds.). Watching American Politics: Articles and Commentaries About Citizens, Politicians, and the News Media. Essex, England: Longman Group, 1981.

1699 _____; and Sanders, Keith R. "Conclusion: Constructing the Realities of a Pluralistic Field," Handbook of Political Communication, eds. Dan D. Nimmo and Keith R. Sanders. Beverly Hills, CA: Sage Publications, 1981, 651-673.

1700 _____; and _____ (eds.). Handbook of Political Communication. Beverly Hills, CA: Sage Publications, 1981.

1701 _____; and _____. "Introduction: The Emergence of Political Communication as a Field," Handbook of Political Communication, eds. Dan D. Nimmo and Keith R. Sanders. Beverly Hills, CA: Sage Publications, 1981, 11-36.

1702 _____; and Savage, Robert L. Candidates and Their Images: Concepts, Methods and Findings. Pacific Palisades, CA: Goodyear Publishing, 1976.

1703 _____; and _____. "Image Typologies in a Senatorial Campaign: A Comparison of Forced vs. Free Distribution Data," Political Methodology, 2 (1975), 293-318.

1704 Nisbet, R. "Public Opinion versus Popular Opinion," The Public Interest, 41 (1975), 168.

1705 Nitz, Lawrence H.; Dawson, Jack; and Phillips, James L. "Machiavellianism and Competitive Social Contacts in a Limited Information Convention Game," Experimental Study of Politics, 5 (1976), 20-41.

1706 Nixon, R. M. The Nixon Presidential Press Conferences. New York: Earl M. Coleman Enterprises, Inc., 1978.

1707 Noelle-Neumann, Elisabeth. "Public Opinion and the Classical Tradition: A Re-evaluation," Public Opinion Quarterly, 43 (1979), 143-156.

1708 _____. "Spiral of Silence: A Theory of Public Opinion," Journal of Communication, 24 (1974), 43-51.

1709 _____. "Turbulences in the Climate of Opinion: Methodological Applications of the Spiral of Silence Theory," Public Opinion Quarterly, 41 (1977), 143-158.

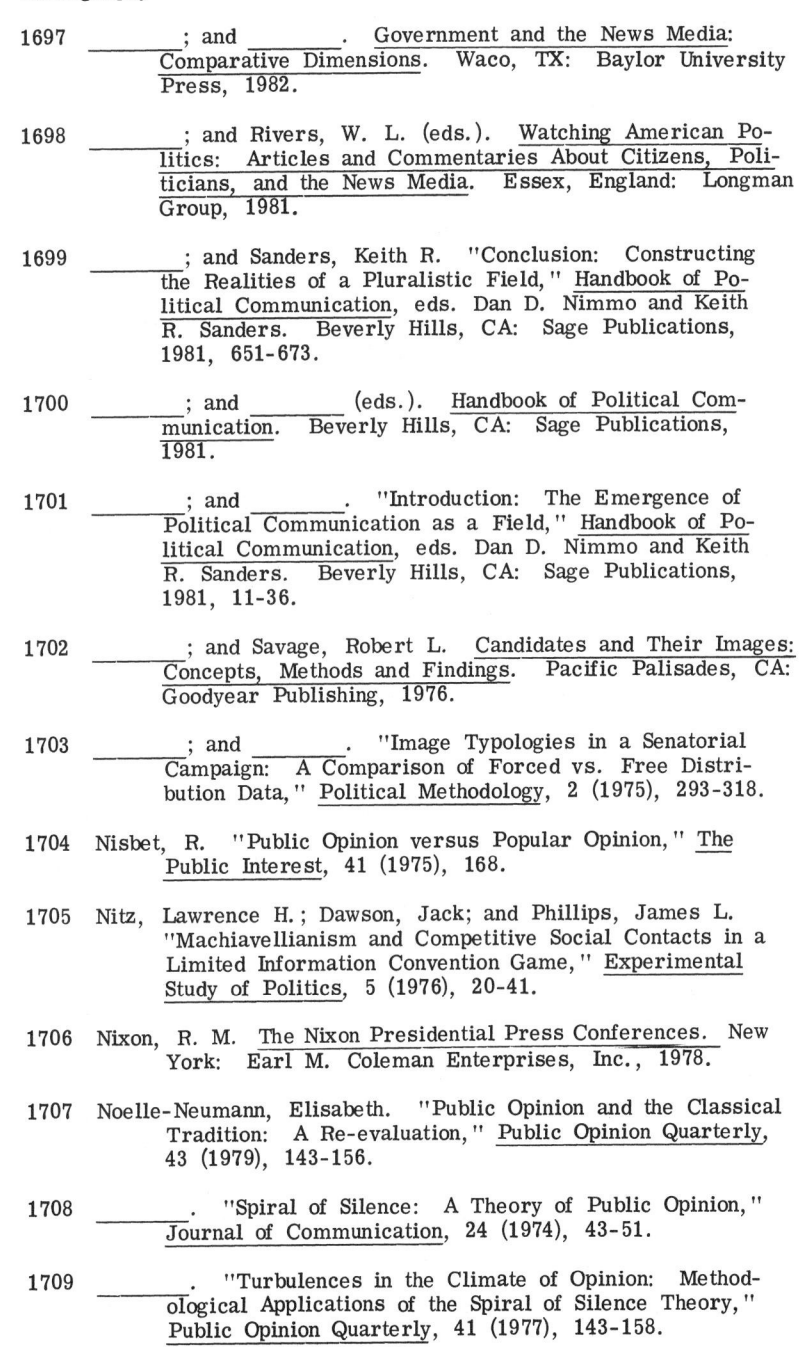

1710 Norrander, Barbara K. "Mass Behavior in Presidential Primaries: Individual and Structural Determinants" (Ph. D. dissertation, Ohio State University, 1982), Dissertation Abstracts International A, 43 (1982), 2780.

1711 Novak, Michael. Choosing Our King: Powerful Symbols in Presidential Politics. New York: Macmillan, 1974.

1712 Nowlan, J. D. Television Charts a New Campaign Map for Illinois. Urbana, IL: Institute of Government and Public Affairs, 1981.

1713 Nygren, Thomas E.; and Jones, Lawrence E. "Individual Differences in Perceptions and Preferences for Political Candidates," Journal of Experimental Social Psychology, 13 (1977), 182-197.

1714 O'Brien, Lawrence F. No Final Victories: A Life in Politics from John F. Kennedy to Watergate. Garden City, NY: Doubleday, 1974.

1715 O'Connor, Thomas F. "The Personalized Campaign: The 1976 Downey Congressional Campaign" (Master's thesis, Adelphi University, 1978), Masters Abstracts, 16 (1978), 127.

1716 O'Keefe, Garrett J. "The Changing Context of Interpersonal Communication in Political Campaigns," Communication Yearbook 5, ed. Michael Burgoon. New Brunswick, NJ: Transaction Books, 1982, 667-681.

1717 _____. "Political Campaigns and Mass Communication," Political Communication, ed. Steven H. Chaffee. Beverly Hills, CA: Sage Publications, 1975.

1718 _____. "Political Malaise and Reliance on Media," Journalism Quarterly, 57 (1980), 122-128.

1719 _____. "The Uses-Gratifications Approach and Political Communication Research," Political Communication Review, 1 (1976), 8-11.

1720 _____; and Atwood, L. Erwin. "Communication and Election Campaigns," Handbook of Political Communication, eds. Dan D. Nimmo and Keith R. Sanders. Beverly Hills, CA: Sage Publications, 1981, 329-357.

1721 _____. and Lui, Jenny. "First Time Voters: Do Media Matter?" Journal of Communication, 30 (1980), 122-129.

1722 _____; and Mendelsohn, Harold. "Media Influences and

Their Anticipation," The Great Debates: Carter vs. Ford, 1976, ed. Sidney Kraus. Bloomington, IN: Indiana University Press, 1979.

1723 _____ ; and _____. "Nonvoting and Role of the Media," Mass Media and Deviance, ed. C. Winnick. Beverly Hills, CA: Sage Publications, 1978.

1724 _____ ; and _____. "Voter Selectivity, Partisanship, and the Challenge of Watergate," Communication Research, 1 (1974), 345-367.

1725 _____ ; _____ ; and Lui, Jenny. "Voter Decision Making: 1972 and 1974," Public Opinion Quarterly, 40 (1976), 320-330.

1726 O'Keefe, M. Timothy; and Sheinkopf, Kenneth G. "The Voter Decides: Candidate Image or Campaign Issue?" Journal of Broadcasting, 18 (1974), 403-412.

1727 Okuda, K. "Hermeneutics and Politics: A Study in Political Symbolism and Communication" (Ph.D. dissertation, University of Toronto, Canada, 1977), Dissertation Abstracts International A, 39 (1978), 2517.

1728 Oneal, Dennis J. "The Treatment of James Earl Carter and Gerald R. Ford during the 1976 Election Campaign by Television Network Commentators Eric Sevareid and Howard K. Smith: An Evaluative Assertion Analysis" (Ph.D. dissertation, University of Southern Mississippi, 1979), Dissertation Abstracts International A, 40 (1980), 5236.

1729 O'Neill, Paul. "A Survey and an Election: The 1978 U.S. Senatorial Primaries in Mississippi," Catalog of Selected Documents in Psychology, 10 (1980), 33-34.

1730 Oppenheimer, B. I. "Interest Groups in the Political Process," Current History, 67 (1974), 75-78.

1731 Ordeshook, Peter C.; and Shepsle, Kenneth A. Political Equilibrium: A Delicate Balance. Hingham, MA: Keuwer Academic Publishers, 1982.

1732 Orman, John M. "Secrecy, Deception, and Presidential Power: John F. Kennedy to Gerald R. Ford" (Ph.D. dissertation, Indiana University, 1979), Dissertation Abstracts International A, 40 (1979), 1057-1058.

1733 Orr, Jack C. "Reports Confront the President: Sustaining a Counterpoised Situation," Quarterly Journal of Speech, 66 (1980), 17-32.

1734 _____; and Burkins, K. E. "The Endorsement of Evasive Leaders: An Exploratory Study," Central States Speech Journal, 17 (1976), 230-239.

1735 Orum, A. M.; and Cohen, R. A. "The Development of Political Orientation among Black and White Children," American Sociological Review, 38 (1973), 62-74.

1736 Osborn, G. C.; and Martin, R. The Role of the British Press in the 1976 American Presidential Election. Hicksville, NY: Exposition Press, 1981.

1737 Osborne, Leonard L. "Patterns of Arrangement in President Kennedy's Major Addresses" (Ph.D. dissertation, University of California, 1978), Dissertation Abstracts International A, 38 (1978), 7022.

1738 _____. "Rhetorical Pattern in President Kennedy's Major Speeches: A Case Study," Presidential Studies Quarterly, 10 (1980), 332-335.

1739 Ostlund, L. E. "Interpersonal Communication Following McGovern's Eagleton Decision," Public Opinion Quarterly, 37 (1973-74), 601-610.

1740 Ostman, Ronald E., et al. "Relation of Questions and Answers in Kennedy's Press Conference," Journalism Quarterly, 58 (1981), 575-581.

1741 Ostroff, David H. "A Participant-Observer Study of TV Campaign Coverage," Journalism Quarterly, 57 (1980), 415-419.

1742 _____. "Television News and Political Campaigns: A Participant-Observation Study of Coverage of the 1978 Ohio Governor's Race in Columbus, Ohio" (Ph.D. dissertation, Ohio University, 1979), Dissertation Abstracts International A, 40 (1979), 2337.

1743 Overacker, Louise. Money in Elections. Salem, NH: Arno, 1974.

1744 Owen, G. "Evaluation of a Presidential Election Game," American Political Science Review, 69 (1975), 947-953.

1745 Owens, J. R.; and Olson, E. C. "Campaign Spending and the Electoral Process in California, 1966-1974," Western Political Quarterly, 30 (1977), 493-512.

1746 Packard, Vance. Hidden Persuaders (rev. ed.). New York: Pocket Books, 1981.

Bibliography

1747 Page, Benjamin I. Choices and Echoes in Presidential Elections: Rational Man and Electoral Democracy. Chicago, IL: University of Chicago Press, 1979.

1748 ———. "Elections and Social Choice: The State of Evidence," American Journal of Political Science, 21 (1977), 639-668.

1749 ———. "Presidential Campaigning: The Rhetoric of Electoral Competition" (Ph. D. dissertation, Stanford University, 1973), Dissertation Abstracts International A, 33 (1973), 6989.

1750 ———. "Theory of Political Ambiguity," American Political Science Review, 70 (1976), 724-752.

1751 Page, G. D. The Scientific Study of Political Leadership. New York: Macmillan, 1977.

1752 Paizis, Suzanne. Getting Her Elected: A Political Woman's Handbook. Sacramento, CA: Cougar Books, 1977.

1753 Palda, K. S. "The Effects of Expenditure on Political Success," Journal of Law and Economics, 18 (1975), 745-780.

1754 Paletz, David L. "Television Drama: The Appeals of the Senate Watergate Hearings," Midwest Quarterly, 21 (1979), 63-70.

1755 ———; and Elson, M. "Television Coverage of the Presidential Conventions: Now You See It, Now You Don't," Political Science Quarterly, 91 (1976), 109-131.

1756 ———; and Entman, Robert M. Media Power Politics. New York: The Free Press, 1981.

1757 ———; and ———. "Presidents, Power and the Press," Presidential Studies Quarterly, 10 (1980), 416-426.

1758 ———; and Vinegar, Richard J. "Presidents On Television: The Effects of Instant Analysis," Public Opinion Quarterly, 41 (1977-78), 488-497.

1759 ———; et al. "Polls in the Media; Content, Credibility, and Consequences," Public Opinion Quarterly, 44 (1980), 495-513.

1760 Palleschi, P. D. "A Game-Theoretic Study of the Rhetoric of the Watergate Affair: June 17, 1972-November 7, 1972" (Ph. D. dissertation, University of Massachusetts, 1977), Dissertation Abstracts International A, 38 (1978), 4447-4448.

1761 Palmgreen, Philip C. "Mass Communication and Political Knowledge: The Effects of Political Level and Mass Media Coverage on Political Learning" (Ph.D. dissertation, University Of Michigan, 1975), Journalism Abstracts, 16 (1978), 19-20.

1762 _____. Mass Media Use and Political Knowledge. Minneapolis, MN: AEJ Publications, 1979.

1763 _____; and Clarke, Peter. "Agenda-Setting with Local and National Issues," Communication Quarterly, 4 (1977), 435-452.

1764 _____; Wenner, Lawrence A.; and Rayburn, J. D., II. "Relations Between Gratifications Sought and Obtained-- A Study of Television News," Communication Research, 7 (1980), 161-192.

1765 Parker, G. How to Win an Impossible Election. Columbia, MO: Civic Enterprises, 1978.

1766 Parker, Glenn R. "Interpreting Candidate Awareness in U.S. Congressional Elections," Legislative Studies Quarterly, 6 (1981), 219-234.

1767 _____. Political Beliefs about the Structure of Government: Congress and the Presidency. Beverly Hills, CA: Sage Publications, 1974.

1768 _____. "Sources of Change in Congressional District Attentiveness," American Journal of Political Science, 24 (1980), 115-124.

1769 _____; and Davidson, Roger H. "Why Do Americans Love their Congressmen So Much More Than their Congress? Legislative Studies Quarterly, 4 (1979), 53-61.

1770 Pateman, Trevor. Television and the February 1974 General Election. New York: Zoetrope, 1977.

1771 Patrick, William L. "Network Television News and Public Opinion Polls" (Ph.D. dissertation, Ohio University, 1975), Dissertation Abstracts International A, 36 (1976), 7030.

1772 Patterson, J. W. "Moral Development and Political Thinking: The Case of Freedom of Speech," Western Political Quarterly, 32 (1979), 7-20.

1773 Patterson, S. C.; et al. Representatives and Represented. New York: Wiley, 1975.

1774 Patterson, Thomas E. The Mass Media Election: How Americans Choose Their President. New York: Praeger, 1980.

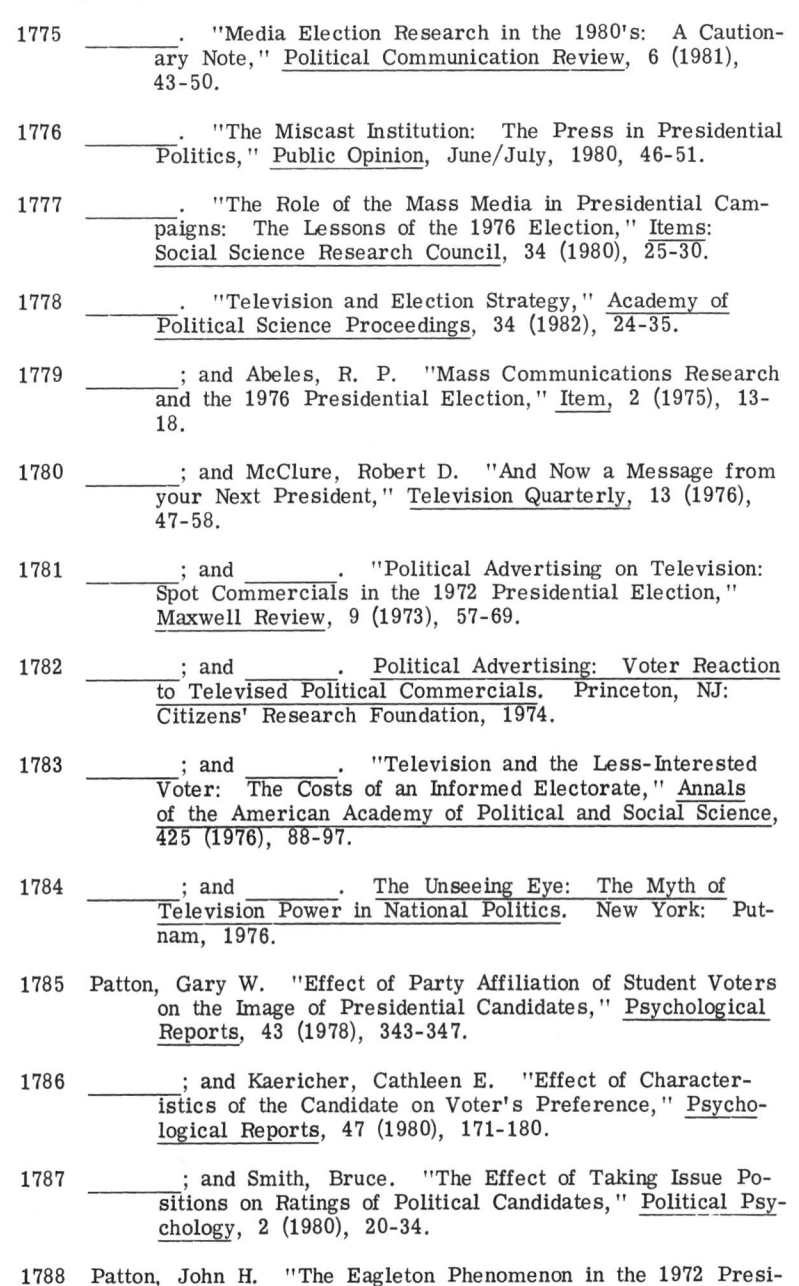

1775 _____. "Media Election Research in the 1980's: A Cautionary Note," Political Communication Review, 6 (1981), 43-50.

1776 _____. "The Miscast Institution: The Press in Presidential Politics," Public Opinion, June/July, 1980, 46-51.

1777 _____. "The Role of the Mass Media in Presidential Campaigns: The Lessons of the 1976 Election," Items: Social Science Research Council, 34 (1980), 25-30.

1778 _____. "Television and Election Strategy," Academy of Political Science Proceedings, 34 (1982), 24-35.

1779 _____; and Abeles, R. P. "Mass Communications Research and the 1976 Presidential Election," Item, 2 (1975), 13-18.

1780 _____; and McClure, Robert D. "And Now a Message from your Next President," Television Quarterly, 13 (1976), 47-58.

1781 _____; and _____. "Political Advertising on Television: Spot Commercials in the 1972 Presidential Election," Maxwell Review, 9 (1973), 57-69.

1782 _____; and _____. Political Advertising: Voter Reaction to Televised Political Commercials. Princeton, NJ: Citizens' Research Foundation, 1974.

1783 _____; and _____. "Television and the Less-Interested Voter: The Costs of an Informed Electorate," Annals of the American Academy of Political and Social Science, 425 (1976), 88-97.

1784 _____; and _____. The Unseeing Eye: The Myth of Television Power in National Politics. New York: Putnam, 1976.

1785 Patton, Gary W. "Effect of Party Affiliation of Student Voters on the Image of Presidential Candidates," Psychological Reports, 43 (1978), 343-347.

1786 _____; and Kaericher, Cathleen E. "Effect of Characteristics of the Candidate on Voter's Preference," Psychological Reports, 47 (1980), 171-180.

1787 _____; and Smith, Bruce. "The Effect of Taking Issue Positions on Ratings of Political Candidates," Political Psychology, 2 (1980), 20-34.

1788 Patton, John H. "The Eagleton Phenomenon in the 1972 Presidential Campaign: A Case Study in the Rhetoric of Paradox," Central States Speech Journal, 24 (1973), 278-287.

1789 _____. "A Government as Good as its People; Jimmy Carter and the Restoration of Transcendence to Politics," Quarterly Journal of Speech, 63 (1977), 249-257.

1790 Paul, Bene L. "Media Use in A California Assembly Campaign" (Master's thesis, San Jose State University, 1976), Journalism Abstracts, 15 (1977), 104-105.

1791 Paysinger, M. A. You May Quote Me--The Politicians. Hicksville, NY: Exposition, 1974.

1792 Peabody, Robert L. "The United States Senate as a Presidential Incubator: Many Are Called But Few Are Chosen," Political Science Quarterly, 91 (1976), 237-258.

1793 Pearl, Arthur. Landslide: The How and Why of Nixon's Victory. Secaucus, NJ: Citadel Press, 1975.

1794 Pedersen, J. T. "Political Involvement and Partisan Change in Presidential Elections," American Journal of Political Science, 22 (1978), 18-30.

1795 Pepper, Robert. "An Analysis of Presidential Primary Election Night Coverage," Educational Broadcasting Review, 7 (1973), 159-166.

1796 _____. "Election Night 1972: TV Network Coverage," Journal of Broadcasting, 18 (1973-74), 27-38.

1797 Perkins, J.; and Fowlkes, D. L. "Opinion Representation versus Social Representation: or, Why Women Can't Run As Women and Win," American Political Science Review, 74 (1980), 92-103.

1798 Perry, James M. Us and Them: How the Press Covered the 1972 Election. New York: Clarkson N. Potter, Inc., 1973.

1799 Perry, Paul. "A Comparison of the Voting Preferences of Likely Voters and Likely Nonvoters," Public Opinion Quarterly, 37 (1973), 99-109.

1800 Perry, W. "Black Political Leadership Styles: The Black Elected Officials of California" (Ph.D. dissertation, United States International University, 1975), Dissertation Abstracts International A, 36 (1975), 1831-1832.

1801 Perwin, C. L. "The Ego, the Self, and the Structure of Political Authority" (Ph.D. dissertation, Princeton University, 1976), Dissertation Abstracts International A, 37 (1976), 3159-3160.

1802　Peters, John G. "The Post-Election Behavior of the American Electorate: A Theory of Electoral Reconciliation" (Ph. D. dissertation, University of Illinois at Urbana-Champaign, 1975), Dissertation Abstracts International A, 36 (1975), 3096.

1803　_____; and Welch, S. "Political Corruption in America: A Search for Definitions and a Theory, or If Political Corruption Is in the Mainstream of American Politics Why Is It Not in the Mainstream of American Politics Research?" American Political Science Review, 72 (1978), 974-984.

1804　Peterzell, Jay. "The Government Shuts Up," Columbia Journalism Review, 21 (1982), 31-37.

1805　Petrick, M. J. "'Equal Opportunities' and 'Fairness' in Broadcast Coverage of Politics," The Annals of the American Academy of Political and Social Science, 427 (1976), 73-83.

1806　Petrockik, John R. "Levels of Issue Voting: The Effect of Candidate-Pairs in Presidential Elections," American Politics Quarterly, 7 (1979), 303-327.

1807　Petrognani, R. "Politics and Imagination," Communication, 5 (1980), 239-243.

1808　Petty, Richard E.; Brock, Timothy C.; and Brock, Sharon S. "Hecklers: Boom or Bust for Speakers?" Public Relations Journal, 34 (1978), 10-14.

1809　_____; and Cocioppo, J. T. "Issue Involvement Can Increase or Decrease Persuasion by Enhancing Message-Relevant Cognitive Responses," Journal of Personality and Social Psychology, 37 (1979), 1915-1926.

1810　Pfautch, Roy. Attitudes toward Campaign Financing. St. Louis: Civic Service, Inc., 1979.

1811　Phelan, John M. Mediaworld: Programming the Public. New York: Seabury Press, 1977.

1812　Phelps, G. A. "Using Hollywood Films to Teach American Campaign Politics: Some Prospects and Problems of Film-Oriented Instruction" (Ph. D. dissertation, Lehigh University, 1978), Dissertation Abstracts International A, 39 (1979), 5127-5128.

1813　Phillipe, Robert. Political Graphics: Art as a Weapon. New York: Abbeville Press, 1982.

1814　Phillips, Kevin P. Mediacracy: American Parties and Politics in the Communication Age. New York: Doubleday, 1975.

1815 _____; and Blackman, Paul H. Electoral Reform and Voter Participation. Washington, D. C.: American Enterprise Institute for Public Policy Research, 1975.

1816 Philport, Joseph C.; and Balon, Robert E. "Candidate Image in a Broadcast Debate," Journal of Broadcasting, 19 (1975), 181-193.

1817 Pierce, John C. "Party, Ideology and Public Evaluations of the Power of Television Newspeople," Journalism Quarterly, 54 (1977), 307-312.

1818 _____; and Sullivan, John L. (eds.). The Electorate Reconsidered. Beverly Hills, CA: Sage Publications, 1980.

1819 _____; et al. The Dynamics of American Public Opinion Patterns and Processes, 1981. Glenview, IL: Scott, Foresman and Co., 1981.

1820 Pierce, Neal R. The New England States: People, Politics and Power in Six New England States. New York: W. W. Norton, 1976.

1821 Pierce, Roy; and Converse, Philip E. "Candidate Visibility in France and the United States," Legislative Studies Quarterly, 6 (1981), 339-371.

1822 Piereson, J. E. "Presidential Popularity and Midterm Voting at Different Electoral Levels," American Journal of Political Science, 19 (1975), 683-694.

1823 _____. "Sources of Candidate Success in Gubernatorial Elections, 1910-1970," Journal of Politics, 39 (1977), 939-958.

1824 _____; and Smith, T. B. "Primary Divisiveness and General Elections Success: A Re-Examination," Journal of Politics, 37 (1975), 555-562.

1825 Pierpoint, R. At the White House: Assignment to Six Presidents. New York: Putnam, 1981.

1826 Pilegge, Joseph C., Jr. "Two-Party Endorsements in a One-Party State," Journalism Quarterly, 58 (1981), 449-453.

1827 Plamenatz, John. "Public Opinion and Political Consciousness," Political Studies, 23 (1975), 342-351.

1828 Pohlmann, Marcus D. "The Electoral Impact of Partisanship and Incumbency Reconsidered: An Extension to Low Salience Elections," Urban Affairs Quarterly, 13 (1978), 495-503.

1829 Polk, Leslie D.; Eddy, John; and Andre, Ann. "Use of Congressional Publicity in a Wisconsin District," Journalism Quarterly, 52 (1975), 543-546.

1830 Pollard, J. E. The Presidents and the Press. New York: Octagon, 1973.

1831 Pollock, Art. "Nixon's Man on the Watergate Panel: Senator Edward Gurney of Florida," Today's Speech, 23 (1975), 7-12.

1832 _____. "Public Broadcasting and Politics: Florida's Politithon '70," Journal of Broadcasting, 18 (1973-74), 39-47.

1833 Pollock, John C. The Politics of Crisis Reporting. New York: Praeger, 1981.

1834 Polsby, Nelson W. "The News Media as an Alternative to Party in Presidential Selection Process," Political Parties in the Eighties, ed. R. A. Goldwin. Washington, D. C.: American Enterprise Institute, 1980.

1835 _____. Political Promises. New York: Oxford, 1974.

1836 _____; and Wildavsky, A. B. Presidential Elections. New York: Scribner, 1980.

1837 Pomper, Gerald M. "Decline of the Party in American Elections (1952-1972)," Political Science Quarterly, 92 (1977), 21-41.

1838 _____. The Election of 1980: Reports and Interpretations. Chatham, NJ: Chatham House Publishers, 1981.

1839 _____. "New Rules and New Games in Presidential Nominations," Journal of Politics, 41 (1979), 784-805.

1840 _____. Voters' Choice: Varieties of American Electoral Behavior. New York: Harper and Row, 1975.

1841 _____; with Lederman, Susan. Elections in America: Control and Influence in Democratic Politics, 2nd ed. New York: Longman, 1980.

1842 Pomper, Marlene M. (ed.). The Election of 1976: Reports and Interpretations by Gerald M. Pomper and Others. New York: David McKay, 1977.

1843 Poor, Peter E. "Television News as a Source of Political Information: A Content Analysis of 'CBS Evening News with Walter Cronkite' Covering the Period of September 1, 1970, to October 15, 1971" (Ph.D. dissertation,

University of Massachusetts, 1975), Dissertation Abstracts International A, 36 (1975), 3994.

1844 Popkin, Samuel L.; et al. "Comment: What Have You Done for Me Lately? Toward An Investment Theory of Voting," American Political Science Review, 70 (1976), 779-805.

1845 Porter, D. T. "An Experimental Investigation of the Effects of Racial Prejudice and Racial Perception upon Communication Effectiveness," Speech Monographs, 41 (1974), 179-184.

1846 Porter, G. S. "Mass Media and the Political Socialization of Children and Adolescents" (Ph.D. dissertation, University of Iowa, 1977), Dissertation Abstracts International A, 38 (1978), 3787.

1847 Porter, Laurinda W. "Rhetorical Visions of America and their Relation to Religious Beliefs in the Rhetoric of Selected 1980 Presidential Candidates (Volumes I and II)" (Ph.D. dissertation, University of Minnesota, 1981), Dissertation Abstracts International A, 42 (1982), 4200.

1848 _____. "The White House Transcripts: Group Fantasy Events Concerning the Mass Media," Central States Speech Journal, 27 (1976), 272-279.

1849 Porter, Sharon B. "A Rhetorical Analysis of the Speaking of Barry Morris Goldwater, 1969-1974" (Ph.D. dissertation, The Louisiana State University and Agricultural and Mechanical College, 1980), Dissertation Abstracts International A, 41 (1981), 4542.

1850 Porter, William E. Assault on the Media: The Nixon Years. Ann Arbor, MI: University of Michigan, 1976.

1851 Powell, Larry. "Voter Needs and Evaluations of Satire," Journalism Quarterly, 55 (1978), 311-318.

1852 _____. "Voting Intention and the Complexity of Political Images: A Pilot Study," Psychological Reports, 40 (1977), 243-246.

1853 _____; and Shelby, A. "Strategy of Assumed Incumbency: A Case Study," Southern Speech Communication Journal, 46 (1981), 105-123.

1854 Powell, Lynda W. "A Bayesian Approach to a Sequential Three Decision Problem: Voting and the Uses of Information in Electoral Choice," Journal of Mathematical Sociology, 6 (1979), 177-198.

1855 Prelutsky, B. "The Selling of the Candidates," Television Quarterly, 13 (1976), 15-18.

1856 The Presidency and the Press. Austin, TX: LBJ School of Public Affairs, University of Texas at Austin, 1976.

1857 Press, Charles. The Political Cartoon. East Brunswick, NJ: Associated University Presses, 1981.

1858 Price, David E.; and Lupfer, Michael. "Volunteers for Gore: The Impact of Precinct-Level Canvass in Three Tennessee Cities," Journal of Politics, 35 (1973), 410-438.

1859 Price, Reynolds. A Palpable God. New York: Atheneum, 1978.

1860 Pride, Richard A.; and Richards, Barbara. "Denigration of Authority? Television News Coverage of the Student Movement," Journal of Politics, 36 (1974), 637-660.

1861 _____; and _____. "Denigration of Political Authority in Television News: The Ecology Issue," Western Political Quarterly, 28 (1975), 635-645.

1862 Prisuta, Robert H. "Mass Media Exposure and Political Behavior," Educational Broadcasting Review, 7 (1973), 167-173.

1863 Prosser, S.; and Converse, J. M. "On Stimson's Interpretation of Declines in Presidential Popularity," Public Opinion Quarterly, 40 (1976), 538-541.

1864 Prucker, Michael J. "Politics and Reform: A Case Study of the Federal Election Campaign Act" (Ph.D. dissertation, State University of New York at Binghamton, 1981), Dissertation Abstracts International A, 42 (1982), 4920.

1865 Purnell, Sandra E. "Politically Speaking, Do Women Exist?" Journal of Communication, 28 (1978), 150-155.

1866 Qualls, James H. "Barber's Typological Analysis of Political Leaders," American Political Science Review, 71 (1977), 182-225.

1867 Quarles, Rebecca C. "Mass Communication and Political Accuracy: A Comparison of First-time and Older Voters" (Ph.D. dissertation, University of Wisconsin-Madison, 1977), Journalism Abstracts, 15 (1977), 22.

1868 _____; "Mass Media Use and Voting Behavior: The Accuracy of Political Perceptions among First Time and Experienced Voters," Communication Research, 6 (1979), 407-436.

1869 Quimby, Rollin W. "Agnew, the Press and the Rhetorical Critic," Western Speech, 39 (1975), 146-154.

1870 _____. "Agnew's Plea Bargain: Between Rhetorics of Consensus and Confrontation," Central States Speech Journal, 28 (1977), 163-172.

1871 Rabinowitz, George. "On the Nature of Political Issues: Insights from a Spatial Analysis (1968 and 1972)," American Journal of Political Science, 22 (1978), 793-817.

1872 _____; et al. "Salience as a Factor in the Impact of Issues on Candidate Evaluation," Journal of Politics, 44 (1982), 41-63.

1873 Rae, Douglas W.; and Eismeier, Theodore J. (eds.). Public Policy and Public Choice. Beverly Hills, CA: Sage Publications, 1979.

1874 Ragan, P. K.; and Dowd, J. J. "The Emerging Political Consciousness of the Aged: A Generational Interpretation," Journal of Social Issues, 30 (1974), 137-158.

1875 Ragsdale, Lyn. "The Fiction of Congressional Elections as Presidential Events," American Politics Quarterly, 8 (1980), 375-398.

1876 _____. "Incumbent Popularity, Challenger Invisibility, and Congressional Voters," Legislative Studies Quarterly, 6 (1981), 201-208.

1877 Raine, Alden S. "Social Conflict Cultural Cleavage, and Political Change: A Contextual Analysis of the 1972 Presidential Election" (Ph.D. dissertation, University of Michigan, 1974), Dissertation Abstracts International A, 35 (1975), 7371.

1878 Rakove, Milton. Don't Make No Waves--Don't Back No Losers, An Insider's Analysis of the Daley Machine. Bloomington, IN: Indiana University Press, 1975.

1879 Ranish, Donald R. "The Rhetoric of a Rebel: George C. Wallace-Campaign Themes and Constituency Responses, 1958-1974" (Ph.D. dissertation, University of California, Santa Barbara, 1975), Dissertation Abstracts International A, 36 (1976), 7611-7612.

1880 Ranney, Austin (ed.). American Elections of Nineteen Eighty. Washington, D. C.: American Enterprise Institute for Public Policy Research, 1981.

1881 _____. "Changing the Rules of the Nominating Game,"

Choosing the President, ed. James D. Barber. Englewood Cliffs, NJ: Prentice-Hall, 1974.

1882 _____. Participation in American Presidential Nominations. Washington, D. C.: American Enterprise Institute for Public Policy Research, 1977.

1883 _____ (ed.). The Past and Future of Presidential Debates. Washington, D. C.: American Enterprise Institute for Public Policy Research, 1979.

1884 _____ (ed.). Presidential Nominating Process: Can It Be Improved? Washington, D. C.: American Enterprise Institute for Public Policy Research, 1980.

1885 Rapoport, Ronald B. "The Sex Gap in Political Persuading: Where the 'Structuring Principle' Works," American Journal of Political Science, 25 (1981), 32-48.

1886 Rarick, David. "Applications of Q-Technique in Political Campaign Research: A Review of Research Findings and Methodological Issues," Political Communication Review, 6 (1981), 27-42.

1887 _____; et al. "The Carter Persona: An Empirical Analysis of the Rhetorical Visions of Campaign '76," Quarterly Journal of Speech, 63 (1977), 258-273.

1888 Rasberry, Robert W. The "Technique" of Political Lying. Washington, D. C.: University Press of America, 1981.

1889 Rasmussen, Karen. "Nixon and the Strategy of Avoidance," Central States Speech Journal, 24 (1973), 193-202.

1890 Rather, Dan; and Gates, Gary P. The Palace Guard. New York: Warner Paperback Library, 1975.

1891 _____; with Mickey Herskowitz. The Camera Never Blinks: Adventures of a TV Journalist. New York: Ballantine Books, 1978.

1892 Raucher, Steven A. "An Analysis of Sensationalism in Network Television News Coverage of Violent Events (Ph. D. dissertation, Wayne State University, 1979).

1893 Raum, Richard D.; and Measell, James S. "Wallace and his Ways: A Study of the Rhetorical Genre of Polarization," Central States Speech Journal, 25 (1974), 28-35.

1894 Raven, B. H. "The Nixon Group," The Journal of Social Issues, 30 (1974), 297-320.

1895 Rawls, James; et al. "Comparison of Wallace, Nixon, and

Humphrey Supporters along Certain Demographic, Attitudinal, and Value-System Dimensions," Psychological Reports, 32 (1973), 35-39.

1896 Reagan, Joey B. "Media Exposure and Community Integration as Predictors of Political Activity" (Ph.D. dissertation, Michigan State University, 1981), Dissertation Abstracts International A, 42 (1982), 3337.

1897 Reagen, J.; and Zenaty, J. "Local News Credibility: Newspapers vs. TV Revisited," Journalism Quarterly, 56 (1979), 168-172.

1898 Real, M. R. "Popular Culture, Media Propaganda, and the 1972 CREEP Campaign," Journal of Popular Culture, 8 (1974), 644-652.

1899 Reardon, Kathleen Kelley. Persuasion: Theory and Context. Beverly Hills, CA: Sage Publications, 1981.

1900 Rebelsky, Freda; Conover, Cheryl; and Chafetz, Patricia. "The Development of Political Attitudes in Young Children," Child Development and Behavior, eds. F. Rebelsky and L. Dorman. New York: Alfred A. Knopf, 1973.

1901 Reeb, Richard H., Jr. "The Role of the Press in American Democracy: The Contemporary Press and the Problem of Objectivity" (Ph.D. dissertation, Claremont Graduate School, 1974), Dissertation Abstracts International A, 35 (1975), 7985.

1902 Reedy, G. E. "The President and the Press: Struggle for Dominance," Annals of the American Academy of Political and Social Science, 427 (1976), 65-72.

1903 Reese, Stephen D.; and Miller, M. Mark. "Political Attitude Holding and Structure: The Effects of Newspaper and Television News," Communication Research, 8 (1981), 167-188.

1904 Reid, John. The Magnificent Society and the Democracy Amendments: How to Free your Congressmen from the Control of the Special Interests. Alameda, CA: Pony X Press, 1981.

1905 Reiter, H. L. "How Accurate are Those Projections? (Attempts by Major News Organizations to Forecast the Presidential Elections Since 1948)," Presidential Studies Quarterly, 12 (1982), 80-83.

1906 _____. "Why Is Turnout Down?" Public Opinion Quarterly, 43 (1979), 297-311.

1907 Reitman, A. The Election Process, 2nd ed. Dobbs Ferry, NY: Oceana Publications, 1980.

1908 Relyea, Harold C.; et al. The Presidency and Information Policy. New York: Center for the Study of the Presidency, 1982.

1909 Renshon, Stanley A. Handbook of Political Socialization. New York: The Free Press, 1977.

1910 _____. "Personality and Family Dynamics in the Political Socialization Process," American Journal of Political Science, 19 (1975), 63-80.

1911 _____. Psychological Needs and Political Behavior: A Theory of Personality and Political Efficacy. New York: The Free Press, 1974.

1912 _____. "The Psychological Origins of Political Efficacy: The Need for Personal Control" (Ph.D. dissertation, University of Pennsylvania, 1974), Dissertation Abstracts International A, 33 (1973), 6420-6421.

1913 Repass, Rex L. "The Role of the Mass Media as Sources of Political Information About Presidential Candidates in 1976 for Voters in Knox County, Tennessee" (Master's thesis, University of Tennessee, 1977), Journalism Abstracts, 16 (1978), 89.

1914 Resnik, Linda I. "An Analysis of the Relationship between Television News Selection and Public Relations Techniques" (Master's thesis, North Texas State University, 1977), Masters Abstracts, 16 (1978), 62.

1915 Reynolds, Henry T. "Rationality and Attitudes Toward Political Parties and Candidates," Journal of Politics, 36 (1974), 983-1005.

1916 Rhode, David W. "Risk Bearing and Progressive Ambition: The Case of the Members of the U.S. House of Representatives," American Journal of Political Science, 23 (1979), 1-26.

1917 Rhodes, S.; and Scarborough, K. "Combatting Stress on the Campaign Trail: A Guide for Campaign Managers and Candidates," Campaigns and Elections, 2 (1981), 17-23.

1918 Rice, Ronald E.; and Paisley, William J. (eds.). Public Communication Campaigns. Beverly Hills, CA: Sage Publications, 1981.

1919 Rice, Tom W. "The Determinants of Candidate Spending in Presidential Primaries: Advice for the States," Presidential Studies Quarterly, 12 (1982), 590-597.

1920 Rich, H. E. "The Acquisition of Political Orientations Among College Students: A Theoretical Model" (Ph.D. dissertation, Purdue University, 1972), Dissertation Abstracts International A, 34 (1973), 431-432.

1921 Ricks, Dana C. "1972 Presidential Campaign Investigation Based on Attitude Measurements of Candidate Images" (Master's thesis, North Texas State University, 1973), Masters Abstracts, 12 (1974), 326-327.

1922 Rigg, Laurence A. "Eight Columnists' Coverage of George McGovern's 1972 Bid for the Presidency" (Master's thesis, University of Florida, 1973), Journalism Abstracts, 12 (1974), 159.

1923 Riggs, Steven F. "A Content Analysis of Newsweek, U.S. News and World Report, and Time's Coverage of the 1980 Presidential Primaries" (Master's thesis, Ball State University, 1980), Journalism Abstracts, 18 (1980), 107-108.

1924 Rippey, J. N. "Use of Polls as a Reporting Tool," Journalism Quarterly, 57 (1980), 642-646+.

1925 Ritter, Kurt W. "American Political Rhetoric and the Jeremiad Tradition: Presidential Nomination Acceptance Addresses, 1960-1976," Central States Speech Journal, 31 (1980), 153-171.

1926 _____. "The 1980 Presidential Debates," Speaker and Gavel, 18 (1981), 12-78.

1927 Rivers, William L. The Other Government: Power and the Washington Media. New York: Universe Books, 1982.

1928 _____; Miller, S. H.; and Gandy, O. "Government and the Media," Political Communication: Issues and Strategies for Research, ed. Steven H. Chaffee. Beverly Hills, CA: Sage Publications, 1975.

1929 _____; and Nyham, M. J. Aspen Notebook on Government and the Media. New York: Praeger, 1973.

1930 Roback, T. H. "Amateurs and Professionals: Delegates to the 1972 Republican National Convention," Journal of Politics, 37 (1975), 436-437.

1931 Roberts, Churchill L. "From Primary to the Presidency: A Panel Study of Images and Issues in the 1976 Election," Western Journal of Speech Communication, 45 (1981), 60-70.

1932 _____. "Media Use and Difficulty of Decision in the 1976

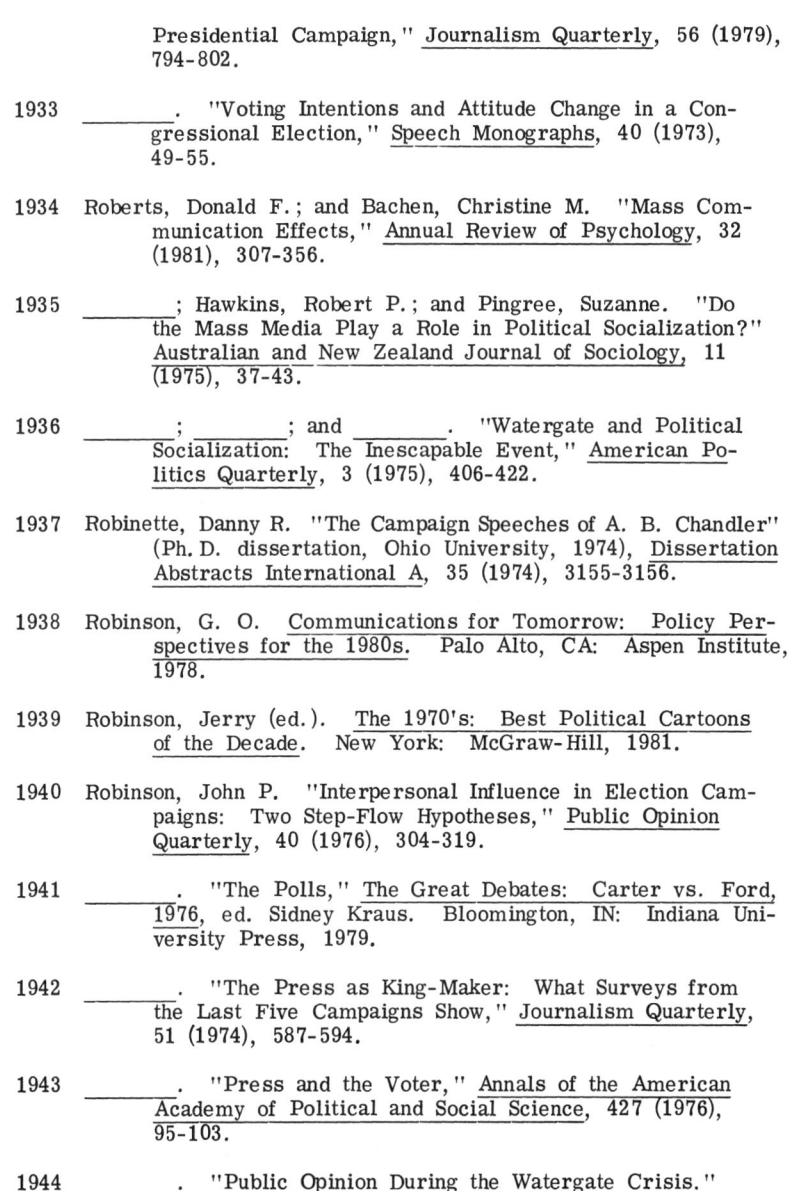

Presidential Campaign," *Journalism Quarterly*, 56 (1979), 794-802.

1933 _____. "Voting Intentions and Attitude Change in a Congressional Election," *Speech Monographs*, 40 (1973), 49-55.

1934 Roberts, Donald F.; and Bachen, Christine M. "Mass Communication Effects," *Annual Review of Psychology*, 32 (1981), 307-356.

1935 _____; Hawkins, Robert P.; and Pingree, Suzanne. "Do the Mass Media Play a Role in Political Socialization?" *Australian and New Zealand Journal of Sociology*, 11 (1975), 37-43.

1936 _____; _____; and _____. "Watergate and Political Socialization: The Inescapable Event," *American Politics Quarterly*, 3 (1975), 406-422.

1937 Robinette, Danny R. "The Campaign Speeches of A. B. Chandler" (Ph.D. dissertation, Ohio University, 1974), *Dissertation Abstracts International A*, 35 (1974), 3155-3156.

1938 Robinson, G. O. *Communications for Tomorrow: Policy Perspectives for the 1980s.* Palo Alto, CA: Aspen Institute, 1978.

1939 Robinson, Jerry (ed.). *The 1970's: Best Political Cartoons of the Decade.* New York: McGraw-Hill, 1981.

1940 Robinson, John P. "Interpersonal Influence in Election Campaigns: Two Step-Flow Hypotheses," *Public Opinion Quarterly*, 40 (1976), 304-319.

1941 _____. "The Polls," *The Great Debates: Carter vs. Ford, 1976*, ed. Sidney Kraus. Bloomington, IN: Indiana University Press, 1979.

1942 _____. "The Press as King-Maker: What Surveys from the Last Five Campaigns Show," *Journalism Quarterly*, 51 (1974), 587-594.

1943 _____. "Press and the Voter," *Annals of the American Academy of Political and Social Science*, 427 (1976), 95-103.

1944 _____. "Public Opinion During the Watergate Crisis." *Communication Research*, 1 (1974), 391-404.

1945 _____; and Jeffries, L. W. "The Changing Role of Newspapers in the Age of Television," *Journalism Monographs*, 63 (1979), 1-31.

1946 _____; and Meadow, Robert. Polls Apart. Cabin John, MD: Seven Locks Press, 1982.

1947 Robinson, Michael J. "American Political Legitimacy in an Era of Electronic Journalism: Reflections on the Evening News," Television as a Social Force: New Approaches to TV Criticism, eds. Douglass Cater and Richard Adler. New York: Praeger, 1975, 97-139.

1948 _____. "The Impact of 'Instant Analysis'," Journal of Communication, 27 (1977), 17-23.

1949 _____. "The Impact of Televised Watergate Hearings," Journal of Communication, 24 (1974), 17-30.

1950 _____. "Prime Time Chic: Between Newsbreaks and Commercials, the Values Are L.A. Liberal," Public Opinion Quarterly, 2 (1979), 42-48.

1951 _____. "Public Affairs Television and the Growth of Political Malaise: The Case of 'The Selling of the Pentagon'," American Political Science Review, 70 (1976), 409-432.

1952 _____. "A Statesman Is Dead: Candidate Images on Network News," What's News, ed. E. Abel. San Francisco: Institute for Contemporary Studies, 1981.

1953 _____. "Television and American Politics 1956-1976," The Public Interest, 48 (1977), 3-39.

1954 _____. "The Three Faces of Congressional Media," The New Congress, ed. Thomas E. Mann and Norman J. Ornstein. Washington, D.C.: American Enterprise Institute, 1981, 55-96.

1955 _____. "The TV Primaries," Wilson Quarterly, Spring, 1977, 80-83.

1956 _____. "TV's Newest Program: The 'Presidential Nominations Game'"; Public Opinion, 1 (1978), 4-46.

1957 _____. "A Twentieth-Century Medium in a Nineteenth-Century Legislature: The Effects of Television on the American Congress," Congress in Change: Evolution and Reform, ed. Norman J. Ornstein. New York: Praeger, 1975.

1958 _____. "Understanding Television's Effects--Experimentation and Survey Research: An Offer One Shouldn't Refuse," Experimental Study of Politics, 4 (1975), 99-133.

1959 _____; and Appel, Kevin R. "Network News Coverage of Congress," Political Science Quarterly, 94 (1979), 407-418.

Bibliography 157

1960 _____; Conover, N.; and Sheehan, M. "The Media at Mid-Year: A Bad Year for McLuhanites?" Public Opinion, June/July, 1980, 41-45.

1961 _____; and McPherson, Karen A. "Television News Coverage Before the 1976 New Hampshire Primary: The Focus of Network Journalism," Journal of Broadcasting, 21 (1977), 177-186.

1962 _____; and Zukin, Clifford. "Television and the Wallace Vote," Journal of Communication, 26 (1976), 79-83.

1963 Robyn, Dorothy L. "A Field Experimental Study of Direct Mail Used in the Paul Simon Congressional Campaign" (Master's thesis, Southern Illinois University, 1976), Journalism Abstracts, 15 (1977), 113.

1964 Roelof, H. Mark. Ideology and Myth in American Politics: A Critique of a National Political Mind. Boston, MA: Little, Brown, 1976.

1965 Rogers, M. K. "Social Psychological Determinants of Political Participation" (Ph.D. dissertation, Claremont Graduate School, 1979), Dissertation Abstracts International B, 41 (1980), 413.

1966 Rogers, Raymonda C. "A Content Analysis of the Coverage Given the 1976 Presidential Primary Campaign in Ten Kentucky Newspapers" (Master's thesis, Murray State University, 1976), Journalism Abstracts, 15 (1977), 113.

1967 Roll, Charles W., Jr.; and Cantril, Albert H. Polls: Their Use and Misuse in Politics, rev. ed. Cabin John, MD: Seven Locks Press, 1980.

1968 Roloff, Michael; and Berger, Charles, (eds.). Social Cognition and Communication. Beverly Hills, CA: Sage Publications, 1982.

1969 Rolt, C. "Private Opinion Polls," Academy of Political Science Proceedings, 34 (1982), 61-74.

1970 Rook, K. S.; et al. "The 'Positivity Bias' in Evaluations of Public Figures: Evidence Against Interpersonal Artifacts," Political Methodology, 5 (1978), 469-500.

1971 Roper, Burns W. "Changing Public Attitudes Toward Television and Other Media 1959-1976," Communications, 4 (1978), 220-238.

1972 _____. "Distorting the Voice of the People," Columbia Journalism Review, 14 (1975), 28-32.

1973 _____. "The Media and the Polls," Public Opinion, February/March, 1980, 46-49.

1974 _____; et al. Polling on the Issues. Cabin John, MD: Seven Locks Press, 1980.

1975 Roper, Elmo B. You and Your Leaders, Their Actions and Your Reactions 1936-1956. Westport, CT: Greenwood Press, 1976.

1976 Roper, W. L. Winning Politics. Radnor, PA: Chilton Book Company, 1978.

1977 Roper Organization. Changing Public Attitudes Toward Television and Other Mass Media, 1959-1976. New York: Television Information Office, 1977.

1978 _____. Evolving Public Attitudes Toward Television and Other Mass Media, 1959-1980. New York: Television Information Office, 1981.

1979 _____. Trends in Public Attitudes Toward Television and Other Mass Media, 1959-1974. New York: Television Information Office, 1975.

1980 _____. What People Think of Television and Other Mass Media, 1959-1972. New York: Television Information Office, 1973.

1981 Rose, B. "Good Evening, Here's What's Happening . . . The Roots of Local Television News," Journal of Popular Film and Television, 7 (1979), 168-180.

1982 Rose, Douglas D. "Citizen Uses of the Ford-Carter Debates," Journal of Politics, 1 (1979), 214-221.

1983 Rose, R. Electoral Participation: A Comparative Analysis. Beverly Hills, CA: Sage Publications, 1980.

1984 Rose, Richard. Electoral Behavior: A Comparative Handbook. New York: Free Press, 1974.

1985 Roseboom, Eugene H.; and Eckes, Alfred E., Jr. A History of Presidential Elections: From George Washington to Jimmy Carter. New York: Macmillan, 1979.

1986 Rosen, C. M. "Legislative Experts and Outsiders: The Two-Step Flow of Communication," Journal of Politics, 36 (1974), 703-730.

1987 _____. "Legislative Influence and Policy Orientation in American State Legislatures," American Journal of Political Science, 18 (1974), 681-691.

Bibliography

1988 Rosenau, James N. Citizenship Between Elections: An Inquiry into the Mobilizable American. New York: The Free Press, 1974.

1989 Rosenau, N. "The Sources of Children's Political Concepts: An Application of Piaget's Theory," New Directions in Political Socialization, eds. D. C. Schwartz and S. K. Schwartz. New York: The Free Press, 1975.

1990 Rosenbaum, W. B.; et al. "Sex Differences in Selective Exposure?" Journal of Social Psychology, 92 (1974), 85-89.

1991 Rosenbloom, David L. The Election Men: Professional Campaign Managers and American Democracy. New York: Quadrangle Books, 1973.

1992 _____. "The Press and the Local Candidate," Annals of the American Academy of Political and Social Science, 427 (1976), 12-22.

1993 Rosenblum, K. E. "'I Know What I Said, I Know What I Meant, I Know What I Did': Three Presidential Press Conferences as Study in the Informal Negotiation of Deviance" (Ph.D. dissertation, University of Colorado at Boulder, 1979), Dissertation Abstracts International A, 40 (1980), 4700-4771.

1994 Rosenfield, L. W. "August 9, 1974: The Victimage of Richard Nixon," Communication Quarterly, 24 (1976), 19-23.

1995 Rosengren, Karl E. "News Diffusion: An Overview," Journalism Quarterly, 50 (1973), 83-91.

1996 _____. "Uses and Gratifications: A Paradigm Outlined," The Uses of Mass Communication, eds. Jay G. Blumler and Elihu Katz. Beverly Hills/London: Sage Publications, 1974.

1997 Rosenman, S. I.; and Rosenman, D. R. Presidential Style. New York: Harper and Row, 1976.

1998 Rosenstone, Steven J. "Forecasting Presidential Elections" (Ph.D. dissertation, University of California, Berkeley, 1979), Dissertation Abstracts International A, 41 (1980), 388.

1999 Rosenthal, A. "Legislative Turnover in the States," State Government, 47 (1974), 148-152.

2000 Rosenthal, Robert E. "A Rhetorical Analysis of the 1972 Presidential Campaign of George Stanley McGovern" (Ph.D. dissertation, Bowling Green State University, 1979),

Dissertation Abstracts International A, 40 (1980), 3627.

2001 Roshco, Bernard. Newsmaking. Chicago, IL: University of Chicago Press, 1976.

2002 Rosinstein, J. "What Became of that Heavy Vote?" Columbia Journalism Review, 15 (1977), 37-39.

2003 Ross, I. The Loneliest Campaign. Westport, CT: Greenwood Press, 1977.

2004 Ross, Mitchell S. The Literary Politicians. Garden City, NY: Doubleday, 1978.

2005 Rothman, Jonathan S. "The Constitutional and Political Implications of Campaign Finance Reform" (Ph.D. dissertation, University of California, Berkeley, 1979), Dissertation Abstracts International A, 40 (1980), 4214-4215.

2006 Rothschild, Michael L. "The Effects of Political Advertising on the Voting Behavior of a Low Involvement Electorate" (Ph.D. dissertation, Stanford University, 1975), Dissertation Abstracts International A, 35 (1975), 7473-7474.

2007 _____. "On the Use of Multiple Methods and Multiple Situations in Political Communications Research," Political Communication: Issues and Strategies for Research, ed. Steven H. Chaffee. Beverly Hills, CA: Sage Publications, 1975, 237-261.

2008 _____. "Political Advertising: A Neglected Policy Issue in Marketing," Journal of Marketing Research, 15 (1978), 58-71.

2009 _____; and Ray, Michael L. "Involvement and Political Advertising Effect," Communication Research, 1 (1974), 264-285.

2010 Rouder, Susan G. "Campaign Impact Through Coalition Building and Political Mobilization" (Ph.D. dissertation, Tufts University, 1981), Dissertation Abstracts International A, 42 (1982), 3741-3742.

2011 Rourke, F. E. "Watergate and the Presidency: Executive Fallibility, Presidential Management Styles," Administration and Society, 6 (1974), 171-178.

2012 Rubin, Alan M. "Child and Adolescent Television Use and Political Socialization," Journalism Quarterly, 55 (1978), 125-129.

2013 _____. "Television in Children's Political Socialization," Journal of Broadcasting, 20 (1976), 51-60.

Bibliography

2014 Rubin, Bernard. Media, Politics and Democracy. New York: Oxford University Press, 1977.

2015 _____ (ed.). Questioning Media Ethics. New York: Praeger, 1978.

2016 _____ (ed.). Small Voices and Great Trumpets: Minorities and the Media. New York: Praeger, 1980.

2017 Rubin, R. L. Press, Party, and Presidency. New York: Norton, 1981.

2018 Rubinoff, Mike R.; and Marsh, Diane T. "Candidates and Colors: An Investigation," Perceptual and Motor Skills, 50 (1980), 868-870.

2019 Rudder, Catherine E. "Why Southerners Vote the Way They Do: Determinants of the Presidential Vote in the South, 1952-1968" (Ph.D. dissertation, Ohio State University, 1973), Dissertation Abstracts International A, 34 (1974), 5274.

2020 Rueter, Theodore (ed.). Transcripts of the 1980 Presidential Debates. Ann Arbor, MI: University Microfilms of Ann Arbor, Michigan.

2021 Ruminske, H. J. "A Content Analysis of Political Coverage in Selected Labor Union Publications During Eight Presidential Campaigns" (Ph.D. dissertation, Ohio University, 1972), Dissertation Abstracts International A, 33 (1973), 6296.

2022 Rundquist, B. S.; Strom, G. S.; and Peters, J. G. "Corrupt Politicians and Their Electoral Support: Some Experimental Observations," American Political Science Review, 71 (1977), 954-963.

2023 Russel, Francis. The President-Makers: From Mark Hanna to Joseph P. Kennedy. Waltham, MA: Little, Brown and Co., 1976.

2024 Russell, Allen A. "The Political Representation of Political Campaign Contributors" (Ph.D. dissertation, University of Michigan, 1980), Dissertation Abstracts International A, 41 (1980), 2277-2278.

2026 Russonello, John M.; and Wolf, Frank. "Newspaper Coverage of the 1976 and 1968 Presidential Campaigns," Journalism Quarterly, 56 (1979), 360-364; 432.

2026 Rutkus, Denis S. "Presidential Television," Journal of Communication, 26 (1976), 73-78.

2027 Ryan, J. P. "Myth and Politics: Political Participation in Three American Subcultures" (Ph. D. dissertation, Northwestern University, 1972), Dissertation Abstracts International A, 33 (1972), 5800-5801.

2028 Ryckman, Richard M.; and Sherman, Martin F. "Locus of Control and Student Reaction to the Watergate Break-in," Journal of Social Psychology, 99 (1976), 305-306.

2029 Sabato, Larry J. "Gubernatorial Politics and the New Campaign Technology," State Government, 53 (1980), 148-152.

2030 _____. The Rise of Political Consultants: New Ways of Winning Elections. New York: Basic Books, 1981.

2031 Saldich, Anne. Electronic Democracy: Television's Impact on the American Political Process. New York: Praeger, 1979.

2032 Salerno, H. F. "Politics, the Media and the Drama," Journal of American Culture, 1 (1978), 189-194.

2033 Sallee, Myrl D. "Political Participation: Self-Esteem, Personal Efficacy, Consciousness, and Political Efficacy as Predictor Variables" (Ph. D. dissertation, University of Nebraska, Lincoln, 1977), Dissertation Abstracts International A, 38 (1978), 4405.

2034 Sanchez-Perez, J. M. Babelism: Social Problems of the Watergate Era. Smithtown, NY: Exposition Press, 1974.

2035 Sandell, Karin L.; and Ostroff, David H. "Political Information Content and Children's Political Socialization," Journal of Broadcasting, 25 (1981), 49-59.

2036 Sanders, E. "On the Costs, Utilities, and Simple Joys of Voting," Journal of Politics, 42 (1980), 854-867.

2037 Sanders, Frederick C., Jr. "The Rhetorical Strategies of Senator Robert Kennedy and Senator Eugene J. McCarthy in the 1968 Presidential Primaries" (Ph. D. dissertation, University of Oregon, 1973), Dissertation Abstracts International A, 34 (1974), 7915.

2038 Sanders, Keith R.; and Atwood, Erwin. "Value Change Induced by Mass Media," Changing Human Values: Individual and Societal, ed. M. Rokeach. New York: Free Press, 1979.

2039 _____; and Kaid, Lynda Lee. "Political Communication

Theory and Research: An Overview 1976-1977," Communication Yearbook 2, ed. Brent Ruben. New Brunswick, NJ: Transaction Books, 1978, 375-389.

2040 _____; and _____. "Political Rallies: Their Uses and Effects," Central States Speech Journal, 32 (1981), 1-11.

2041 _____; and Pace, Thomas J. "The Influence of Speech Communication on the Image of a Political Candidate: 'Limited Effects' Revisited," Communication Yearbook 1, ed. Brent Ruben. New Brunswick, NJ: Transaction Books, 1977.

2042 Sanders, Marion K. The Lady and the Vote. Westport, CT: Greenwood Press, 1974.

2043 Sanoff, Alvin P. "The Perils of Polling 1980," Washington Journalism Review, 3 (1981), 32-35.

2044 Sarris, Andrew. Politics and Cinema. New York: Columbia University Press, 1978.

2045 Sather, Lawrence A. "Biography as Rhetorical Criticism: An Analysis of John F. Kennedy's 1960 Presidential Campaign by Selected Biographers" (Ph.D. dissertation, Washington State University, 1974), Dissertation Abstracts International A, 35 (1975), 6845-6846.

2046 Sauls, Samuel J. "Prelude to Red Lion: History and Analysis of the Proposed Red Lion et al., vs. FCC and the Democratic National Committee Challenge of the Fairness Doctrine" (Master's thesis, North Texas State University, 1980), Masters Abstracts, 19 (1981), 73.

2047 Savage, Robert L. "The Diffusion of Information Approach," Handbook of Political Communication, eds. Dan D. Nimmo and Keith R. Sanders. Beverly Hills, CA: Sage Publications, 1981, 101-119.

2048 _____. "From Selective Distortion Through Minimal Effects to Media Election: Four Decades of Media/Voting Research," Political Communication Review, 6 (1981), 1-12.

2049 Sawyer, Thomas C. "The Mass Communication Roles of the Republican National Chairman in the 1972 Campaign" (Ph.D. dissertation, Ohio State University, 1973), Dissertation Abstracts International A, 34 (1974), 7261.

2050 Sayre, N. "Reflections on the Tube," Columbia Journalism Review, 19 (1980), 29-35.

2051 Scaff, L. A. "Two Concepts of Political Participation," Western Political Quarterly, 28 (1975), 447-462.

2052 Scarrow, Harold A.; with Borman, Steve. "The Effects of Newspaper Endorsements on Election Outcomes: A Case Study," Public Opinion Quarterly, 43 (1979), 388-393.

2053 Scaturo, Douglas J. "Issue Relevance as a Source of Political Involvement," Journal of Social Psychology, 101 (1977), 59-67.

2054 Schaffner, Paul; and Wandersman, Abraham. "Familiarity Breeds Success: A Field Study of Exposure and Voting Behavior," Personality and Social Psychology Bulletin, 1 (1974), 88-90.

2055 _____; _____; and Stang, David. "Candidate Name Exposure and Voting: Two Field Studies," Basic and Applied Social Psychology, 2 (1981), 195-203.

2056 Schandler, Herbert Y. The Unmaking of a President: Lyndon Johnson and Vietnam. Princeton, NJ: Princeton University, 1977.

2057 Scheele, H. Z. "Campaign 1980: Reflections on the Role of Political Communications," Vital Speeches, 47 (1981), 269-274.

2058 Scheibal, William J. "A Communicative Analysis of the Role of Television Coverage of the 1968 Democratic National Convention" (Master's thesis, North Texas State University, 1974), Masters Abstracts, 13 (1975), 101.

2059 _____. "A Comparative Analysis of Newspaper and Television Coverage of the 1976 Democratic National Convention" (Ph.D. dissertation, University of Texas at Austin, 1978), Dissertation Abstracts International A, 39 (1978), 1927-1928.

2060 Scherer, C. W. "Differential Knowledge Gain from a Media Campaign: A Field Experiment" (Ph.D. dissertation, University of Wisconsin-Madison, 1977), Dissertation Abstracts International A, 38 (1978), 7008.

2061 Schiller, H. I. The Mind Managers. Boston, MA: Beacon Press, 1973.

2062 Schlesinger, Arthur M., Jr. The Imperial Presidency. New York: Popular Library, Inc., 1964.

2063 _____. "Politics and the American Language," American Scholar, 43 (1974), 553-562.

2064 _____; and Israel, Fred L. (eds.). The Coming to Power: Critical Presidential Elections in American History. New York: Chelsea House, 1981.

Bibliography

2065 Schlesinger, J. A. "Primary Goals of Political Parties: A Clarification of Positive Theory," American Political Science Review, 69 (1975), 840-849.

2066 Schluter, W. "Campaign Finance Disclosure; from the Back Room to the Spotlight," State Government, 47 (1974), 153-155.

2067 Schmidt, B. C., Jr. "Access to the Broadcast Media: The Legislative Precedents: Diversity in Broadcasting," Journal of Communication, 28 (1978), 60-68.

2068 Schmitt, Carl M. "Voting Behavior in Western Democracies: A Cross National Study of Factors Influencing Voter Turnout and Partisanship in the United States, Great Britain, and Germany" (Ph.D. dissertation, New York University, 1976), Dissertation Abstracts International A, 37 (1977), 6076.

2069 Schneider, Pamela J. "Political Campaign Management Styles: A 1972 Field Study" (Ph.D. dissertation, University of Michigan, 1973), Dissertation Abstracts International A, 34 (1974), 615.

2070 Schrag, Robert L.; Hudson, Richard A.; and Bernabo, Lawrence M. "Television's New Humane Collectivity," Western Journal of Speech Communication, 45 (1981), 1-12.

2071 Schramm, Martin. Running for President 1976: The Carter Campaign. New York: Stein and Day, 1977.

2072 Schramm, Wilbur. Men, Messages and Media: A Look at Human Communication. New York: Harper and Row, 1973.

2073 Schreibman, Faye. "TV News Coverage of Elections: A Guide to Archival Collections," Campaigns and Elections, 2 (1981), 27-29.

2074 Schuetz, Janet. "Communicative Competence and the Bargaining of Watergate," Journal of Western Speech Communication, 42 (1978), 105-115.

2075 Schuster, Camille P. "A Critique of Candidates' Styles in the 1976 Presidential Campaign" (Ph.D. dissertation, Ohio State University, 1977), Dissertation Abstracts International A, 38 (1978), 6402.

2076 Schuster, Gary. "An Interview with Jim Brady," Washington Journalism Review, 2 (1981), 36-38.

2077 Schutz, Charles E. Political Humor: From Aristophanes to Sam Ervin. Cranbury, NJ: Associated Presses, Inc., 1977.

2078 Schwalbe, T. "A Multidimensional Approach to Political Participation," (Ph. D. dissertation, University of Southern California, 1980), Dissertation Abstracts International A, 40 (1980), 5237.

2079 Schwartz, D. A. "How Fast Does News Travel?" Public Opinion Quarterly, 37 (1973-74), 625-627.

2080 Schwartz, David C. Political Alienation and Political Behavior. Chicago: Aldine, 1973.

2081 Schwartz, John E.; and Volgy, Thomas. "On Television Viewing and Citizen's Political Attitudes, Activity and Knowledge: Another Look at the Media's Impact on Politics," Western Political Quarterly, 33 (1980), 153-166.

2082 Schwartz, Tony. Media: The Second God. New York: Random House, 1982.

2083 _____. The Responsive Chord. Garden City, NY: Doubleday, 1973.

2084 Schwartzman, Edward. Campaign Craftsmanship: A Professional's Guide to Campaigning for Elective Office. New York: Universe Books, 1973.

2085 Schweitzer, D. "How to Buy Media (in Political Campaigns): Getting the Most for Your Money," Campaigns and Elections, 2 (1981), 34-39.

2086 Sears, David O. "Political Socialization," Handbook of Political Science: Micropolitical Theory, Vol. 2, eds. Fred I. Greenstein and Nelson W. Polsby. Reading, MA: Addison-Wesley, 1975.

2087 _____; and Chaffee, Steven H. "Uses and Effects of the 1976 Debates: An Overview of Empirical Studies," The Great Debates: Carter vs. Ford, 1976, ed. Sidney Kraus. Bloomington, IN: Indiana University Press, 1979.

2088 _____; and Whitney, Richard E. "Political Persuasion," Handbook of Communication, eds. Ithiel de Sola Pool, et al. Chicago: Rand McNally College Publishing Company, 1973.

2089 _____; et al. "Self-interest vs. Symbolic Politics in Policy Attitudes and Presidential Voting," American Political Science Review, 74 (1980), 670-684.

2090 Sears, John. "The Press Elects the President"; and Diamond, Edwin, "Not Really," Washington Journalism Review, 2 (1980), 32-37.

Bibliography

2091 Segall, M. H. Human Behavior and Public Policy-Political Psychology. Elmsford, NY: Pergamon Press, 1977.

2092 Seiden, Martin H. Who Controls the Mass Media?: Popular Myths and Economic Realities. New York: Basic Books, 1974.

2093 Seigel, Paul J. "An Analysis of the Factors that Determine the Success of Congressional Campaigns" (Master's thesis, Western Michigan University, 1977), Masters Abstracts, 16 (1978), 114.

2094 Semlak, William D. "Effect of Media Use in Foreign Student Perceptions of U.S. Political Leaders," Journalism Quarterly, 56 (1979), 153-156+.

2095 _____. "A Rhetorical Analysis of George S. McGovern's Campaign for the 1972 Democratic Presidential Nomination" (Ph.D. dissertation, University of Minnesota, 1973), Dissertation Abstracts International A, 34 (1974), 7370.

2096 Seroka, J. "Incumbency and Reelection: Governors vs. U.S. Senators," State Government, 53 (1980), 161-165.

2097 Seroka, K. B., et al. "Precise Procedures for Optimizing Campaign Communication," Communication Yearbook 1, ed. Brent Ruben. New Brunswick, NJ: Transaction Books, 1977.

2098 Serow, Ann G. "Mass Media and National Politics: The Question of Bias in News Reporting" (Ph.D. dissertation, University of Connecticut, 1975), Dissertation Abstracts International A, 35 (1975), 7372.

2099 Servan-Schreiber, Jean-Jacques. The Power to Inform. New York: McGraw-Hill, 1974.

2100 Sevener, Donald J. "Editorial and Opinion Page Coverage of the Presidential Election Campaign of 1972 by Five Michigan Daily Newspapers" (Master's thesis, Michigan State University, 1973), Journalism Abstracts, 12 (1974), 167-168.

2101 Seymour-Ure, Colin. The American Presidency: Power and Communication. New York: Macmillan, 1982.

2102 _____. The Political Impact of Mass Media. Beverly Hills, CA: Sage Publications, 1974.

2103 _____. "Presidential Power, Press Secretaries and Communication," Political Studies, 28 (1980), 253-270.

2104 Shaffer, C. "The Press Secretary in the Office of the Mayor of New York City: 1898-1972" (Ph. D. dissertation, New York University, 1973), Dissertation Abstracts International A, 34 (1973), 1348.

2105 Shaffer, W. R. "Simple and Inexpensive Election Prediction: A Practical Alternative," Western Political Quarterly, 28 (1975), 506-515.

2106 Shannon, W. Wayne. Party, Constituency, and Congressional Voting: A Study of Legislative Behavior in the United States House of Representatives. Westport, CT: Greenwood Press, 1981.

2107 Shapiro, Andrew O. Media Access: Your Rights to Express Your Views on Radio and Television. Boston, MA: Little, Brown, and Co., 1976.

2108 Sharp, P. R. "Challenger Campaigns for the United States House of Representatives: A Study of Indiana Democrats in 1972" (Ph. D. dissertation, Georgetown University, 1973), Dissertation Abstracts International A, 35 (1974), 543-544.

2109 Shaw, Donald L.; and Clemmer, C. L. "News and the Public Response," The Emergence of American Political Issues, eds. Donald L. Shaw and Maxwell E. McCombs. St. Paul, MN: West Publishing Co., 1977.

2110 _____; and McCombs, Maxwell E. (eds.). The Emergence of American Political Issues: The Agenda-Setting Function of the Press. St. Paul, MN: West Publishing Co., 1977.

2111 Shaw, M. "Reinstatement: The American Presidential Election of 1976," Parliamentary Affairs, 30 (1977), 241-257.

2112 Shawe, Janice G. "Reporter Bias: Do Journalists Judge Black and White Politicians by a Different Set of Criteria?" (Master's thesis, California State University, Fullerton, 1978), Masters Abstracts, 16 (1978), 247.

2113 Sheffield, Carole J. "The Campaign to Mobilize the Newly Enfranchised in the 1972 Presidential Election: An Interest Group Analysis of the National Movement for the Student Vote and the Youth Citizenship Fund, Inc." (Ph. D. dissertation, Miami University, 1973), Dissertation Abstracts International A, 34 (1974), 6723-6724.

2114 Sheffield, James F.; and Goering, Lawrence K. "Winning and Losing: Candidate Advantage in Local Elections," American Politics Quarterly, 6 (1978), 453-468.

2115 Sheingold, C. A. "Social Networks and Voting: The Resurrection of a Research Agenda," American Sociological Review, 38 (1973), 712-720.

2116 Sheinkopf, Kenneth G. "Family Communication Patterns and Anticipatory Socialization," Journalism Quarterly, 51 (1973), 24-30.

2117 _____; Atkin, Charles K.; and Bowen, Lawrence. "How Political Party Workers Respond to Political Advertising," Journalism Quarterly, 50 (1973), 334-339.

2118 Shepard, Lee. "Does Campaign Spending Really Matter?" Public Opinion Quarterly, 41 (1977), 196-205.

2119 Shepherd, R. "Leadership, Public Opinion and the Referendum," Political Quarterly, 46 (1975), 25-35.

2120 Shields, M. "Using Television: Political Campaigns," Politics Today, 5 (1978), 12-13.

2121 Shields, Mark. "Confidential--Memo to the Candidate," Washington Journalism Review, 2 (1980), 48-49.

2122 Shienbaum, K. E. "Ideology versus Rhetoric in American Politics" (Ph.D. dissertation, New York University, 1973), Dissertation Abstracts International A, 34 (1974), 7848-7849.

2123 Shikiar, Richard. "Authoritarianism and Political Behavior: The 1972 Election," Psychological Reports, 36 (1975), 874.

2124 _____. "Multidimensional Perceptions of the 1972 Presidential Election," Multivariate Behavioral Research, 11 (1976), 259-263.

2125 _____. "The Perception of Politicians and Political Issues: A Multidimensional Scaling Approach," Multivariate Behavioral Research, 9 (1974), 461-477.

2126 _____; Wiggins, Nancy H.; and Fishbein, Martin. "The Prediction of Political Evaluation and Voting Preference: A Multidimensional Analysis," Journal of Research in Personality, 10 (1976), 424-436.

2127 Shoemaker, Pamela J. "The Perceived Legitimacy of Deviant Political Groups: Two Experiments on Media Effects," Communication Research, 9 (1982), 249-286.

2128 Shostek, H. "Structural Dimensions of Television Editorial Effectiveness," Journalism Quarterly, 52 (1975), 37-43.

2129 Shukovsky, Paul R. "Political Verbal Behavior" (Master's thesis, Western Michigan University, 1973), Masters Abstracts, 11 (1973), 477.

2130 Shupe, Ralph E., Jr. "Agenda-Setting in the Electronic Age: The Trend of Network News Toward Coverage of Campaign Trivia in Presidential Campaigns" (Master's thesis, University of Maryland, 1978), Journalism Abstracts, 17 (1979), 111.

2131 Shyles, Leonard C. "An Analysis of Images, Issues, and Presentational Methods of Televised Political Spot Advertisements in 1980's Presidential Primaries" (Ph.D. dissertation, Ohio State University, 1981), Dissertation Abstracts International A, 42 (1982), 2920.

2132 Siberman, J.; and Yochum, G. "The Role of Money in Determining Election Outcomes," Social Science Quarterly, 58 (1978), 671-682.

2133 Siegel, P. "Protecting Political Speech: Brandenburg vs. Ohio Updated," Quarterly Journal of Speech, 67 (1981), 69-80.

2134 Sies, Dennis E. "The Presidency and Television: A Study of Six Administrations" (Ph.D. dissertation, University of Cincinnati, 1978), Dissertation Abstracts International A, 39 (1979), 5704-5705.

2135 Sigal, Leon V. "Newsmen and Campaigners: Organization Men Make the News," Political Science Quarterly, 93 (1978), 465-470.

2136 _____. Reporters and Officials: The Organization and Politics of Newsmaking. Lexington, MA: Lexington Books, 1973.

2137 Sigelman, Lee. "The Dynamics of Presidential Support: An Overview of Research Findings," Presidential Studies Quarterly, 9 (1979), 206-216.

2138 _____. "Gauging the Public Response to Presidential Leadership," Presidential Studies Quarterly, 10 (1980), 427-433.

2139 _____. "Presidential Popularity and Presidential Elections," Public Opinion Quarterly, 43 (1979), 532-534.

2140 _____. "Question-order Effects on Presidential Popularity," Public Opinion Quarterly, 45 (1981), 199-207.

2141 _____; and Miller, Lawrence. "Understanding Presidential Rhetoric: The Vietnam Statements of Lyndon Johnson," Communication Research, 5 (1978), 25-56.

2142 _____; and Sigelman, Carol K. "Politics of Popular Culture: Campaign Cynicism and the Candidate," Sociology and Social Research, 58 (1974), 272-277.

2143 _____; and _____. "Presidential Leadership of Public Opinion: From 'Benevolent Leader' to 'Kiss of Death'?" Experimental Study of Politics, 7 (1981), 1-22.

2144 Silberman, J.; and Yochum, G. "Role of Money in Determining Election Outcomes," Social Science Quarterly, 58 (1978), 671-682.

2145 Silver, Howard J. "Presidential Power and the Post-Watergate Presidency," Presidential Studies Quarterly, 8 (1978), 199-213.

2146 Silver, Morris. "A Demand Analysis of Voting Costs and Voting Participation," Social Science Research, 2 (1973), 111-124.

2147 Silverthorne, C. P.; and Mazmanian, L. "Effects of Heckling and Media of Presentation on the Impact of a Persuasive Communication," Journal of Social Psychology, 96 (1975), 229-236.

2148 Simmons, Robert O., Jr. "The Impact of Television's 1976 Election Night Coverage on Basic Political Attitudes and Cognitions" (Master's thesis, University of Michigan, 1981), Masters Abstracts, 21 (1983), 98.

2149 Simmons, S. J. The Fairness Doctrine and the Media. Berkeley CA: University of California Press, 1978.

2150 Simons, Herbert W. "On Politicians, Critics, and Reified Myths," Human Communication Research, 8 (1982), 386-388.

2151 _____; Chesebro, James W.; and Orr, C. Jack. "A Movement Perspective on the 1972 Presidential Campaign," Quarterly Journal of Speech, 59 (1973), 168-179.

2152 _____; and Leibowitz, K. "Shifts in Candidate Images," The Great Debates: Ford versus Carter, 1976, ed. Sidney Kraus. Bloomington, IN: Indiana University Press, 1979.

2153 _____; and Mechling, Elizabeth W. "The Rhetoric of Political Movements," Handbook of Political Communication, eds. Dan D. Nimmo and Keith R. Sanders. Beverly Hills, CA: Sage Publications, 1981, 417-444.

2154 Simpson, Dick. Winning Elections: A Handbook in Participatory Politics. Athens, OH: Swallow Press, 1982.

2155 Singer, Aaron (ed.). Campaign Speeches of American Presidential Candidates, 1928-1972. New York: Frederick Ungar Publishing Co., Inc., 1976.

2156 Singleton, Donald L. "The Role of Broadcasting in Presidential Popularity: An Exploration in Presidential Power" (Ph.D. dissertation, University of Oklahoma, 1977), Dissertation Abstracts International A, 39 (1978), 1176-1177.

2157 Sisatto, S. "Political Climate and Communication," Communications International Journal of Communication Research, 5 (1979), 67-77.

2158 Siune, K.; and Kline, F. Gerald. "Communication, Mass Political Behavior, and Mass Society," Political Communication: Issues and Strategies for Research, ed. Steven H. Chaffee. Beverly Hills, CA: Sage Publications, 1975.

2159 Skellie, Fred A. "Political Belief Systems, Issues, Candidates, and Youth" (Ph.D. dissertation, Johns Hopkins University, 1973), Dissertation Abstracts International A, 34 (1974), 7332.

2160 Slack, Jennifer D. Communication Technologies and Society: Concepts of Causality and Politics of Technical Intervention. Norwood, NJ: Ablex Publishing, 1982.

2161 Slater, I. "Orwell, Marcuse and the Language of Politics," Political Studies, 23 (1975), 459-474.

2162 Slater, William T. "The White House Press Corps During the Ford Administration" (Ph.D. dissertation, Stanford University, 1978), Dissertation Abstracts International A, 39 (1978), 527.

2163 Sloan, L. R.; Love, R. E.; and Ostrom, T. M. "Political Heckling: Who Really Loses?" Journal of Personality and Social Psychology, 30 (1974), 518-525.

2164 Smith, Craig R. "Addendum to 'Contemporary Political Speech Writing'," Southern Speech Communication Journal, 42 (1977), 191-194.

2165 _____. "Contemporary Political Speech Writing," Southern Speech Communication Journal, 42 (1976), 52-67.

2166 _____. "The Republican Keynote Address of 1968: Adaptive Rhetoric for the Multiple Audience," Western Speech, 39 (1975), 32-39.

2167 _____. "Ronald Reagan's Attempt to Build a National Majority," Central States Speech Journal, 30 (1979), 98-102.

2168 Smith, Gary D. "The Pulse of Presidential Popularity: Kennedy in Crisis" (Ph. D. dissertation, University of California, Los Angeles, 1978), Dissertation Abstracts International A, 38 (1978), 6915.

2169 Smith, H. E.; and Norris, L. Newsmakers: The Press and the Presidents. Reading, MA: Addison-Wesley, 1974.

2170 Smith, James R. "A Factor Analytic Study of Student and Adult Judgments of Television News" (Ph. D. dissertation, The Pennsylvania State University, 1975), Dissertation Abstracts International A, 36 (1976), 7031.

2171 Smith, Kim A. "Effects of a Political Event on the Political Socialization Process: The 1976 Presidential Debates" (Ph. D. dissertation, University of Wisconsin-Madison, 1978), Journalism Abstracts, 17 (1979), 34-35.

2172 Smith, P. A. Electing a President. New York: Praeger, 1982.

2173 Smith, Raymond. "The Carter-Ford Debates: Some Perceptions from Academe," Central States Speech Journal, 28 (1977), 250-257.

2174 Smith, Robert R. "Mythic Elements in Television News," Journal of Communication, 29 (1979), 75-82.

2175 Smith-Lovin, Lynn. "Individual Political Participation: The Effects of Social Structure and Communication Behavior," Pacific Sociological Review, 22 (1979), 23-50.

2176 Smoger, Gerson H. "Organizing Political Campaigns: A Survey of 19th and 20th Century Trends" (Ph. D. dissertation, University of Pennsylvania, 1982), Dissertation Abstracts International A, 43 (1982), 915.

2177 Smolka, R. G.; and Rossotti, J. E. Registering Voters by Mail. Washington, D. C.: American Enterprise Institute for Public Policy Research, 1975.

2178 Snapper, Bruce L. "Alienation as a Transmitter of Political Values" (Master's thesis, California State University, Long Beach, 1974), Masters Abstracts, 12 (1974), 146-147.

2179 Snider, G. A. "Assessing the Candidate Preference Function," American Journal of Political Science, 23 (1979), 732-754.

2180 Sniderman, Paul M. Personality and Democratic Politics. Berkeley, CA: University of California Press, 1975.

2181 _____; et al. "Stability of Support for the Political System: The Initial Impact of Watergate," American Politics Quarterly, 3 (1975), 437-457.

2182 Sobel, Robert. The Manipulators: America in the Media Age. Garden City, NY: Doubleday, 1976.

2183 Soderlund, Walter C.; and Wagenberg, Ronald H. "A Content Analysis of Editorial Coverage of the 1972 Electoral Campaigns in Canada and the United States," Western Political Quarterly, 28 (1975), 85-107.

2184 Sohn, Ardyth B. "A Longitudinal Analysis of Agenda-Setting Effects" (Ph.D. dissertation, Southern Illinois University, 1976), Dissertation Abstracts International A, 37 (1977), 5416-5417.

2185 _____. "A Longitudinal Analysis of Local Non-Political Agenda-Setting Effects," Journalism Quarterly, 55 (1978), 325-333.

2186 Sohn, H. L. "The Relationship of Newspaper Issue Agendas to the Current and Anticipated Issue Agendas of Community Leaders, Non-Leaders, and Newspaper Staff" (Ph.D. dissertation, Southern Illinois University, 1976), Dissertation Abstracts International A, 34 (1977), 5417.

2187 Soule, John W.; and Marx, Paul. "Cognitive Dissonance and Public Reaction to Watergate," Experimental Study of Politics, 5 (1976), 1-19.

2188 Spadaro, Robert N. "Political Constraints on Public Policy: The Folkways of Politicians," Human Relations, 29 (1976), 287-305.

2189 _____. "Some Folkways of Political Leaders: The Rules of the Game," Journal of Applied Psychology, 59 (1974), 125-126.

2190 Spear, Joseph C. "The President and the Press: A Critical Analysis of the Nixon Administration's Policy toward the News Media" (Master's thesis, American University, 1973), Masters Abstracts, 12 (1974), 126-127.

2191 Spencer, Wallace H. "Presidential Communication: Information and Decision Making" (Ph.D. dissertation, University of Washington, 1977), Dissertation Abstracts International A, 38 (1977), 1631.

2192 Spero, Robert. The Duping of the American Voter: Dishonesty and Deception in Presidential Television Advertising. New York: Harper and Row, 1980.

2193 Spragens, William C. "The Myth of the Johnson 'Credibility Gap'," Presidential Studies Quarterly, 10 (1980), 629-635.

2194 _____. The Presidency and the Mass Media in the Age of Television. Lanham, MD: University Press of America, 1979.

2195 _____. "A Rivalry for Influence: National Convention Delegates View the Mass Media," International Behavioural Scientist, 5 (1973), 50-64.

2196 _____; with Terwood, C. A. From Spokesman to Press Secretary: White House Media Operations. Lanham, MD: University Press of America, 1980.

2197 Srinivasan, Seetha. "The Role of Press Secretary James C. Hagerty in the Development of Political Public Relations" (Master's thesis, University of Florida, 1979), Journalism Abstracts, 17 (1979), 114.

2198 Staats, Elmer B. "Impact of the Federal Election Campaign Act of 1971," Annals of the American Academy of Political and Social Science, 425 (1976), 88-97.

2199 Stanwick, Kathy; and Li, Christine. The Political Participation of Women in the United States: A Selected Bibliography, 1950-1976. Metuchen, NJ: Scarecrow Press, Inc., 1977.

2200 Star, Meyer W. "The Cognitive Organization of Mass Media Images: A Multidimensional Scaling Approach" (Ph.D. dissertation, University of South Carolina, 1976), Dissertation Abstracts International B, 37 (1976), 1976-1977.

2201 Starr, D. P. "Adulterous Ghostwriting," Quarterly Journal of Speech, 62 (1976), 288.

2202 Steck, Joan O. "Press Commentary and the 1972 Presidential Election: An Analysis of Selected Columnists" (Ph.D. dissertation, University of Wisconsin-Madison, 1980), Dissertation Abstracts International A, 41 (1980), 1819.

2203 Steeper, F. T. "Public Response to Gerald Ford's Statements on Eastern Europe in the Second Debate," The Presidential Debates: Media, Electoral, and Policy Perspectives, eds. George F. Bishop, Robert G. Meadow, and Marilyn Jackson-Beeck. New York: Praeger, 1978.

2204 Stehle, Timothy E. "The Agenda-Setting Function of Newspapers: A Path Analysis Using Individual-Level Measures" (Master's thesis, Indiana University, 1980), Journalism Abstracts, 18 (1980), 120.

2205 Steinberg, Arnold. The Political Campaign Handbook. Lexington, MA: D. C. Heath, 1976.

2206 _____. Political Campaign Management: A Systems Approach. Lexington, MA: Lexington Books, 1976.

2207 Steindorf, Jeffrey A. "Judging Politicians by Their Moral Rationales: The Effect of Judge's Own Moral Reasoning" (Ph.D. dissertation, Northern Illinois University, 1976), Dissertation Abstracts International B, 37 (1977), 6410-6411.

2208 Steinfatt, Thomas M.; et al. "News Diffusion of the George Wallace Shooting: The Apparent Lack of Interpersonal Communication as an Artifact of Delayed Measurement," Quarterly Journal of Speech, 59 (1973), 401-412.

2209 Steininger, M.; and Majdanik, D. "Alienation, Liberalism-Conservatism, and Presidential Preference," Psychological Reports, 34 (1974), 382.

2210 Stephens, Mitchell. "Clout: Murdoch's Political Post," Columbia Journalism Review, 21 (1982), 44-46.

2211 Stevenson, Robert K. "An Empirical Study of the Nature of Machiavellianism as Uncovered in the White House Tapes" (Master's thesis, California State University, Fullerton, 1976), Masters Abstracts, 14 (1976), 120.

2212 Stevenson, Robert L.; and Greene, Mark T. "A Reconsideration of Bias in the News," Journalism Quarterly, 57 (1980), 115-121.

2213 _____; and Laing, Robert B. "The Audience for the Television Network News," Journal of Broadcasting, 20 (1976), 159-168.

2214 _____; and White, K. P. "The Cumulative Audience of Television Network News," Journalism Quarterly, 57 (1980), 477-481.

2215 _____; et al. "Untwisting The News Twisters: A Replication of Efron's Study," Journalism Quarterly, 50 (1973), 211-219.

2216 Stewart, Charles J. "Voter Perception of Mudslinging in Political Communication," Central States Speech Journal, 26 (1975), 279-286.

2217 Stewart, Debra W. (ed.). Women in Local Politics. Metuchen, NJ: Scarecrow Press, Inc., 1980.

2218 Stewart, J. "Congress on the Air: Issues and Alternatives," Journal of Communication, 25 (1974), 82-90.

2219 Stewart, W. H. Alabama and the 1976 Presidential Election. University, AL: University of Alabama Press, 1977.

2220 Stimson, James A. "Beliefs Systems: Constraint, Complexity, and the 1972 Election," American Journal of Political Science, 19 (1975), 393-417.

2221 _____. "Public Support for American Presidents: A Cyclical Model," Public Opinion Quarterly, 40 (1976), 1-21.

2222 Stoess, Jean L. "Reporting the 1976 General Election in Nevada: A History and Analysis of the News Election Service" (Master's thesis, University of Nevada, 1978), Journalism Abstracts, 17 (1979), 116.

2223 Stogdill, R. M. Handbook of Leadership. New York: The Free Press, 1974.

2224 Stone, Gerald. "Tracing the Time-Lag in Agenda-Setting," Studies in Agenda-Setting, ed. Maxwell E. McCombs and Gerald Stone. Syracuse, NY: Newhouse Communication Research Center, 1976.

2225 _____; and McCombs, Maxwell E. "Tracing the Time Lag in Agenda-Setting," Journalism Quarterly, 58 (1981), 51-55.

2226 Stone, William F. The Psychology of Politics. New York: The Free Press, 1974.

2227 Stovall, James G. "Foreign Policy Issue Coverage in the 1980 Presidential Campaign," Journalism Quarterly, 59 (1982), 531-540.

2228 Straffin, P. D. "Bandwagon Curve," American Journal of Political Science, 21 (1977), 695-709.

2229 Strand, P. J.; and Hofstetter, C. Richard. "Television News Coverage of the 1972 Election: A Convergent and Discriminant Validation of Some Selected Indicators," Political Methodology, 4 (1977), 507-522.

2230 Stroud, Kandy. How Jimmy Won: The Victory Campaign from Plains to the White House. West Caldwell: William Morrow, 1977.

2231 Strouse, James C. The Mass Media, Public Opinion and Public Policy Analysis. Columbus, OH: Charles E. Merrill Publishing Co., 1975.

2232 Strum, P. Presidential Power and American Democracy. Santa Monica, CA: Goodyear Publishing, 1979.

2233 Sudman, Seymour. "The Presidents and the Polls," Public Opinion Quarterly, 46 (1982), 301-310.

2234 Sudol, Ronald A. "The Rhetoric of Strategic Retreat: Carter and the Panama Canal Debate," Quarterly Journal of Speech, 65 (1979), 379-391.

2235 Suedfeld, Peter; Rank, Darylynn; and Borrie, Roderick A. "Frequency of Exposure and Evaluation of Candidates and Campaign Speeches," Journal of Applied Social Psychology, 5 (1975), 118-126.

2236 Sullivan, John L.; and Minns, D. R. "'The Benevolent Leader Revisited': Substantive Finding or Methodological Artifact?" American Journal of Political Science, 20 (1976), 763-772.

2237 _____; and _____. "Ideological Distance Between Candidates: An Empirical Examination," American Journal of Political Science, 20 (1976), 439-468.

2238 _____; Pierson, James; and Marcus, George E. Political Tolerance and American Democracy. Chicago, IL: University of Chicago Press, 1982.

2239 _____; and Uslaner, E. M. "Congressional Behavior and Electoral Marginality," American Journal of Political Science, 22 (1978), 536-553.

2240 Sundquist, James L. The Decline and Resurgence of Congress. Washington, D. C.: Brookings, 1981.

2241 Surlin, Stuart H.; and Gordon, Thomas. "How Values Affect Attitudes Toward Direct Reference Political Advertising," Journalism Quarterly, 54 (1977), 89-98.

2242 _____; and _____. "Selective Exposure and Retention of Political Advertising," Journal of Advertising Research, 5 (1976), 32-44.

2243 Swanson, David L. "And That's the Way it Was? Television Covers the 1976 Presidential Campaign," Quarterly Journal of Speech, 63 (1977), 239-248.

2244 _____. "A Constructivist Approach," Handbook of Political Communication, eds. Dan D. Nimmo and Keith R. Sanders. Beverly Hills, CA: Sage Publications, 1981, 169-191.

2245 _____. "The Continuing Evolution of the Uses and Gratifications Approach," Communication Research, 6 (1979), 3-7.

2246 _____. "Information Utility: An Alternative Perspective

Bibliography

in Political Communication," Central States Speech Journal, 27 (1976), 95-101.

2247 _____. "On the Symbolist Insight in the Study of Political Communication," Human Communication Research, 8 (1982), 379-382.

2248 _____. "Political Communication: A Revisionist View Emerges," Quarterly Journal of Speech, 64 (1978), 211-232.

2249 _____. "Political Communication Research and the Uses and Gratifications Model: A Critique," Communication Research, 6 (1979), 37-53.

2250 _____. "Political Information, Influence, and Judgment in the 1972 Presidential Campaign," Quarterly Journal of Speech, 59 (1973), 130-142.

2251 _____. "The Uses and Misuses of Uses and Gratifications," Human Communication Research, 3 (1977), 214-221.

2252 Swanson, Linda L.; and Swanson, David L. "The Agenda-Setting Function of the First Ford-Carter Debate," Communication Monographs, 45 (1978), 347-353.

2253 Swerdlow, Joel. "The Decline of the Boys on the Bus," Washington Journalism Review, 3 (1981), 15-19.

2254 Swinyard, William R.; and Coney, Kenneth A. "Promotional Effects on a High- versus Low-Involvement Electorate," Journal of Consumer Research, 5 (1978), 41-48.

2255 Syme, G. J. "Voting Preference and Frequency Estimation of Political Statements," European Journal of Social Psychology, 8 (1978), 121-124.

2256 Szybillo, G. J.; and Hartenbaum, R. F. "Political Advertising the the Broadcast Media," Journal of Advertising, 5 (1976), 42-46.

2257 Taebel, D. A. "Effect of Ballot Position on Electoral Success," American Journal of Political Science, 19 (1975), 519-526.

2258 Tan, Alexis S. "Evaluation of Newspapers and Television by Blacks and Mexican-Americans," Journalism Quarterly, 55 (1978), 673-681.

2259 _____. "Mass Media Exposure, Public Affairs Knowledge, and Black Militancy," Journalism Quarterly, 53 (1976), 271-279.

2260 _____. "Mass Media Use, Issue Knowledge and Political Involvement," Public Opinion Quarterly, 44 (1980), 241-248.

2261 _____. "Political Participation, Diffuse Support and Perceptions of Political Efficacy as Predictors of Mass Media Use," Communication Monographs, 48 (1981), 133-145.

2262 Tankard, James W.; et al. "Nonverbal Cues and Television News," Journal of Communication, 27 (1977), 106-111.

2263 Tardy, Charles H.; Gaughan, B.; Hemphill, M.; and Crockett, Nan. "Media Agendas and Political Participation," Journalism Quarterly, 58 (1981), 624-627.

2264 Tatalovich, R. "Electoral Votes and Presidential Campaign Trails, 1932-1976," American Politics Quarterly, 7 (1979), 489-496.

2265 Taylor, A., III. "Mudslinging in Michigan," Columbia Journalism Review, 15 (1977), 43.

2266 Taylor, D. G. "Pluralistic Ignorance and the Spiral of Silence: A Formal Analysis," Public Opinion Quarterly, 46 (1982), 311-335.

2267 Tebbel, John. The Media in America. New York: Thomas Y. Crowell Co., 1974.

2268 Tedin, K. L. "The Influence of Parents on the Political Attitudes of Adolescents," American Political Science Review, 68 (1974), 1579-1592.

2269 Teer, F.; and Spence, J. D. Political Opinion Polls. Atlantic Highlands, NJ: Humanities Press, 1973.

2270 Tefft, Diane P. "Communication and Cognition Effects from Poll Questions" (Master's thesis, University of Washington, 1975), Journalism Abstracts, 13 (1975), 137-138.

2271 Television and Behavior: Ten Years of Scientific Progress and Implications for the Eighties: Volume I, Summary Report. Washington, D. C.: Government Printing Office, 1982.

2272 Tercheck, Ronald. "Incentives and Voter Participation: a Research Note," Political Science Quarterly, 94 (1979), 135-140.

2273 Tetlock, Philip E. "Personality and Isolationism: Content Analysis of Senatorial Speeches," Journal of Personality and Social Psychology, 41 (1981), 737-743.

Bibliography

2274 _____. "Pre- to Post-Election Shifts in Presidential Rhetoric: Impression Management of Cognitive Adjustment," Journal of Personality and Social Psychology, 41 (1981), 207-212.

2275 Thayer, George. Who Shakes the Money Tree? American Campaign Financing Practices from 1789 to the Present. New York: Simon & Schuster, 1974.

2276 Thomas, David A. "A Qualitive Content Analysis of Richard M. Nixon's Treatment of Selected Issues in his Presidential Campaign Oratory in the 1960 and 1968 Elections" (Ph. D. dissertation, Michigan State University, 1973), Dissertation Abstracts International A, 34 (1973), 3600-3601.

2277 Thomas, Helen. Dateline: White House. New York: Macmillan, 1975.

2278 Thompson, Hunter S. Fear and Loathing on the Campaign Trail. San Francisco, CA: Straight Arrow Press, 1973.

2279 Thompson, Wayne N. "Barbara Jordan's Keynote Address: Fulfilling Dual and Conflicting Purposes," Central States Speech Journal, 30 (1979), 272-277.

2280 Thorson, Esther; and Thorson, Stuart J. "Perceptual-Cognitive Aspects of Political Socialization: An Experimental Approach," Experimental Study of Politics, 5 (1976), 42-84.

2281 Tichenor, P. J.; and Wackman, D. B. "Mass Media and Community Public Opinion," American Behavioral Scientist, 16 (1973), 593-606.

2282 Tidmarch, C. M.; and Carpenter, D. "Congressmen and the Electorate, 1968 and 1972," Journal of Politics, 40 (1978), 479-487.

2283 Tiemens, Robert K. "Television's Portrayal of the 1976 Presidential Debates: An Analysis of Visual Content," Communication Monographs, 45 (1978), 363-370.

2284 Tillinghast, Diana S. "Information Seeking on Watergate and President Nixon's Resignation and Attitudes Toward Nixon and the Mass Media" (Ph. D. dissertation, Michigan State University, 1976), Dissertation Abstracts International A, 37 (1977), 5424-5425.

2285 Tipton, Leonard; Haney, Roger D.; and Baseheart, John. "Media Agenda-Setting in City and State Election Campaigns," Journalism Quarterly, 52 (1975), 15-22.

2286 Todd, Rusty; and Brody, Richard A. "Mass Media and Stability of Party Identification: Are There Floating Partisans?" Communication Research, 7 (1980), 275-294.

2287 Toggerson, S. K. "Media Coverage and Information-Seeking Behavior," Journalism Quarterly, 58 (1981), 89-93.

2288 Tollison, Robert; Crain, Mark; and Pautler, Paul. "Information and Voting: An Empirical Note," Public Choice, 24 (1975), 43-49.

2289 Tonkin, H. "Equalizing Language: The Politics of Language," Journal of Communication, 29 (1979), 124-133.

2290 Tracey, M. "'Yesterday's Men'--A Case Study in Political Communication," Mass Communication and Society, eds. J. Curran, M. Gurevitch and J. Woollacott. London, England: Edward Arnold in Association with The Open University Press, 1977.

2291 Tracey, Michael. The Production of Political Television. Boston, MA: Routledge and Kegan Paul, Ltd., 1977.

2292 Trent, Judith. "Presidential Surfacing: The Ritualistic and and Crucial First Act," Communication Monographs, 45 (1978), 281-292.

2293 _____. "A Synthesis of Methodologies Used in Studying Political Communication," Central States Speech Journal, 26 (1975), 278-279.

2294 _____; and Trent, Jimmie D. "The Rhetoric of the Challenger: George Stanley McGovern," Central States Speech Journal, 25 (1974), 11-18.

2295 Truhon, Stephen A.; and McKinney, John P. "Children's Drawings of the Presidential Candidates," Journal of Genetic Psychology, 134 (1979), 157-158.

2296 Tucker, R. C. "Personality and Political Leadership," Political Science Quarterly, 92 (1977), 383-393.

2297 Tunstall, Jeremy. The Media are American: Anglo-American Media in the World. New York: Columbia University Press, 1977.

2298 _____; and Walker, David. Media Made in California: Hollywood, Politics, and the News. New York: Oxford University Press, 1981.

2299 Tursky, B. "Evaluation of the Cognitive Component of Political Issues by Use of Classical Conditioning," Journal of Personality and Social Psychology, 34 (1976), 865-873.

Bibliography

2300 Twentieth Century Fund. With the Nation Watching: A Report of the Twentieth Century Fund Task Force on Televised Presidential Debates. Lexington, MA: Lexington Books, 1979.

2301 Twer, Doran J. "Presidential Spot Advertising: A Descriptive Study" (Master's thesis, University of Pennsylvania, 1976), Journalism Abstracts, 14 (1976), 179.

2302 Valley, David B. "A History and Analysis of Democratic Presidential Nomination Acceptance Speeches to 1968" (Ph. D. dissertation, University of Illinois at Urbana-Champaign, 1972), Dissertation Abstracts International A, 33 (1973), 5873.

2303 _____. "Significant Characteristics of Democratic Presidential Nomination Acceptance Speeches," Central States Speech Journal, 25 (1974), 56-62.

2304 Van Jones, Billy. "Attitude Change Toward the Candidates of the 1980 Presidential Election," Journal of Social Psychology, 116 (1982), 297-298.

2305 Vanleuven, J. K. "The Prediction of Attitudes from Values: A Public Opinion Approach" (Ph. D. dissertation, Washington State University, 1976), Dissertation Abstracts International B, 38 (1977), 1475-1476.

2306 VanSickle, C. K. "The Oral Communication of Senator Sam J. Ervin, Jr., in the Watergate Hearings: A Study in Consistency" (Ph. D. dissertation, Michigan State University, 1976), Dissertation Abstracts International A, 37 (1976), 3268.

2307 Vatz, Richard E. "Presidential Rhetoric: A Study of Rhetoric, Ethos, and Public Opinion" (Ph. D. dissertation, University of Pittsburgh, 1976), Dissertation Abstracts International A, 37 (1976), 3268-3269.

2308 _____. "Public Opinion and Presidential Ethos," Western Speech Communication Journal, 40 (1976), 196-206.

2309 Veblen, Eric. The Manchester "Union Leader" in New Hampshire Elections. Hanover, NH: New England University Press, 1975.

2310 Vedung, Evert. Political Reasoning. Beverly Hills, CA: Sage Publications, 1982.

2311 Vermeer, Jan P. "Campaign Propaganda and the Press: Campaign Press Releases in the 1973 New Jersey Gubernatorial Campaign" (Ph. D. dissertation, Princeton University,

1979), Dissertation Abstracts International A, 40 (1979), 1671.

2312 _____. For Immediate Release, Candidate Press Releases in American Political Campaigns. Westport, CT: Greenwood Press, 1982.

2313 Vernon, George L. "Dogmatism as a Variable in Political Economic Conservatism, Candidate Preference, and Abstract Thinking Ability" (Master's thesis, University of Louisville, 1974), Masters Abstracts, 13 (1975), 45.

2314 Vickers, James R. "The Role of Images in the 1972 California Democratic Primary" (Master's thesis, California State University, Northridge, 1973), Journalism Abstracts, 12 (1974), 185-186.

2315 Vidich, A. J. "Political Legitimacy in Bureaucratic Society: An Analysis of Watergate," Social Research, 42 (1975), 778-811.

2316 Volgy, Thomas J.; and Schwarz, J. E. "On Television Viewing and Citizens' Political Attitudes, Activity and Knowledge: Another Look at the Impact of Media on Politics," Western Political Quarterly, 33 (1980), 153-166.

2317 Wackman, D. B.; et al. "Chain Newspaper Autonomy as Reflected in Presidential Campaign Endorsements," Journalism Quarterly, 52 (1975), 411-420.

2318 Wagner, Dale E. "Public Financing of Federal Elections: Enactment and Recision of the 1966 Long Act" (Ph.D. dissertation, University of Maryland, 1975), Dissertation Abstracts International A, 36 (1976), 6931.

2319 Wagner, Randolph G. "Public Response to Watergate" (Ph.D. dissertation, Yale University, 1981), Dissertation Abstracts International A, 42 (1981), 2842.

2320 Wakshley, Jacob J.; and Edison, Nadyne G. "Attraction, Credibility, Perceived Similarity, and the Image of Public Figures," Communication Quarterly, 27 (1980), 27-34.

2321 Walk, Kenneth D.; and Lupfer, Michael B. "Presidential Debate as a Civics Lesson," Public Opinion Quarterly, 42 (1978), 342-353.

2322 Walker, A. S. "A Study of Relationships Between Mass Media, Community Involvement and Political Participation" (Ph.D. dissertation, Indiana University, 1976), Dissertation Abstracts International A, 37 (1977), 4680-4681.

2323 Walker, J. "Presidential Campaigns: Reforming the Reforms," Wilson Quarterly, 5 (1981), 88-101.

2324 Walker, Stephen G.; and Murphy, Timothy G. "The Utility of the Operational Code in Political Forecasting," Political Psychology, 3 (1981-82), 24-60.

2325 Walker, Thomas G. "Leader Selection and Behavior in Small Political Groups," Small Group Behavior, 7 (1976), 363-368.

2326 Wallenstein, M. H. "Political Poster Appeal: A Partial Audience Typology" (Master's thesis, Kent State University, 1976).

2327 Wanat, John. "The Dynamics of Presidential Popularity Shifts," American Politics Quarterly, 10 (1982), 181-196.

2328 _____. "Political Broadcast Advertising and Primary Election Voting," Journal of Broadcasting, 18 (1974), 413-422.

2329 Wander, Philip. "Cultural Criticism," Handbook of Political Communication, eds. Dan D. Nimmo and Keith R. Sanders. Beverly Hills, CA: Sage Publications, 1981, 497-528.

2330 Wang, Chia-hua. "U.S. Presidential Press Secretaries in the Truman-Carter Years" (Master's thesis, University of Missouri, 1981), Journalism Abstracts, 19 (1981), 91-92.

2331 Ware, P. D.; and Tucker, R. K. "Heckling as Distractions: An Experimental Study of its Effect on Source Credibility," Speech Monographs, 41 (1974), 185-188.

2332 Wasburn, P. C. "Authoritarianism and Political Participation," Journal of Political and Military Sociology, 3 (1975), 165-177.

2333 Washington, J. "The American Political Drama" (Ph.D. dissertation, University of Tennessee, 1976), Dissertation Abstracts International A, 37 (1977), 5337.

2334 Waters, Judith A. "The Image of the President: Components of the Political Leadership Role" (Ph.D. dissertation, City University of New York, 1976), Dissertation Abstracts International B, 38 (1977), 421.

2335 Watson, Margaret J. "The Effect of Feelings and Various Forms of Feedback Upon Conflict in a Political Group Problem-Solving Situation" (Ph.D. dissertation, University of Colorado, 1973), Dissertation Abstracts International A, 34 (1974), 4012.

2336 Watson, R. A. The Presidential Contest. New York: Wiley, 1980.

2337 Wattenberg, Martin P. "From Parties to Candidates: Examining the Role of the Media," Public Opinion Quarterly, 46 (1982), 216-227.

2338 Watzlawick, Paul. How Real is Real? Confusion, Disinformation and Communication. New York: Random House, 1976.

2339 Wayne, S. J. The Road to the White House. New York: St. Martin's Press, 1980.

2340 Wead, D. "Interpersonal Networks and Political Behavior," American Journal of Political Science, 26 (1982), 117-143.

2341 _____. Reagan, In Pursuit of the Presidency. Plainfield, NJ: Logos Int., 1980.

2342 Weaver, David H. "Audience Need for Orientation and the Media Effects," Communication Research, 7 (1980), 361-376.

2343 _____. "Media Agenda-Setting and Media Manipulation," Mass Communication Review Yearbook, 3, eds. D. Charles Whitney, Ellen Wartella, and Sven Windahl. Beverly Hills, CA: Sage Publications, 1982, 537-554.

2344 _____. "Political Issues and Voter Need for Orientation," The Emergence of American Political Issues: The Agenda-Setting Function of the Press, ed. Donald L. Shaw and Maxwell E. McCombs. St. Paul, MN: West Publishing Co., 1977.

2345 _____; and Buddenbaum, J. M. "Newspapers and Television: A Review of Research on Uses and Effects," Mass Communication Review Yearbook, 1, ed. H. de Bock. Beverly Hills, CA: Sage Publications, 1980.

2346 _____; Graber, Doris A.; McCombs, Maxwell E.; and Eyal, Chaim. Media Agenda-Setting in a Presidential Election: Issues, Images, Interest. New York: Praeger, 1981.

2347 _____; McCombs, Maxwell E.; and Spellman, Charles. "Watergate and the Media: A Case Study of Agenda-Setting," American Politics Quarterly, 3 (1975), 458-472.

2348 _____; and Wilhoit, Cleveland. "News Magazine Visibility of Senators," Journalism Quarterly, 51 (1974), 67-72.

Bibliography 187

2349 _____; and _____. "News Media Coverage of U.S. Senators in Four Congresses, 1953-1974," Journalism Monographs, 67 (1980), 1-34.

2350 _____; _____; and Reide, P. "Personal Needs and Media Use," ANPA News Research Report, 21 (1979), 2-7.

2351 Weaver, Ruth A. "Political Message Targeting and System Implementation: An Analysis of Effectiveness" (Ph.D. dissertation, University of Missouri-Columbia, 1980), Dissertation Abstracts International A, 42 (1981), 912.

2352 Weaver, S. "From Candidate to President," Public Interest, 50 (1978), 161-167.

2353 Webb, C.; and Mockus, J. "A Guide to Recruiting and Managing Campaign Volunteers," Campaigns and Elections, 2 (1981), 18-23.

2354 Wegner, Daniel M.; Wenzlaff, R.; Kerker, R. M.; and Beattie, A. E. "Incrimination Through Innuendo: Can Media Questions Become Public Answers?" Journal of Personality and Social Psychology, 40 (1981), 822-832.

2355 Weil, Gordon L. The Long Shot: George McGovern Runs for President. New York: Norton, 1974.

2356 Weiner, Michael J.; and Lurey, Edward. "The 'Lost Letter Technique' as a Predictor of the 1972 Presidential Election," Journal of Psychology, 84 (1973), 195-197.

2357 Weingast, D. E. We Elect a President. New York: Messner, 1973.

2358 Weiss, Ann E. Polls and Surveys: A Look at Public Opinion Research. New York: Franklin Watts, 1979.

2359 Weiss, C. H. "What America's Leaders Read," Public Opinion Quarterly, 38 (1974), 1-22.

2360 Weiss, W. "Review of the Uses of Mass Communications: Current Perspective on Gratifications Research," Public Opinion Quarterly, 40 (1976), 132-133.

2361 Weissberg, Robert. "Political Efficacy and Political Illusion," Journal of Politics, 37 (1975), 469-487.

2362 _____. Political Learning, Political Choice and Democratic Citizenship. Englewood Cliffs, NJ: Prentice-Hall, 1974.

2363 Weitzel, Allen R. "Contemporary Campaign Communication: A Case Study of a Nevada State Senate Race" (Ph.D. dissertation, University of Southern California, 1974),

Dissertation Abstracts International A, 34 (1974), 7371-7372.

2364 Welch, Susan (ed.). Public Opinion: Its Formation, Measurement, and Impact. Palo Alto, CA: Mayfield Publishing Co., 1975.

2365 Welch, W. P. "The Effectiveness of Expenditures in State Legislative Races," American Politics Quarterly, 4 (1976), 333-356.

2366 Wellings, Constance. "Personal Trust and Political Trust: An Examination of a Relationship" (Master's thesis, Florida Atlantic University, 1972), Masters Abstracts, 11 (1973), 64.

2367 Wendt, Hans W.; and Muncy, Carole A. "Studies of Political Character: Factor Patterns of 24 U.S. Vice-Presidents," Journal of Psychology, 102 (1979), 125-131.

2368 Wenglinsky, M. "Television Nation," Columbia Forum, 3 (1974), 12-16.

2369 Wenner, Lawrence A. "Political News on Television: A Uses and Gratifications Study" (Ph.D. dissertation, University of Iowa, 1977), Dissertation Abstracts International A, 39 (1978), 12-13.

2370 Westley, B. "Setting the Political Agenda: What Makes It Change?" Journal of Communication, 26 (1976), 43-47.

2371 Whale, John. The Half-Shut Eye: Television and Politics in Britain and America. Westport, CT: Greenwood Press, 1981.

2372 Whalen, Ardyce C. "The Presentation of Image in Ella T. Grasso's Campaign," Central States Speech Journal, 27 (1976), 207-211.

2373 Whalen, Joan C. "The Identification of Formal 'Topoi' in the 1960 Presidential Campaign Speeches of Vice-President Richard M. Nixon" (Master's thesis, California State University, Fullerton, 1976), Masters Abstracts, 14 (1976), 54.

2374 Wheeler, M. E.; and Reed, S. K. "Response to Before and After Watergate Caricatures," Journalism Quarterly, 52 (1975), 134-136.

2375 Wheeler, Michael. Lies, Damn Lies and Statistics: The Manipulation of Public Opinion in America. New York: Liveright Publishing Corp., 1976.

Bibliography

2376 _____. "Reining in Horserace Journalism," Public Opinion. February/March, 1980, 41-55.

2377 White, B. "Maryland: Getting the Governor," Columbia Journalism Review, 14 (1975), 12-14.

2378 White, David. "The Parrot Language of Politics," New Society, 54 (1980), 8-10.

2379 White, Karen M. "Political Efficacy and Media Use, 1976 Political Campaigns" (Master's thesis, University of Texas, 1980), Journalism Abstracts, 18 (1980), 127.

2380 White, Ray. "Government VIP's Rate the Washington Press," Washington Journalism Review, 4 (1982), 37-40.

2381 White, Theodore H. Breach of Faith: The Fall of Richard Nixon. New York: Atheneum, 1975.

2382 _____. The Making of the President 1972. New York: Atheneum, 1973.

2383 Whitney, D. Charles. "Status Inconsistency and Attention to Public Affairs in Mass Media," Journalism Quarterly, 57 (1980), 138-141.

2384 Wides, Jeffery W. "Perceived Economic Competency and the Ford/Carter Election," Public Opinion Quarterly, 43 (1979), 535-543.

2385 Wiegele, Thomas C. "Modes of Stress and Disturbance in Elite Political Behavior: Psychological Variables in Political Decision Making," Psychopathology and Political Leadership, ed. R. S. Robins. New Orleans: Tulane Studies in Political Science, 1977.

2386 _____. "Physiologically Based Content Analysis: An Application in Political Communication," Communication Yearbook 2, ed. Brent D. Ruben. New Brunswick, NJ: Transaction Books, 1978, 423-436.

2387 Wilcox, A. R. Public Opinion and Political Attitudes. New York: Wiley, 1974.

2388 Wildman, Robert W., II; and Wildman, Robert W. "Note on Application of the Semantic Differential to the Electoral Process," Psychological Reports, 38 (1976), 1185-1186.

2389 Wiles, Charles R. "An Analysis of Political Opinion Leadership Among 18 to 20 Year Old College Students" (Ph.D. dissertation, Southern Illinois University, 1974), Dissertation Abstracts International A, 35 (1975), 7857-7858.

2390 Wilhoit, G. Cleveland; and Auh, Taik S. "Newspaper Endorsement and Coverage of Public Opinion Polls in 1970," Journalism Quarterly, 51 (1974), 654-658.

2391 _____; and Drew, D. "The Politics, Community Participation and the Profile of the Editorial Writer," Journalism Quarterly, 50 (1973), 638-644.

2392 _____; and Weaver, David H. Newsroom Guide to Polls and Surveys. NY: American Newspaper Publishers Association, 1980.

2393 William, Charles H. "The Gatekeeper Function of the Governor's Staff," Western Political Quarterly, 33 (1980), 87-93.

2394 Williams, F.; Dordick, H. S.; and Horstmann, P. "Where Citizens Go for Information," Journal of Communication, 27 (1977), 95-99.

2395 Williams, Frederick. The Communications Revolution. Beverly Hills, CA: Sage Publications, 1982.

2396 Williams, Wenmouth, Jr.; and Larsen, David C. "Agenda-Setting in an Off-Election Year," Journalism Quarterly, 54 (1977), 744-749.

2397 _____; and Semlak, William. "Campaign '76: Agenda-Setting During the New Hampshire Primary," Journal of Broadcasting, 22 (1978), 531-540.

2398 _____; and _____. "Structural Effects of TV Coverage on Political Agendas," Journal of Communication, 28 (1978), 114-119.

2399 Wilson, C. Edward; and Howard, Douglas M. "Public Perception of Media Accuracy," Journalism Quarterly, 55 (1978), 73-76.

2400 Wilson, Chris; and Williams, Ederyn. "Watergate Words: A Naturalistic Study of Media and Communication," Communication Research, 4 (1977), 169-178.

2401 Wilson, G. L. "Strategy of Explanation: Richard M. Nixon's August 8, 1974, Resignation Address," Communication Quarterly, 24 (1976), 14-20.

2402 Wimmer, Roder D. "Mass Media and the Older Voter: 1972," Journal of Broadcasting, 20 (1976), 313-322.

2403 _____. "A Multivariate Analysis of the Use and Effects of the Mass Media in the 1968 Presidential Election" (Ph.D. dissertation, Bowling Green State University, 1976), Dissertation Abstracts International A, 37 (1977), 4681.

Bibliography 191

2404 Windhauser, John W. "A Comparative Content Analysis of How the Ohio Metropolitan Daily Press Reported the 1971 Ohio Municipal Election Campaigns: An Index of Press Coverage" (Ph.D. dissertation, Ohio University, 1975), Journalism Abstracts, 13 (1975), 39-40.

2405 _____. "How the Metropolitan Press Covered the 1970 General Election Campaigns in Ohio," Journalism Quarterly, 53 (1976), 264-270.

2406 _____. "Reporting of Campaign Issues in Ohio Municipal Election Races," Journalism Quarterly, 54 (1977), 332-340.

2407 _____. "Reporting of Ohio Municipal Elections by the Ohio Metropolitan Daily Press," Journalism Quarterly, 54 (1977), 552-565.

2408 _____; and Stempel, Guido H., III. "Reliability of Six Techniques for Content Analysis of Local Coverage," Journalism Quarterly, 56 (1979), 148-152.

2409 Winsor, Jerry L. "A Rhetorical Analysis of George S. McGovern's Campaign for Reelection in 1974" (Ph.D. dissertation, University of Nebraska-Lincoln, 1975), Dissertation Abstracts International A, 36 (1976), 4858.

2410 Winter, James P. "Contingent Conditions and the Agenda-Setting Function," Mass Communication Review Yearbook, Vol. 2, ed. G. Cleveland Wilhoit. Beverly Hills, CA: Sage Publications, 1981.

2411 _____. "Differential Media-Public Agenda-Setting Effects for Selected Issues, 1948-1976" (Ph.D. dissertation, Syracuse University, 1981), Dissertation Abstracts International A, 42 (1981), 1841-1842.

2412 Winter, Ralph K., Jr. Watergate and the Law; Political Campaigns and Presidential Power. Washington, D.C.: American Enterprise Institute for Public Policy Research, 1974.

2413 _____; and Bolton, John R. Campaign Financing and Political Reform. Washington, D.C.: American Enterprise Institute for Public Policy Research, 1974.

2414 Wirsing, R. "Political Power and Information: A Cross-Cultural Study," American Anthropologist, 75 (1973), 153-170.

2415 Wirthlin, Richard; Breglio, Vincent; and Beal, Richard. "Campaign Chronicle," Public Opinion, 4 (1981), 43-49.

2416 Witcover, Jules. *Marathon: The Pursuit of the Presidency 1972-1976.* New York: Viking, 1977.

2417 _____. *The Resurrection of Richard Nixon.* New York: G. P. Putnam's Sons, 1979.

2418 _____. "The Trials of a One-Candidate Campaign," *Columbia Journalism Review,* 11 (1973), 9-30.

2419 Witherspoon, P. D. "The Rhetoric of Gerald R. Ford: A Multi-dimensional Analysis of Presidential Communication" (Ph.D. dissertation, University of Texas at Austin, 1977), *Dissertation Abstracts International A,* 38 (1978), 3807.

2420 Witker, Kristi. *How to Lose Everything in Politics Except Massachusetts.* New York: Mason and Lipscomb, 1974.

2421 Woelfel, John C. "Changes in Interpersonal Communication Patterns as a Consequence of Need for Information," *Communication Research,* 4 (1977), 235-256.

2422 Wolfe, Donald T. "Southern Strategy: Race, Region, and Republican Presidential Politics, 1964 and 1968" (Ph.D. dissertation, Johns Hopkins University, 1974), *Dissertation Abstracts International A,* 35 (1975), 7990.

2423 Wolfinger, Raymond E.; and Rosenstone, Steven J. *Who Votes?* New Haven, CT: Yale University Press, 1980.

2424 _____; _____; and McIntoch, R. A. "Presidential and Congressional Voters Compared," *American Politics Quarterly,* 9 (1981), 245-255.

2425 Womack, David L. "ABC, CBS, and NBC Live Television Interviews Conducted During the 1972 Democratic National Convention: An Audio Content Analysis" (Master's thesis, University of Mississippi, 1974), *Journalism Abstracts,* 13 (1975), 151.

2426 _____; and Hoar, Jere R. "Treatment of Candidates in Convention Floor Interviews," *Journalism Quarterly,* 58 (1981), 300-302.

2427 Woo, Lillian C. *The Campaign Organizer's Manual.* Durham, NC: Carolina Academic Press, 1980.

2428 Woodward, Bob; and Bernstein, Carl. *All the President's Men.* New York: Simon & Schuster, 1974.

2429 Woodward, Gary C. "Prime Ministers and Presidents: A Survey of the Differing Rhetorical Possibilities of High Office," *Communication Quarterly,* 27 (1979), 41-49.

2430 Wooten, J. Dasher: The Roots and Rising of Jimmy Carter. New York: Summit Books, 1978.

2431 Worchel, Stephen; Andreoli, Virginia; and Eason, Joe. "Is the Medium the Message? A Study of the Effects of Media, Communication, and Message Characteristics on Attitude Change," Journal of Applied Social Psychology, 5 (1975), 157-172.

2432 Wright, Charles. "Functional Analysis and Mass Communication Revisited," The Uses of Mass Communications, eds. Jay G. Blumler and Elihu Katz. Beverly Hills, CA: Sage Publications, 1974.

2433 Wright, D. K. "Survey Shows Politicians Favor Commercial Printing," Journalism Quarterly, 51 (1974), 520-521.

2434 Wright, Gerald C., Jr. "Black Voting Turnout and Education in the 1968 Presidential Election," Journal of Politics, 37 (1975), 563-568.

2435 Wright, J. D. "Alienation and Political Negativism: New Evidence from National Surveys," Sociology and Social Research, 60 (1976), 111-134.

2436 _____. "Does Acquiescence Bias the Index of Political Efficacy?" Public Opinion Quarterly, 39 (1975), 219-226.

2437 Wright, Thomas L.; and Arbuthnot, Jack. "Interpersonal Trust, Political Preference, and Perception of the Watergate Affair," Personality and Social Psychology Bulletin, 1 (1974), 168-170.

2438 _____; _____; and Silber, Robert. "Interpersonal Trust and Attributions of Source Credibility: Evaluations of a Political Figure in a Crisis," Perceptual and Motor Skills, 44 (1977), 943-950.

2439 Yalch, R. F. "Pre-election Interview Effects on Voter Turnout," Public Opinion Quarterly, 40 (1976), 331-336.

2440 Yarnell, Steven M. "Explaining Congressional Campaign Behavior: An Information Processing Perspective" (Ph.D. dissertation, Ohio State University, 1978), Dissertation Abstracts International A, 39 (1978), 3121.

2441 Yiannakis, D. E. "House Members' Communication Styles: Determinants and Consequences" (Ph.D. dissertation, University of Rochester, 1980), Dissertation Abstracts International A, 41 (1980), 390.

2442 Yorke, Harvey; and Doherty, Liz. The Candidate's Handbook for Winning Local Elections. Novato, CA: Harvey Yorke, 1982.

2443 Young, H. P. "The Allocation of Funds in Lobbying and Campaigning," Behavioral Science, 23 (1978), 21-31.

2444 Zais, James P. "A Theory of Presidential Nominations," (Ph.D. dissertation, University of Illinois at Urbana-Champaign, 1976), Dissertation Abstracts International A, 37 (1977), 6734-6735.

2445 Zanna, Mark P.; et al. "Student Political Campaigners: Who Campaigns and What Effect Does It Have on Them?" Journal of Applied Social Psychology, 3 (1973), 371-384.

2446 _____; and del Vecchio, Steven M. "Perceived Credibility of Television News: A Matter of Viewer's Attitudes and the Position Taken by the Media," European Journal of Social Psychology, 3 (1973), 213-216.

2447 _____; and _____. "Viewer's Political Orientation and the Appropriateness of TV Newscaster Behavior," Journal of Social Psychology, 93 (1974), 311-312.

2448 _____; Klosson, Ellen C.; and Darley, John M. "How Television News Viewers Deal with Facts that Contradict Their Beliefs: A Consistency and Attribution Analysis," Journal of Applied Social Psychology, 6 (1976), 159-176.

2449 Zarefsky, David. "Subordinating the Civil Rights Issue: Lyndon Johnson in 1964," Southern Speech Communication Journal, 48 (1983), 103-118.

2450 Zashin, E.; and Chapman, P. C. "The Uses of Metaphor and Analogy: Toward a Renewal of Political Language," Journal of Politics, 36 (1974), 290-326.

2451 Zechmeister, K.; and Druckman, D. "Determinants of Resolving a Conflict of Interest: A Simulation of Political Decision-Making," Journal of Conflict Resolution, 17 (1973), 63-87.

2452 Zeidenstein, H. Direct Election of the President. Lexington, MA: Lexington Books, 1973.

2453 Zillman, Dolf; Bryant, Jennings; and Cantor, Joanne R. "Brutality of Assault in Political Cartoons Affecting Humor Appreciation," Journal of Research in Personality, 7 (1974), 334-345.

2454 Zimmer, Troy A. "The Impact of Watergate on the Public's Trust in People and Confidence in the Mass Media," Social Science Quarterly, 59 (1979), 743-751.

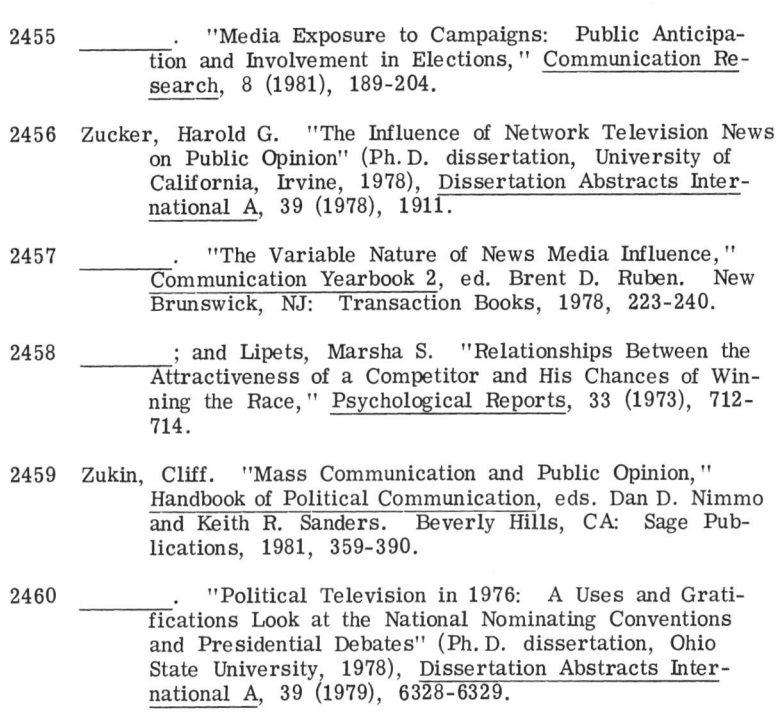

Bibliography

2455 _____. "Media Exposure to Campaigns: Public Anticipation and Involvement in Elections," Communication Research, 8 (1981), 189-204.

2456 Zucker, Harold G. "The Influence of Network Television News on Public Opinion" (Ph.D. dissertation, University of California, Irvine, 1978), Dissertation Abstracts International A, 39 (1978), 1911.

2457 _____. "The Variable Nature of News Media Influence," Communication Yearbook 2, ed. Brent D. Ruben. New Brunswick, NJ: Transaction Books, 1978, 223-240.

2458 _____; and Lipets, Marsha S. "Relationships Between the Attractiveness of a Competitor and His Chances of Winning the Race," Psychological Reports, 33 (1973), 712-714.

2459 Zukin, Cliff. "Mass Communication and Public Opinion," Handbook of Political Communication, eds. Dan D. Nimmo and Keith R. Sanders. Beverly Hills, CA: Sage Publications, 1981, 359-390.

2460 _____. "Political Television in 1976: A Uses and Gratifications Look at the National Nominating Conventions and Presidential Debates" (Ph.D. dissertation, Ohio State University, 1978), Dissertation Abstracts International A, 39 (1979), 6328-6329.

2461 _____. "A Reconsideration of the Effects of Information on Partisan Stability," Public Opinion Quarterly, 41 (1977), 244-254.

GUIDE TO THE LITERATURE

Bibliographies serve an important function, but sophisticated scholars realize that such works are no substitute for continuous efforts to stay abreast of new materials in any discipline. To that end, this section offers recommendations on the best sources of new developments in the field of political campaign communication.

Professional and Scholarly Journals

As was true when the first volume of this bibliography was published, the largest number of articles related to political science can be found in Journalism Quarterly (JQ) and Public Opinion Quarterly (POQ). POQ is published by the American Association for Public Opinion Research (AAPOR) and has a heavy survey research emphasis when covering political communication. JQ, on the other hand, reflects the interests of the Association for Education in Journalism in concentrating its articles on print and broadcast coverage of politics. Each issue of JQ also includes a regular bibliography of articles and books on mass communication.

Although most of the articles on political communication still appear in communication, broadcast, and journalism periodicals, the traditional political science journals have increased their recognition of the area's importance in such journals as the American Journal of Political Science, American Political Science Review, and Western Political Quarterly. The psychology, sociology, education, and business journals still offer useful insights but on a less frequent basis. Table 1 contains a rank-order listing of the journals which have contributed the most articles to this bibliography.

In the past ten years, several new journals have been founded. Foremost among those contributing to the political communication field is Communication Research, containing many high quality articles. American Politics Quarterly has proved a useful source of additional articles, and Presidential Studies Quarterly has provided helpful analyses of relationships between the press and the executive branch of government. The Political Communication Division of the International Communication Association began in 1975 to sponsor Political Communication Review (PCR).[1] PCR contains book reviews, review articles, bibliographic essays, and annotated bibliographies designed to keep political communication scholars informed of new developments.

Table 1

Major Professional and Scholarly Journals with Articles on Political Campaign Communication, 1973-1982.*

    Journalism Quarterly
    Public Opinion Quarterly
    American Journal of Political Science
    American Political Science Review
    Journal of Politics
    American Politics Quarterly
    Journal of Communication
    Communication Research
    Western Political Quarterly
    Presidential Studies Quarterly
    Central States Speech Journal
    Columbia Journalism Review
    Quarterly Journal of Speech
    Political Science Quarterly
    Journal of Broadcasting
    Communication Monographs
    Communication Quarterly
    Social Science Quarterly
    Southern Speech Communication Journal
    Annals of the American Academy of Political and Social Science
    Psychological Reports
    Political Communication Review
    Political Studies
    Washington Journalism Review
    Western Journal of Speech Communication

*These journals are listed in order of the number of articles in the bibliography. Only journals which produced 12 or more entries are listed.

Guide to the Literature

Of interest to scholars with practical campaign interests is Campaigns and Elections,[2] an excellent new journal which blends scholarly findings with observations by campaign professionals.

Books and Reports

The number of books devoted to the political communication area has increased three-fold, providing more than 650 entries in this volume, compared to the 196 entries in the volume covering 1950-1972. Most new-book entries can be obtained from Books in Print.

Another indispensable source for books is Communication Booknotes[3] (formerly Mass Media Booknotes), a monthly publication which reviews new books. The book review sections of major journals are also helpful, particularly those of Journal of Communication, American Political Science Review, and Political Communication Review. The "Book Notes" section of Washington Monthly is a good source of current popular books with relevance to political communication.

All political communication scholars should also be aware of the excellent Communication Yearbook series sponsored by the International Communication Association and published by Sage Publications (Box 5024, Beverly Hills, CA 90210). Each yearbook volume contains several political communication articles and essays. The new Political Communication Yearbook[4] series which commenced in 1984 is also an additional source of research articles.

Reports published by private associations and government agencies are difficult to track down. However, a few resources in this category are worth constant attention. The Monthly Catalogue of government documents continues to be the best source for locating materials published by the Government Printing Office. The National Association of Broadcasters publishes useful political broadcast media reports, such as the Political Broadcast Catechism.[5] An excellent reference service is provided by the Campaign Practices Report.[6] This reference service provides constant updates on campaign, broadcast, and finance regulations.

Unpublished Material

Unpublished material in political campaign communication falls into two major categories: (1) dissertations and theses and (2) convention papers. Dissertations are the least difficult to locate since Dissertation Abstracts International regularly includes abstracts of doctoral dissertations from most major universities. For a fee, University Microfilms[7] will conduct a key-word search of doctoral dissertations for researchers. Master's thesis information is less comprehensively collected, but the best sources are Masters Abstracts and Journalism Abstracts.

Papers presented at the conventions of professional and scholarly organizations are an excellent source of timely information on political communication, all the more valuable because such papers tend to preview the work which will eventually make its way into the scholarly journals. Unfortunately, no centralized location indexes all of these paper sources, and none are included in this volume.

Locating such works can be difficult and time-consuming. The associations which will yield the best return for the effort are the International Communication Association, the American Association for Public Opinion Research, the Speech Communication Association, the Association for Education in Journalism, the Southwest Social Science Association, the American Political Science Association, the Midwest Political Science Association, the Midwest Association for Public Opinion Research, and the other regional associations of the communication and political science disciplines. Acquisition of papers is obviously simplified by convention attendance, but one can usually obtain copies of convention programs and contact the authors for papers. The American Political Science Association publishes an advance copy of its fall convention program in the spring issue of its newsletter PS. Information on other convention dates and locations can usually be found in the newsletters of the relevant associations or by writing directly to the association.

Another source of convention paper citations is the Education Resources Information Service (ERIC).[8] The ERIC system stores abstracts of many documents including convention papers, speeches, and unpublished reports. Keyword searches are available through this computerized system.

Indexes and Abstracting Services

Despite the time-lag involved, indexes and abstracting services are essential in uncovering relevant political communication literature, especially in a field with such wide interdisciplinary boundaries. The traditional indexing systems noted in the introduction to this work continue to be important sources of bibliographic citations. Of greatest utility are the Social Science Index, Psychological Abstracts, and the Humanities Index. Between them, these three indexes cover the majority of the journals which publish political campaign communication articles. Beginning in 1978, Communication Abstracts[9] has provided a broad interdisciplinary coverage of the communication field, abstracting over 100 academic journals. Current Contents[10] publishes weekly listings of the Table of Contents from major journals. The Social and Behaviorial Sciences edition is the most useful for political communication scholars.

Guide to the Literature

However, the best indexes are seldom comprehensive, and all suffer from the limitations of their individual subject categorization systems. One partial solution to this problem may be the increased availability of computerized reference services which allow researchers to choose their own key words for search purposes or which provide citation searches. An outstanding guide to such data bases is Online Bibliographic Databases: A Directory and Sourcebook,[11] listing 200 different services and information on how to use them.

Two particularly worthwhile computerized data bases are DIALOG[12] and BRS/After Dark.[13] DIALOG includes over 175 data sets such as Books in Print, Congressional Information Service, Comprehensive Dissertation Index, Conference Papers Index, Congressional Record Abstracts, ERIC, PAIS International, Sociological Abstracts, and American Political Science Documents. The Bibliographic Retrieval Service offers BRS/After Dark as means of providing users access to the system in evening hours at reduced rates. This system contains numerous collections in the sociology, medical, education, and psychology fields, as well as the Social Science Citation Index. Initial hookup and user fees vary considerable among systems. Libraries often subscribe to such bases, and most can be accessed with any microcomputer which has a modem and a smart terminal program.

In conclusion, researchers can expect computerized data bases to make bibliographic updating in political campaign communication easier and more efficient. At the same time, researchers continue to have little access to non-print resources on political communication, although some suggestions for locating such materials can be found in the recent Handbook of Political Communication.[14]

Notes

1. Political Communication Review is currently available to members of the Political Communication Division of the International Communication Association (8140 Burnet Road, P. O. Box 9589, Austin, TX 78766). To purchase individual copies and sets of back issues contact: Lynda Lee Kaid, Editor; Political Communication Review; Department of Communication; University of Oklahoma; Norman, OK 73019.

2. Campaign and Elections, Suite 602, National Press Building, Washington, D. C. 20045.

3. To subscribe to Communication Booknotes, write: Professor Chris Sterling, Editor; Communication Booknotes; 4507 Airlie Way; Annandale, VA 22003 ($10 per year).

4. The Political Communication Yearbook series is being edited by

Dan Nimmo, Keith R. Sanders, and Lynda Lee Kaid; and is being published by the Southern Illinois University Press (Carbondale, Illinois, 62901).

5. National Association of Broadcasters; 1771 N Street, NW; Washington, D.C. 20036.

6. Congressional Quarterly, Inc.; 1414 22nd St., NW; Washington, D.C. 20037 ($324 per year).

7. University Microfilms, 313 North First St., Ann Arbor, MI 48106.

8. U.S. Office of Education; 400 Maryland Ave., NW; Washington, D.C. 20202. The Speech Communication Association (5105 Backlick Road, Suite E; Annandale, VA 22003) coordinates the speech communication module of ERIC.

9. Communication Abstracts in published by Sage Publications, Box 5024, Beverly Hills, CA 90210 (quarterly--$36 per year).

10. Current Contents, Institute for Scientific Information, 3501 Market St., University City Science Center, Philadelphia, PA 19104.

11. James L. Hall and Marjorie J. Brown. Online Bibliographic Databases: A Directory and Sourcebook. Detroit, MI: Gale Research, 1983 ($90).

12. DIALOG Information Resources, Inc., Marketing Department, 3460 Hillview Ave., Palo Alto, CA 94304 (800/227-1927).

13. BRS/After Dark, 1200 Rt. 7, Latham, NY 12110 (800/833-4707).

14. Lynda Lee Kaid. "Guide to the Literature," Handbook of Political Communication, eds. Dan D. Nimmo and Keith R. Sanders. Beverly Hills, CA: Sage Publications, 1981, 693-701.

INDEX

Advertising. See Political Advertising
Advertising Agencies. See Professional Campaign Consultants--Advertising Agencies
Agenda-Setting Function of the Mass Media 33, 110, 171, 172, 181, 208, 288, 427, 586, 688, 803, 811, 837, 1060, 1100, 1174, 1206, 1496, 1497, 1498, 1499, 1500, 1501, 1502, 1503, 1504, 1505, 1522, 1584, 1598, 1650, 1763, 2109, 2110, 2130, 2184, 2185, 2186, 2204, 2224, 2225, 2252, 2263, 2285, 2342, 2343, 2344, 2346, 2347, 2370, 2396, 2397, 2398, 2410, 2411
Aging, political aspects 1224, 1874, 2401
Agnew, Spiro 187, 311, 510, 522, 752, 777, 791, 792, 1869, 1870
Alabama 2219
Anderson, John 339, 578, 941
Apologia/Apologetic Discourse (see also Speeches/Speaking) 853, 968, 1194, 1285
Attitude Change (see also Cognitive Dissonance; Social Judgment) 1430, 1515, 1516, 1532, 1561, 1563, 1593, 1603, 1607, 1899, 1933, 1968, 2087, 2299, 2304, 2305, 2431
Authoritarianism and Politics 304, 305, 962, 963, 964, 1356, 1471, 2123, 2333

Baker, Howard 21, 1662
Balance/Balance Theories See Cognitive Dissonance; Selective Exposure
Ballots 263, 505, 805, 2257
Bandwagon Effect/Curve 411, 505, 2228
Bias. See Mass Media--Bias; Newspapers in/and Politics--Bias; Television in/and Politics--Bias
Bibliographies 307, 593, 650, 851, 882, 969, 1167, 1176, 1179, 2199
Blacks in/and Politics 11, 54, 191, 436, 656, 1078, 1380, 1381, 1401, 1416, 1672, 1735, 1800, 1845, 2112, 2258, 2259, 2434
Brady, Jim 2076
Broadcasting. See Mass Media; Political Broadcasting; Radio in/and Politics; Television in/and Politics
Brooke, Edward W. 980
Brown, Jerry 1328, 1329, 1387
Buttons. See Campaign Paraphernalia--Buttons

Cable TV. See Television in/and Politics--Cable TV
California 515, 1299, 1328, 1329, 1745, 1753, 1919, 2118
Campaign Expenditures 7, 9, 42, 477, 509, 528, 584, 835, 874, 934, 1113, 1116, 1137, 1145, 1666, 1743, 1745, 1753, 1919, 2118

Campaign Management. See Political Campaigns--Campaign Management; Professional Campaign Consultants--Campaign Management
Campaign Paraphernalia
  Buttons 739, 954
  Graphics 1813
  Literature 1595, 1596
  Posters 2326
  Printing 2433
Campaign Spending. See Campaign Expenditures; Finance
Campaigns. See Congressional Campaigns/Elections; Gubernatorial Campaigns/Elections; Political Campaigns; Presidential Campaigns; State and Local Campaigns/Elections
Candidates. See Political Candidates; names of particular candidates
Canvassing (see also Local and Precinct Level Campaigning) 31, 116, 125, 155, 609, 1192, 1462, 1595, 1858
Carter, James (see also Debates--Carter-Ford; Debates--Carter-Reagan) 56, 339, 367, 378, 400, 587, 588, 689, 823, 824, 949, 979, 1140, 1177, 1206, 1282, 1334, 1372, 1389, 1602, 1728, 1789, 1887, 2071, 2230, 2234, 2430
Cartoons, political 278, 323, 591, 749, 906, 993, 1218, 1551, 1857, 1939, 1453
Challengers. See Political Candidates--Challengers
Chandler, Albert B. 1937
Channels of Communication (see also particular channels--Radio; Television, Newspapers, etc.) 1511
Charisma (see also Image) 282, 306, 378, 848
Chronopolitics 1258
Clement, Frank 295, 296
Coalitions, political 622, 766, 914, 1033, 2010
Coattails, political 1118, 1283, 1621
Cognition, Cognitive See Political Cognitions/Knowledge; Information
Cognitive Dissonance (see also Selective Exposure) 112, 522, 573, 758, 898, 1240, 1411, 1603, 2187
Communication, political aspects
  General 93, 94, 147, 254, 289, 342, 435, 439, 446, 466, 483, 514, 636, 655, 712, 768, 770, 826, 950, 977, 1013, 1014, 1059, 1061, 1161, 1171, 1454, 1541, 1565, 1617, 1686, 1688, 1807, 1918, 1938, 2057, 2097, 2157, 2290, 2363
  Interpersonal 308, 340, 392, 425, 609, 734, 768, 819, 946, 1015, 1108, 1165, 1398, 1715, 1716, 1739, 1940, 1986, 2208, 2340, 2421
  Mass Communication 264, 369, 383, 391, 405, 423, 561, 573, 574, 585, 592, 658, 659, 768, 972, 1108, 1687, 1717, 1934, 2459
  Research and Theory 221, 258, 333, 334, 335, 336, 337, 338, 415, 417, 523, 546, 552, 612, 643, 810, 918, 935, 957, 972, 1038, 1046, 1110, 1197, 1207, 1311, 1316, 1449, 1465, 1515, 1536, 1594, 1685, 1687, 1688, 1689, 1692, 1693, 1699, 1700, 1701, 1720, 1775, 2007, 2039, 2048, 2102, 2158, 2248, 2293, 2329, 2345
Computers (see also Technology) 556
Congress 36, 92, 128, 242, 243, 351, 374, 458, 724, 760, 815, 816, 923, 929, 1023, 1085, 1106, 1183, 1202, 1246, 1269,

Index 205

1286, 1289, 1463, 1484, 1598, 1599, 1600, 1634, 1767, 1769, 1773, 1792, 1829, 1904, 1916, 1954, 1957, 1959, 2218, 2239, 2240, 2282, 2348, 2349, 2441
Congressional Campaigns/Elections (see also Incumbency) 6, 40, 77, 107, 110, 191, 354, 375, 433, 455, 501, 509, 519, 575, 583, 669, 670, 698, 702, 709, 742, 854, 961, 1008, 1030, 1031, 1032, 1034, 1086, 1099, 1113, 1115, 1116, 1118, 1119, 1129, 1136, 1210, 1228, 1238, 1312, 1338, 1342, 1385, 1425, 1426, 1439, 1443, 1444, 1445, 1446, 1484, 1510, 1523, 1533, 1596, 1670, 1703, 1715, 1729, 1766, 1768, 1822, 1875, 1876, 1933, 1963, 2093, 2096, 2106, 2108, 2424, 2440
Conkling, Roscoe 1057
Constituents/Constituency 458, 519, 1012, 1023, 1106, 1202, 1286
Constructivist Approach 2244, 2247
Conventions (see also Nominating Process; Presidential Campaigns--Nominations)
  General 149, 370, 567, 713, 1096, 1121, 1287, 1386, 1388, 1705, 1930, 2166, 2195, 2279, 2302, 2303, 2425, 2426, 2460
  Newspaper Coverage 75, 346, 2059
  Television Coverage 346, 711, 1236, 1755, 2059, 2974, 3020
Credibility. See Mass Media--Credibility
Cynicism. See Political Alienation, Political Trust, Political Efficacy

Daley, Richard J. 75, 1878
Debates
  General 1, 5, 50, 183, 184, 214, 228, 229, 232, 290, 402, 412, 418, 562, 563, 581, 600, 648, 831, 832, 893, 938, 947, 985, 996, 1005, 1111, 1112, 1187, 1278, 1326, 1361, 1544, 1546, 1816, 1883, 1926, 2020, 2300, 2321, 2460
  Carter-Ford 1, 5, 14, 168, 184, 237, 290, 347, 348, 540, 562, 570, 581, 600, 707, 803, 813, 895, 920, 947, 965, 985, 1160, 1272, 1304, 1305, 1306, 1402, 1526, 1528, 1542, 1543, 1570, 1586, 1587, 1628, 1643, 1722, 1892, 1941, 2087, 2152
  Carter-Reagan 214, 1926, 2171, 2173, 2203, 2252, 2283
  Humphrey-McGovern 775, 1529
  Kennedy-Nixon 1, 1273, 1542, 1543
Decision Making 262, 368, 421, 562, 658, 659, 820, 2191, 2451
Diffusion, of political information 235, 413, 1995, 2047, 2079, 2208
Direct Mail 519, 1596, 1963
Dirty Politics 721, 2216
Docudramas 1043, 1181
Documentaries 1951
Dogmatism and Politics 649, 1147, 1357, 2313
Drama--Dramatization, in politics (see also Fantasy) 198, 204, 480, 481, 484, 2333
Drinan, Rev. Robert F. 1312

Eagleton, Thomas 58, 276, 434, 666, 1037, 1281, 1411, 1739, 1788
Economic Variables, in political campaigns 77, 725, 1268, 1560, 1614
Editorials. See Newspapers in/and Politics--Editorials

Efficacy. See Political Efficacy
Eisenhower, Dwight D. 916
Election Eve Reporting. See Predictions
Election Forecasting. See Predictions; Polling/Polls
Elections (see also Congressional Campaigns/Elections; Gubernatorial Campaigns/Elections; Presidential Campaigns/Elections; State and Local Campaigns/Elections) 190, 238, 463, 841, 842, 927, 1001, 1218, 1257, 1327, 1479, 1601, 1637, 1638, 1673, 1720, 1748, 1765, 1822, 1873, 1908
Electoral Behavior. See Voter Behavior
Electoral College 219, 2264
Entertainers, in politics 111
Ervin, Samuel 2306
Esch, Marvin Lionel 698
Evers, Charles 78

Fairness Doctrine (see also Regulation) 366, 788, 1805, 2046, 2149
Family, in political campaigning 1216, 1217
Fantasy, in politics 276, 277, 278, 523, 524, 997, 1351, 1613, 1694, 1695, 1848
Film in/and Politics 111, 451, 673, 1627, 1680, 1812, 2044
Finance (see also Campaign Expenditures) 8, 17, 18, 19, 42, 43, 44, 45, 46, 47, 51, 73, 192, 216, 433, 515, 536, 539, 575, 646, 676, 822, 846, 858, 859, 1020, 1022, 1041, 1117, 1149, 1245, 1349, 1407, 1431, 1432, 1482, 1483, 1510, 1580, 1743, 1745, 1810, 1864, 2005, 2024, 2066, 2132, 2144, 2198, 2275, 2318, 2413, 2443
First Amendment/Free Speech 788, 1772, 2133
Florida 715, 1344, 1346, 1831, 1832
Ford, Gerald (see also Debates--Carter-Ford) 79, 647, 796, 1206, 1413, 1728, 2162, 2203, 2419
Foreign Policy/Affairs, in politics 524, 1225, 1317, 1506, 1625, 1626, 1656, 1659, 1660, 1661, 1833, 2227

Gallup Poll 807, 808, 809
Georgia 998
Gergen, Dave 700
Ghostwriting. See Speechwriting
Godwin, Mills, Jr. 896
Goldwater, Barry M. 1849
Government and the Media 128, 129, 185, 196, 242, 243, 244, 256, 269, 601, 602, 844, 1260, 1464, 1697, 1804, 1927, 1928, 1929, 2099, 2393
Grasso, Ella T. 2372
Groups, political influence; in decision making 363, 883, 1250, 1300, 2127, 2325, 2335
Gubernatorial Campaigns/Elections 44, 143, 211, 299, 571, 668, 847, 1186, 1823, 2029, 2096, 2311, 2377

Hawaii 470
Heckling 166, 195, 974, 1808, 2147, 2163, 2331
Horserace Journalism 320, 402, 924, 2130

Humor, in politics 1075, 1851, 2077, 2453
Humphrey, Hubert H. (see also Debates--Humphrey-McGovern) 474, 1895

Ideology, political 91, 124, 127, 1018, 1680, 1817, 1950, 1964, 2122, 2209, 2237, 2313, 2422
Illinois 375, 1182, 1712, 1878
Images, political (see also Political Candidates--Images) 70, 160, 344, 401, 1017, 1054, 1186, 1214, 1251, 1252, 1264, 1282, 1330, 1419, 1450, 1454, 1470, 1564, 1575, 1635, 1680, 1690, 1691, 1695, 1696, 1702, 1703, 1726, 1785, 1786, 1816, 1852, 1855, 1872, 1921, 1952, 2152, 2200, 2320, 2372, 2437, 2438
Impeachment 603
Inaugurals 113, 277, 298, 437, 441, 442, 577, 735, 736, 1024, 1282, 1549, 1550
Incumbency 6, 885, 1115, 1129, 1210, 1396, 1604, 1605, 1670, 1828, 1853, 1876, 2096
Indiana 1008, 2108
Information
   General (Political) 280, 564, 565, 652, 653, 811, 812, 873, 1035, 1070, 1150, 1538, 1561, 1579, 1664, 1671, 2191, 2246, 2250, 2288, 2461
   Access to and Availability of 376, 517, 1034, 1035, 1664, 2338, 2414
   Processing 438, 733, 753, 922, 1356
   Seeking/Usage 96, 177, 424, 472, 1511, 1651, 1854, 2287, 2421
   Sources 108, 109, 1843, 1913, 2394, 2461
Instant Analysis 293, 1005, 1180, 1758, 1948
Interest Groups (see also Lobbying) 461, 705, 1393, 1428, 1431, 1432, 1730, 1904, 2113
Interpersonal Communication. See Communication, political aspects-- Interpersonal
Interviewing, in politics 1280
Iranian Hostage Crisis 59, 277
Issue Voting 171, 321, 380, 397, 871, 872, 1148, 1339, 1557, 1566, 1806
Issues, political 396, 579, 1148, 1244, 1251, 1357, 1539, 1575, 1583, 1588, 1726, 1734, 1787, 1809, 1871, 1872, 2053, 2125, 2159, 2227, 2299, 2344

Jefferson, Thomas 298
Johnson, Lyndon B. 318, 440, 508, 750, 793, 921, 1131, 1319, 1378, 1591, 2056, 2141, 2193, 2449
Jordan, Barbara 2279
Journalism. See News, Newspapers; Television News

Kennedy, Edward 361, 367, 450, 604, 823
Kennedy, John F. (see also Debates--Kennedy-Nixon) 216, 535, 720, 750, 1075, 1203, 1216, 1222, 1225, 1606, 1714, 1737, 1738, 1740, 2045, 2168
Kennedy, Robert F. 1337, 2037
Kentucky, 1906
Kissinger, Henry 479

Knowledge Gap 628, 696, 825

Lambert, Louis 1186
Lance, Bert 830
Language, in politics (see also Metaphor; political, mass media)
  248, 511, 657, 889, 894, 1074, 1132, 1636, 1734, 1888, 2063,
  2161, 2289, 2378, 2400, 2450
Law. See Regulation
Leaders/Leadership 306, 316, 362, 763, 915, 941, 1000, 1191,
  1240, 1751, 2223, 2296, 2325, 2334, 2389
Legitimacy/Legitimation 422, 595, 645, 713, 848
Literature, political (see also Campaign Paraphernalia--Literature)
  337, 1146, 1161, 1517
Lobbying (see also Interest Groups) 36, 92, 533, 1428, 2443
Local Campaigns/Elections. See State and Local Campaigns/Elections
Local and Precinct Level Campaigning 121, 280, 281, 332, 503,
  616, 626, 1071, 1072, 1087, 1192

Machiavellianism. See Personality Variables
Magazines 667, 703, 704, 716, 777, 1421, 1923, 2348
Malaise. See Political Alienation, Political Efficacy, Political Trust
Marginals/Marginality. See Political Competition
Marketing, in politics 1267
Mass Communication. See Communication, political aspects--Mass
  Communication; Mass Media
Mass Media (see also Magazines; Newspapers in/and Politics; Radio
  in/and Politics; Television in/and Politics)
  General 2, 35, 41, 60, 85, 106, 138, 179, 209, 239, 253, 269,
    327, 404, 416, 451, 462, 476, 537, 622, 671, 677, 678,
    683, 684, 697, 714, 717, 731, 753, 755, 768, 788, 795,
    812, 817, 827, 856, 864, 887, 951, 952, 955, 958, 959,
    991, 1073, 1080, 1089, 1183, 1195, 1253, 1254, 1255, 1268,
    1274, 1275, 1276, 1277, 1310, 1358, 1365, 1447, 1466,
    1475, 1508, 1547, 1553, 1555, 1558, 1561, 1562, 1587,
    1599, 1600, 1687, 1688, 1690, 1697, 1698, 1717, 1721,
    1723, 1746, 1756, 1759, 1761, 1762, 1774, 1777, 1790,
    1804, 1811, 1814, 1833, 1834, 1848, 1850, 1898, 1901,
    1913, 1942, 1943, 1971, 1972, 1977, 1978, 1979, 1980,
    1992, 2014, 2015, 2016, 2032, 2038, 2049, 2061, 2072,
    2090, 2092, 2098, 2099, 2121, 2127, 2129, 2147, 2182,
    2195, 2200, 2231, 2258, 2259, 2267, 2281, 2284, 2286,
    2287, 2297, 2298, 2322, 2337, 2354, 2359, 2394, 2399,
    2400, 2402, 2431, 2432, 2457
  Bias 682, 685, 1045, 1047, 1048, 1049, 1088, 1901, 2212, 2215,
    2354, 2399
  Coverage 59, 118, 119, 164, 193, 249, 346, 385, 416, 455, 486,
    520, 541, 578, 613, 667, 701, 800, 830, 877, 888, 910, 913,
    924, 1047, 1048, 1172, 1281, 1328, 1329, 1439, 1537, 1539,
    1558, 1625, 1626, 1630, 1761, 1798, 1859, 2021, 2135, 2136,
    2222, 2227, 2253, 2278, 2376, 2415
  Credibility 660, 1641, 1642, 1897, 2454
  Exposure 64, 101, 181, 331, 430, 471, 502, 628, 1109, 1237,
    1335, 1503, 1592, 1718, 1862, 1896, 2259, 2455

Impact of 72, 97, 126, 186, 340, 373, 385, 414, 415, 448, 457, 473, 706, 1196, 1341, 1347, 1362, 1707, 1708, 1709, 2459
Use 53, 90, 178, 182, 261, 421, 426, 445, 500, 623, 719, 1063, 1867, 1868, 1932, 1995, 2060, 2094, 2260, 2261, 2350, 2379, 2383, 2403
Massachusetts 980
McCarthy, Eugene 626, 1042, 2037
McCarthy, Joe--McCarthyism 165, 905
McGovern, George (see also Debates--Humphrey-McGovern) 52, 609, 632, 909, 975, 1053, 1093, 1364, 1513, 1514, 1548, 1552, 1564, 1739, 1922, 2000, 2095, 2294, 2355, 2409, 2420
Message Evaluation 294, 340, 518, 2431
Metaphor; political, mass media 1547, 1590, 2450
Michigan 982, 1141, 1206, 2100, 2265
Minorities in/and Politics (see also Blacks in/and Politics; Women in/and Politics) 162, 667, 714, 1359, 2016, 2258
Mississippi 373
Missouri 1095
Moss, Geoffrey 1632
Movements, Political 2151, 2153
Muckrakers 639, 731
Mudslinging (see also Dirty Politics) 2216, 2265
Music, preferences and politics 1473
Muskie, Edmund 148, 836
Myth--Mythmaking, in politics 159, 199, 482, 866, 1691, 1695, 1964, 2027, 2150, 2174

Name Identification/Familiarity. See Political Candidates--Recognition
Nevada 1266, 2222, 2363
New Hampshire 1042, 1961, 2309, 2397
New Jersey 2311
New Politics. See Politics--New
New York 1057
News 2, 22, 57, 58, 80, 95, 141, 187, 239, 331, 342, 368, 448, 469, 476, 478, 542, 639, 661, 685, 686, 746, 760, 814, 825, 930, 937, 1011, 1082, 1088, 1198, 1336, 1359, 1371, 1415, 1494, 1598, 1599, 1600, 1694, 1697, 1698, 1791, 1833, 1897, 2001, 2098, 2099, 2112, 2212, 2298, 2457
News Conferences 188, 479, 508, 783, 1131, 1222, 1301, 1437, 1440, 1669, 1706, 1733, 1734, 1740, 1993
Newspapers in/and Politics
  General 115, 142, 279, 420, 456, 521, 647, 661, 764, 878, 986, 1468, 1500, 1503, 1623, 1736, 1903, 1945, 2186, 2204, 2210, 2345
  Bias 2098
  Campaign and Election Coverage 1, 78, 191, 299, 317, 703, 704, 715, 791, 1026, 1429, 1469, 1491, 1492, 1493, 1494, 1512, 1585, 1922, 1966, 2025, 2100, 2309, 2392, 2404, 2405, 2406, 2407, 2408
  Editorials 493, 506, 692, 794, 804, 953, 1056, 1095, 1263, 1266, 1318, 1474, 1490, 1491, 1657, 1658, 1659, 1660, 1661, 1826, 2052, 2183, 2202, 2309, 2317, 2390, 2391
  Information Source 22, 123, 357, 891, 1592, 1593

Nixon, Richard M. (see also Debates--Kennedy-Nixon) 4, 115, 136, 160, 188, 205, 245, 318, 431, 440, 447, 493, 545, 603, 665, 750, 752, 833, 866, 909, 936, 952, 960, 968, 976, 999, 1024, 1053, 1102, 1120, 1194, 1203, 1253, 1256, 1259, 1298, 1318, 1364, 1375, 1397, 1400, 1485, 1564, 1635, 1669, 1706, 1731, 1793, 1850, 1889, 1890, 1894, 1895, 1898, 1994, 2129, 2190, 2276, 2284, 2373, 2381, 2382, 2401, 2417
Nominating Process (see also Conventions; Presidential Campaigns--Nomination) 38, 39, 194, 223, 346, 567, 635, 759, 849, 1033, 1457, 1530, 1839
North Dakota 961

Ohio 703, 1083, 1084, 1512, 1742, 2404, 2405, 2406, 2407
Opinion Leaders 64, 240, 878, 991, 1354
Orben, Robert 432

Party Affiliation. See Political Party
Personality Variables, in political behavior 1262, 1380, 1569, 1705, 1801, 1895, 1911, 1965, 2180, 2211, 2273, 2296, 2320, 2385, 2437, 2438
Persuasion 98, 1313, 1515, 1516, 1899, 1918, 2088
Petitions/Petition Signing 223, 819
Photographs 23
Pinkney, Arnold 1084
Political Activity. See Political Participation
Political Advertising 95, 100, 104, 158, 206, 245, 247, 285, 286, 287, 288, 294, 364, 482, 605, 606, 607, 610, 629, 630, 631, 668, 730, 757, 852, 874, 945, 992, 1053, 1081, 1132, 1137, 1151, 1152, 1154, 1162, 1163, 1164, 1168, 1169, 1178, 1186, 1315, 1331, 1412, 1413, 1487, 1495, 1519, 1540, 1545, 1562, 1574, 1640, 1649, 1726, 1781, 1782, 1783, 1784, 2006, 2008, 2009, 2083, 2084, 2085, 2117, 2131, 2192, 2241, 2242, 2250, 2256, 2301, 2328
Political Agendas 465, 467
Political Alienation 319, 525, 839, 981, 1065, 1181, 1380, 1381, 1382, 1383, 1648, 1718, 2080, 2178, 2209, 2435
Political Ambition 1396, 1916
Political Attitudes (see also Political Alienation; Political Efficacy; Political Involvement/Interest; Political Trust) 15, 84, 87, 114, 147, 226, 230, 234, 315, 321, 377, 380, 395, 543, 548, 553, 571, 917, 1004, 1007, 1029, 1159, 1210, 1220, 1238, 1241, 1291, 1292, 1293, 1366, 1438, 1452, 1453, 1473, 1508, 1518, 1656, 1683, 1903, 1915, 1920, 2038, 2081, 2142, 2148, 2178, 2207, 2238, 2305, 2316, 2387
Political Authority 84, 87, 142, 145, 189, 306, 1801
Political Behavior (see also Voting Behavior) 124, 267, 291, 468, 475, 527, 642, 751, 851, 1091
Political Beliefs (see also Political Attitudes; Political Cognitions) 53, 72, 74, 82, 112, 145, 226, 324, 331, 571, 596, 769, 917, 942, 1028, 1036, 1094, 1104, 1126, 1155, 1240, 2159, 2220
Political Broadcasting (see also Radio in/and Politics; Television in/and Politics) 9, 90, 152, 153, 154, 254, 259, 283, 325, 366, 406, 787, 1114, 1234, 1392, 1609, 1633, 1668

Index

Political Campaigns
  General 98, 167, 268, 450, 460, 752, 780, 987, 998, 1062, 1066, 1209, 1384, 1424, 1433, 1531, 1582, 1611, 1717, 1750, 1835, 1976, 2049, 2121, 2154, 2351, 2412, 2415, 2416, 2418, 2420, 2445
  Management 34, 35, 83, 86, 105, 162, 516, 1208, 1209, 1363, 1404, 1424, 1448, 1481, 1611, 1618, 1619, 1917, 2069, 2154, 2176, 2205, 2206, 2351, 2353
Political Candidates (see also Blacks in/and Politics--Candidates; Women in/and Politics--Candidates)
  General 167, 313, 617, 858, 1133, 1213, 1235, 1251, 1330, 1369, 1443, 1567, 1731, 2075, 2097, 2337, 2352, 2418
  Challengers 1032, 2159
  Characteristics 24, 207, 681, 724, 867, 1252, 1786, 2018, 2458
  Evaluations of 65, 68, 177, 207, 313, 319, 548, 560, 854, 1190, 1320, 1480, 1488, 2126, 2235, 2304
  Images/Perceptions of (see also Images) 3, 290, 354, 367, 388, 494, 495, 547, 564, 823, 824, 994, 995, 1141, 1143, 1144, 1175, 1177, 1241, 1320, 1487, 1691, 1702, 1703, 1713, 1784, 1785, 1786, 1787, 1921, 2041, 2125
  Issue Position 68, 496, 564, 899
  Recognition 6, 854, 876, 1168, 1766, 1821, 1876, 2054, 2055
  Selection/Preference 304, 305, 454, 582, 653, 871, 2179, 2313
Political Change 81
Political Cognitions/Knowledge (see also Political Learning; Agenda-Setting) 101, 116, 180, 229, 426, 502, 507, 555, 677, 748, 1157, 1221, 1224, 1237, 1238, 1410, 1503, 1505, 1579, 1590, 1612, 1761, 1762, 1809, 1951, 1968, 2060, 2081, 2148, 2259, 2316
Political Competence 13, 719
Political Competition 528, 589, 681, 1099, 1142
Political Consultants. See Professional Campaign Consultants; Political Campaigns--Management
Political Corruption (see also Watergate) 435, 797, 926, 1616, 1732, 1803, 2022
Political Efficacy 11, 55, 74, 526, 756, 1534, 1592, 1911, 2033, 2261, 2361, 2379, 2436
Political Information. See Information; Political Cognitions/Knowledge
Political Institutions 380
Political Involvement/Interest 82, 169, 393, 550, 557, 767, 970, 1078, 1109, 1211, 1430, 1794, 2006, 2009, 2053, 2254, 2455
Political Knowledge. See Information; Political Cognitions/Knowledge
Political Learning (see also Political Cognitions/Knowledge; Political Socialization) 120, 229, 537, 888, 948, 1761, 2362
Political Life 198, 353, 408, 1369
Political Linkage 1615, 1624
Political Lying 1323
Political Machine 1288
Political Participation 54, 74, 82, 88, 91, 117, 170, 326, 425, 467, 501, 555, 756, 862, 1124, 1125, 1126, 1204, 1219, 1322, 1325, 1340, 1357, 1358, 1455, 1526, 1581, 1592, 1645, 1646, 1647, 1648, 1653, 1815, 1896, 1965, 1983, 1988, 2027, 2033, 2051, 2077, 2154, 2175, 2199, 2261, 2263, 2272, 2322, 2332

Political Party 10, 190, 486, 505, 536, 538, 539, 589, 675, 676, 677, 741, 742, 822, 861, 881, 970, 982, 1067, 1072, 1185, 1192, 1201, 1294, 1296, 1330, 1331, 1342, 1368, 1403, 1410, 1414, 1423, 1455, 1458, 1482, 1556, 1567, 1620, 1785, 1794, 1814, 1817, 1818, 1819, 1820, 1828, 1834, 2065, 2068, 2106, 2117, 2186, 2337, 2461
Political Power (see also Presidential--Power) 189, 316, 579, 869, 1019
Political Psychology (see also Authoritarianism and Politics; Dogmatism and Politics) 3, 273, 274, 367, 388, 389, 390, 454, 546, 548, 572, 587, 588, 761, 763, 778, 867, 907, 908, 935, 971, 979, 1000, 1016, 1076, 1091, 1092, 1104, 1133, 1261, 1262, 1516, 1636, 1667, 2091, 2226
Political Rhetoric. See Rhetoric, political
Political Rallies 1175, 2040, 2041
Political Socialization 10, 11, 32, 93, 94, 102, 103, 126, 180, 307, 324, 329, 395, 414, 423, 500, 504, 543, 553, 561, 576, 593, 594, 596, 600, 723, 756, 768, 984, 1078, 1108, 1125, 1126, 1134, 1146, 1220, 1275, 1418, 1456, 1538, 1656, 1735, 1846, 1900, 1909, 1910, 1935, 1936, 1989, 2012, 2013, 2035, 2086, 2116, 2171, 2268, 2280, 2295
Political Sociology 201, 213, 393, 818, 928, 1103, 1104
Political Speaking. See Speeches/Speaking, political
Political Support. See Political Participation
Political Trust 11, 13, 37, 74, 526, 767, 1204, 1585, 2142, 2366, 2437, 2454
Political Values. See Political Attitudes
Politicians 66, 140, 157, 182, 340, 352, 353, 761, 763, 1040, 1223, 1323, 1571, 1791, 2004, 2150
Politics
  General 201, 271, 302, 328, 400, 857, 989
  New 470, 569
  Practical. See Professional Campaign Consultants
  State and Local. See State and Local Campaigns/Elections
Polling/Polls (see also Gallup Poll; Predictions) 35, 61, 62, 150, 151, 194, 246, 320, 372, 381, 382, 411, 534, 544, 580, 582, 583, 694, 695, 722, 727, 728, 771, 807, 808, 809, 863, 864, 1098, 1158, 1291, 1292, 1293, 1295, 1303, 1307, 1308, 1367, 1370, 1399, 1572, 1573, 1610, 1759, 1771, 1924, 1941, 1946, 1967, 1969, 1973, 1974, 1975, 2043, 2269, 2270, 2356, 2358, 2364, 2375, 2390, 2392
Positivity Bias, of political figures (see also Political Socialization) 1320, 1321, 1418, 1970, 2087, 2236
Posters. See Campaign Paraphernalia--Posters
Powell, Jody 699
Predictions
  General 322, 580, 582, 1998, 2105, 2324
  Election Eve Reports 266, 330, 687, 1905
Presidency
  General 309, 349, 410, 572, 598, 619, 798, 890, 915, 939, 989, 1004, 1006, 1009, 1039, 1077, 1135, 1155, 1184, 1212, 1229, 1232, 1242, 1243, 1247, 1301, 1376, 1397, 1559, 1629, 1676, 1677, 1678, 1711, 1767, 1997, 2062, 2101, 2429

Index

and the Press 128, 129, 270, 275, 440, 478, 512, 662, 699, 789, 930, 931, 932, 933, 973, 999, 1011, 1055, 1183, 1225, 1302, 1319, 1372, 1373, 1374, 1476, 1555, 1604, 1605, 1733, 1756, 1757, 1758, 1776, 1825, 1830, 1856, 1869, 1902, 1908, 1993, 2014, 2017, 2026, 2031, 2103, 2134, 2162, 2169, 2190, 2191, 2194, 2196, 2197, 2277, 2330, 2380

Presidential--
Character 137, 197, 216, 398, 475, 971, 1866, 1997
Image (see also Images; Political Candidates--Images) 129, 216, 358, 394, 637, 745, 1203, 2307, 2308, 2334
Performance 355, 797, 1284, 2011, 2193
Popularity 176, 318, 951, 952, 1226, 1227, 1228, 1360, 1440, 1614, 1822, 1863, 2137, 2138, 2139, 2140, 2143, 2156, 2168, 2221, 2233, 2327
Power 485, 513, 838, 966, 967, 988, 1044, 1442, 1597, 1644, 1676, 1677, 1732, 1757, 1890, 2101, 2103, 2145, 2156, 2232, 2412

Presidential Campaigns/Elections
General 12, 40, 62, 71, 79, 85, 88, 89, 122, 133, 134, 135, 138, 179, 197, 250, 300, 301, 310, 370, 379, 409, 444, 779, 891, 902, 903, 925, 1010, 1230, 1231, 1233, 1283, 1284, 1332, 1339, 1343, 1348, 1350, 1463, 1477, 1486, 1507, 1532, 1560, 1617, 1711, 1744, 1747, 1749, 1774, 1776, 1777, 1794, 1835, 1836, 1837, 1840, 1841, 1880, 1985, 2003, 2019, 2021, 2064, 2075, 2090, 2151, 2172, 2209, 2264, 2323, 2336, 2339, 2341, 2356, 2357, 2422, 2424, 2434, 2452
1952 Election 241, 554
1960 Election 193, 771, 1075, 1182
1964 Election 692, 771, 790, 1026
1968 Election 195, 611, 626, 708, 732, 771, 781, 892, 1026, 1120, 1375, 1408, 1895, 2403, 2434
1972 Election 148, 241, 286, 308, 364, 380, 580, 624, 627, 703, 704, 849, 885, 901, 909, 964, 1026, 1045, 1047, 1048, 1072, 1120, 1296, 1335, 1512, 1537, 1539, 1562, 1564, 1566, 1567, 1588, 1603, 1608, 1651, 1798, 1877, 2100, 2124, 2220, 2356
1976 Election 112, 146, 186, 222, 278, 304, 313, 320, 346, 421, 422, 429, 438, 497, 595, 858, 859, 900, 948, 1140, 1144, 1206, 1207, 1237, 1430, 1619, 1736, 1842, 1966, 2111, 2219, 2384
1980 Election 304, 313, 317, 339, 401, 604, 634, 641, 725, 829, 913, 962, 1143, 1170, 1290, 1452, 1589, 1618, 1838, 1880
Nomination (see also Conventions; Nominating Process) 1399, 1478, 1839, 1881, 1882, 1884, 1956, 2444
Press Conferences. See News Conferences
Press Releases 107, 806, 1166, 2311, 2312
Press Secretaries 358, 1319, 1377, 1555, 2076, 2103, 2104, 2196, 2197, 2330
Primary Elections 116, 148, 179, 222, 535, 568, 871, 872, 934, 944, 1051, 1096, 1221, 1333, 1337, 1343, 1349, 1391, 1399, 1457, 1459, 1512, 1530, 1596, 1608, 1620, 1655, 1710, 1729, 1795, 1824, 1919, 1923, 1955, 1956, 1961, 1966, 2037, 2397
Professional Campaign Consultants
General/Organizational 251, 252, 314, 449, 638, 701, 802, 911, 912, 940, 1066, 1363, 1575, 2023, 2030, 2084, 2027, 2442

Advertising Agencies 610, 2085
Campaign Management (see also Political Campaigns--Management) 428, 1003, 1017, 1127, 1481, 1917, 1991, 2069, 2135, 2136, 2205, 2206
Media Consultants 821, 1377, 1448, 1690, 2030
Propaganda 156, 241, 265, 674, 1331, 1610, 1898, 2129, 2311
Public Affairs 25, 178, 233, 331, 1220, 1951
Public Opinion 61, 62, 200, 202, 220, 224, 246, 291, 387, 443, 499, 513, 529, 534, 691, 694, 695, 705, 729, 771, 799, 850, 860, 886, 991, 1058, 1097, 1105, 1297, 1298, 1305, 1340, 1341, 1405, 1406, 1440, 1472, 1533, 1539, 1610, 1688, 1704, 1707, 1708, 1709, 1819, 1827, 2119, 2231, 2281, 2305, 2307, 2308, 2356, 2358, 2364, 2375, 2387, 2389, 2456, 2459
Public Policy 224, 244, 466, 651, 728, 841, 1139, 1873, 1938, 2188, 2231
Public Relations 241, 250, 801, 1914, 2197
Public Television 103, 132, 754, 1832

Q-Methodology 333, 334, 335, 337, 338, 339, 401, 1454, 1886

Radio and/in Politics 2107
Rationality, in voting behavior 9, 212, 232, 319, 396, 790, 1193, 1408, 1409, 1622, 1747, 1915
Reagan, Ronald (see also Debates--Carter-Reagan) 298, 339, 350, 442, 634, 745, 824, 1055, 2167, 2341
Reasoning, political 1210, 2310, 2313
Recruitment 390, 2353
Referendum 2119
Reform
  General 1815
  Broadcast 257, 303, 325
  Campaign/Election 42, 45, 48, 49, 776, 840, 1041, 1117, 1349, 1805, 1864, 2005, 2323, 2413
Regulation (see also Finance; Reform)
  Broadcast 325, 366, 788, 843, 1271, 1529, 1668, 2046, 2067, 2107
  Campaign/Election 8, 16, 49, 161, 283, 325, 487, 788, 875, 1025, 1145, 1489, 1615, 1810
Religion and Politics 1589, 1847
Representation. See Political Accountability
Research and Theory. See Communication, political aspects--Research and Theory
Responsiveness. See Political Accountability
Rhetoric, political (see also Language in Politics; Speeches, political; Rhetorical Strategies) 56, 115, 127, 148, 159, 203, 216, 236, 295, 298, 398, 410, 447, 452, 453, 508, 510, 511, 524, 535, 644, 665, 689, 690, 693, 708, 735, 736, 743, 744, 745, 750, 762, 793, 796, 833, 865, 896, 904, 919, 921, 926, 949, 961, 974, 976, 978, 1008, 1027, 1057, 1093, 1102, 1122, 1136, 1256, 1548, 1549, 1550, 1551, 1662, 1737, 1738, 1749, 1760, 1789, 1847, 1849, 1879, 1887, 1893, 1925, 2000, 2045, 2095, 2122, 2141, 2166, 2234, 2274, 2292, 2294, 2307, 2409, 2419, 2429

Index

Rhetorical Strategies 21, 52, 205, 343, 344, 345, 378, 781, 849, 997, 1334, 1378, 1460, 1889, 2037

School Election. See State and Local Campaigns/Elections
Selective Exposure (see also Cognitive Dissonance) 144, 1175, 1990
Senate. See Congress; Congressional Campaigns/Elections
Simon, Paul 1963
Slogans 597
Social Judgment Theory, in politics 897, 898, 900, 901, 1244, 1607
Source Credibility 63, 166, 294, 518, 542, 770
Speeches, political 21, 295, 296, 311, 374, 403, 792, 836, 837, 1068, 1175, 1233, 1282, 1285, 1514, 1532, 1679, 1737, 1738, 1849, 1925, 1937, 2040, 2041, 2155, 2166, 2235, 2273, 2276, 2302, 2303, 2373, 2386, 2401
Speechwriting, political 431, 432, 545, 608, 2164, 2165, 2201
Spiral of Silence (see also Public Opinion) 1707, 1708, 1709, 2266
State Legislatures/Legislators 1332, 1334, 1346, 1416, 1417, 1468, 1531, 1987, 1999
State and Local Campaigns/Elections (see also Gubernatorial Campaigns/Elections) 105, 178, 211, 263, 292, 341, 371, 477, 521, 556, 557, 638, 806, 877, 879, 953, 970, 1012, 1013, 1069, 1071, 1079, 1083, 1084, 1123, 1128, 1130, 1138, 1149, 1270, 1407, 1490, 1491, 1492, 1568, 1582, 1595, 1790, 1820, 1828, 1992, 1999, 2114, 2363, 2365, 2372, 2404, 2405, 2406, 2407, 2409, 2442
Stevenson, Adlai E., III 375
Stokes, Carl 1083
Strategy and Tactics in Political Campaigns 83, 86, 603, 690, 829, 1127
Subliminal Politics 1189, 1695
Surveys/Survey Research, in politics 227, 230, 231, 234
Symbols 598, 627, 1203, 1727, 1813

Technology, campaign (see also Computers) 1090, 1322, 2029, 2160, 2395
Television Advertising. See Political Advertising
Television News (see also Television in/and Politics--Campaign and Election Coverage) 26, 27, 28, 30, 57, 59, 102, 131, 141, 222, 245, 365, 491, 547, 551, 615, 625, 640, 664, 666, 765, 773, 774, 785, 786, 834, 936, 937, 1045, 1049, 1050, 1051, 1052, 1053, 1064, 1101, 1156, 1189, 1317, 1324, 1344, 1347, 1352, 1353, 1354, 1355, 1394, 1429, 1494, 1495, 1500, 1576, 1608, 1669, 1694, 1728, 1741, 1742, 1764, 1770, 1771, 1774, 1776, 1777, 1778, 1783, 1784, 1795, 1796, 1817, 1843, 1860, 1861, 1891, 1892, 1903, 1914, 1947, 1952, 1955, 1956, 1959, 1960, 1971, 1975, 1978, 1979, 1980, 1981, 2126, 2130, 2156, 2170, 2174, 2213, 2214, 2215, 2229, 2262, 2369, 2425, 2426, 2446, 2447, 2448, 2456, 2459
Television in/and Politics
General 99, 103, 111, 132, 210, 284, 297, 312, 329, 350, 386, 407, 408, 456, 488, 489, 490, 492, 530, 614, 618, 621, 710,

726, 747, 754, 772, 828, 838, 845, 855, 868, 879, 919, 956, 957, 969, 983, 986, 1002, 1067, 1134, 1153, 1158, 1211, 1213, 1215, 1331, 1398, 1435, 1436, 1441, 1578, 1604, 1605, 1674, 1675, 1712, 1774, 1784, 1855, 1945, 1947, 1948, 1950, 1951, 1953, 1957, 1958, 1960, 1962, 2031, 2050, 2070, 2081, 2082, 2083, 2085, 2120, 2271, 2291, 2316, 2345, 2368, 2371, 2460
Bias (see also Television News) 67, 1045, 1048, 1394
Cable-TV 1173
Campaign and Election Coverage (see also Television News) 359, 365, 497, 624, 635, 703, 704, 1045, 1053, 2059, 2073, 2148, 2243, 2291, 2398, 2425, 2426
Commentary 1318, 2128
Credibility 1336, 1338
Information Source 22, 891, 1054
Interview Shows 29, 1353
Tennessee 1858, 1913
Texas 905, 996, 1121, 1490, 1491, 1492, 1493
Ticket-Splitting 109, 373, 471, 472, 718, 1420, 1451, 1569
Trust. See Political Trust
Turnout 31, 155, 280, 319, 880, 1393, 1462, 1723, 1799, 1906, 2002, 2068, 2423, 2434, 2439

Uses and Gratifications, of political information 173, 174, 175, 255, 260, 261, 384, 659, 672, 922, 1197, 1199, 1200, 1355, 1359, 1379, 1516, 1520, 1521, 1527, 1535, 1536, 1642, 1719, 1764, 1851, 1996, 2087, 2245, 2249, 2251, 2350, 2360, 2369, 2460

Vice-President 2367, 2373
Vietnam 115, 921, 1378, 1591, 2056, 2141, 2432
Virginia 896
Voter Behavior 20, 24, 63, 65, 97, 109, 114, 178, 179, 207, 271, 315, 355, 360, 363, 369, 377, 379, 459, 463, 464, 498, 499, 509, 517, 549, 590, 611, 620, 652, 653, 663, 679, 680, 737, 738, 740, 758, 794, 850, 870, 881, 882, 928, 942, 943, 1016, 1021, 1028, 1029, 1035, 1039, 1103, 1107, 1148, 1188, 1205, 1235, 1238, 1239, 1249, 1252, 1258, 1264, 1265, 1270, 1320, 1351, 1360, 1398, 1409, 1410, 1423, 1427, 1461, 1554, 1556, 1557, 1615, 1620, 1631, 1664, 1665, 1681, 1682, 1684, 1721, 1725, 1726, 1786, 1799, 1802, 1815, 1818, 1836, 1837, 1838, 1840, 1841, 1842, 1844, 1854, 1862, 1868, 1873, 1876, 1943, 1983, 1984, 2019, 2036, 2054, 2055, 2068, 2089, 2115, 2146, 2255, 2288, 2340, 2385, 2423
Voter Competence. See Voter Behavior
Voter Registration 2177

Wallace, George C. 391, 599, 644, 675, 693, 708, 734, 781, 1026, 1655, 1879, 1893, 1895, 1962, 2208
Waller, William 78
Watergate 37, 76, 84, 87, 132, 152, 175, 205, 217, 218, 226, 394, 419, 493, 559, 566, 633, 645, 647, 654, 660, 665, 754, 755, 767, 818, 884, 968, 981, 984, 997, 1004, 1010, 1059, 1260, 1263, 1307, 1308, 1309, 1314, 1345, 1401, 1523, 1524, 1527, 1580, 1635, 1663, 1676, 1714, 1724, 1754, 1760, 1831, 1848,

1888, 1936, 1944, 2011, 2028, 2034, 2074, 2145, 2181, 2187, 2211, 2284, 2306, 2315, 2319, 2347, 2374, 2381, 2400, 2412, 2428, 2437, 2438, 2454

West Virginia 535

Wisconsin 1012, 1013, 1829

Women in/and Politics 69, 163, 225, 272, 399, 531, 532, 558, 723, 1247, 1248, 1364, 1390, 1417, 1434, 1563, 1568, 1577, 1683, 1752, 1797, 1865, 1885, 2042, 2199, 2217

Yorty, Samuel W. 268

Young Voters (see also Political Socialization) 1650, 1651, 1652, 1654, 1721, 1785, 1867, 1868, 1920, 2113, 2159, 2170, 2389, 2445

3 1222 00274 7031

NO LONGER THE PROPERTY
OF THE
UNIVERSITY OF R.I. LIBRARY